# BLACK&DECKER

## HOME IMPROVEMENT LIBRARY™

# *Easy* Wood
# Furniture Projects

## *32 Step-by-Step Projects for the Home*

CREATIVE
PUBLISHING
international

Minnetonka, Minnesota

# Credits

*Executive Editor:* Bryan Trandem
*Associate Creative Director:* Tim Himsel
*Managing Editor:* Jennifer Caliandro
*Project Manager:* Michelle Skudlarek
*Lead Editor:* Daniel London
*Editor:* Susan Wichmann
*Technical Editor:* Philip Schmidt
*Copy Editor:* Janice Cauley
*Senior Art Director:* Kevin Walton
*Mac Designers:* Patti Goar, Jonathan Hinz,
    Jon Simpson, Brad Webster

*Vice President of Photography & Production:*
    Jim Bindas
*Studio Services Manager:* Marcia Chambers
*Photo Services Coordinator:* Carol Osterhus
*Photographers:* Tate Carlson, Andrea Rugg
*Set Builder:* Dan Widerski
*Production Manager:* Helga Thieland
*Manager, Production Services:* Kim Gerber

Copyright© 1999
Creative Publishing international, Inc.
5900 Green Oak Drive
Minnetonka, MN 55343
1-800-328-3895
All rights reserved
Printed on American paper by: R. R. Donnelly & Sons Co.
10 9 8 7 6 5 4 3 2 1

*President:* Iain Macfarlane
*Director, Creative Development:* Lisa Rosenthal
*Executive Managing Editor:* Elaine Perry

Created by: The Editors of Creative Publishing international, Inc.,
in cooperation with Black & Decker.
**BLACK&DECKER** is a trademark of the Black & Decker
Corporation and is used under license.

Library of Congress
Cataloging-in-Publication Data

Easy wood furniture projects: 32 step-by-step projects
for the home.

p. cm. — (Black & Decker home improvement library)
ISBN 0-86573-630-8 (softcover)
1. Furniture making. 2. Woodwork Patterns. I. Creative
Publishing International. II. Series.
TT194.E25 1999
684.1'04--dc21
99-24778

# Contents

## Family Room Projects

## Home Office Projects

## Bedroom Projects

## Kitchen Projects

# Introduction

This is a book of plans. For each of the 32 projects that follow, you will find a complete cutting list, a lumber-shopping list, a detailed construction drawing, full-color photographs of major steps and clear, easy-to-follow directions that guide you through each project.

You don't need a lot of experience working with the hand tools and portable power tools used to make the furniture in this book. But if you haven't used any of the tools before, it is a good idea to practice using them on scraps of wood before you tackle the actual projects.

Because you build the furniture yourself, you can select lumber and hardware to match a certain room decor or complement another furnishing. You can also finish the pieces any way you want to create just the right accent.

Read the sections that follow to become familiar with the tools and materials needed for the projects. Woodworking Techniques (pages 6 to 9) introduces you to some simple, time-tested methods used by woodworkers everywhere.

## Tools You Will Use

At the start of each project, a set of symbols shows which power tools are used to complete the project as it is shown. In some cases, optional tools, such as a power miter saw, may be suggested for speedier work. You will also need a set of basic hand tools: hammer, screwdrivers, tape measure, level, combination square, framing square, compass, wood chisels, nail set, putty knife, utility knife, straightedge, C-clamps and pipe or bar clamps. Where required, specialty hand tools are listed for each project.

**Circular saw** *to make straight cuts. For long cuts, use a straight-edge guide. Install a carbide-tipped combination blade for most projects.*

**Drill** *for drilling holes and driving screws. Accessories help with sanding and grinding tasks. Use a corded or cordless drill with variable speed.*

**Jig saw** *for making contoured and internal cuts and for short straight cuts. Use the recommended blade for each type of wood or cutting task.*

**Power sander** *to prepare wood for a finish and to smooth sharp edges. Owning several power sanders (⅓-sheet, ¼-sheet and belt) is helpful.*

**Router** *to cut structural grooves (rabbets) in wood. Also ideal for making a variety of decorative edges and roundover cuts.*

## Safety Tips

•*Always wear eye and hearing protection when operating power tools and performing any other dangerous woodworking activities.*

•*Choose a well-ventilated work area when cutting or shaping wood and when using finishing products.*

# Materials Used in This Book

## Sheet goods:

*AB PLYWOOD:* A smooth, paintable plywood, usually made from pine or fir. The better (A) side is sanded and free from knots and defects.

*BIRCH PLYWOOD:* A sturdy plywood with birch veneer on both sides. Excellent for painting but attractive enough for stain or clear finish.

*OAK PLYWOOD:* A plywood with high-quality oak veneers. A workable, stainable product that blends well with solid oak lumber.

*LAUAN PLYWOOD:* A relatively inexpensive plywood with a smooth mahogany veneer on one side. The natural color varies widely.

*MEDIUM-DENSITY FIBERBOARD (MDF):* A smooth board made from compressed wood fibers. It is highly workable and resists warping.

*HARDBOARD:* A dense fiberboard with one hard, smooth side.

## Dimension lumber:
*The "nominal" size of lumber is usually larger than the actual size. For example, a 1 × 4 board measures ¾" × 3½".*

*SELECT PINE:* Finish-quality pine that is mostly free of knots and other imperfections.

*#2-OR-BETTER PINE:* A grade lower than select but more commonly available.

*RED OAK:* A common, durable hardwood, oak is popular for its color, straight grain and solid appearance.

*ASPEN:* A soft, workable hardwood. Aspen is good for painting but should be sealed for an even stain.

*CEDAR:* A lightweight softwood with a natural resistance to moisture. Smooth cedar is best for furniture.

## Other wood products:

*WOOD MOLDINGS:* Available in a vast range of styles and sizes. Most types of molding are available in a variety of woods.

*VENEER EDGE TAPE:* Self-adhesive wood veneer sold in ¾"-wide strips. Applied to plywood edges with a household iron.

*WOOD PLUGS:* ⅜"-dia. × ¼"-thick disks with a slightly conical shape.

## Fasteners and adhesives:

*WOOD SCREWS:* Steel, zinc-coated steel, brass or brass-coated steel screws with a heavy shank and fine threads. Steel screws are stronger than brass but can stain acidic wood, such as oak, if exposed to moisture. The gauge number refers to shank diameter.

*DECK SCREWS:* Similar to wallboard screws, these have a light shank and coarse threads, making them ideal for fastening soft woods.

*FINISH NAILS AND BRADS:* Thin-shank, steel nails with a small, cup-shaped head. They are driven below the surface with a nail set.

*WIRE NAILS:* Small, steel nails with a flat, round head.

*WOOD GLUE:* Yellow (or "carpenter's") glue is good for indoor furniture projects. Application and drying time depend on the product.

*CERAMIC TILE ADHESIVE:* Multipurpose thin-set mortar or latex mastic. Both are applied with a V-notch trowel.

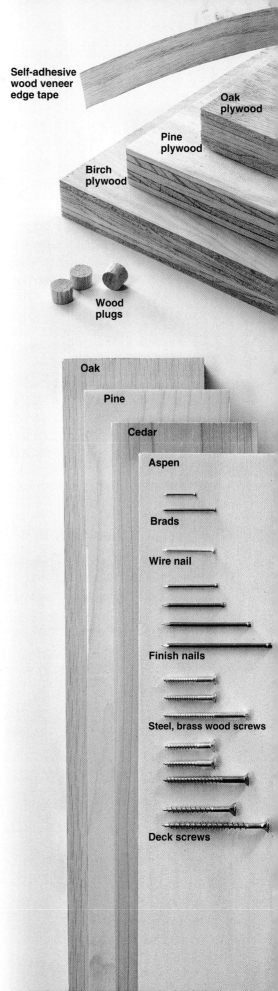

Self-adhesive wood veneer edge tape

Oak plywood

Pine plywood

Birch plywood

Wood plugs

Oak

Pine

Cedar

Aspen

Brads

Wire nail

Finish nails

Steel, brass wood screws

Deck screws

# Tips for Applying Finishing Products

Test your finishes on a scrap taken from the same boards used in the project, and experiment with different applications. Check product labels for compatibility of different finishes, and follow manufacturer's directions. Remember to finish all wood surfaces—including undersides of tabletops and insides of drawers—to prevent warping caused by uneven moisture absorption. Apply two or three thin coats of a protective topcoat, like polyurethane, over bare, painted or stained wood. Penetrating oils, such as tung oil, provide protection and a low-gloss, "bare wood" look.

# Woodworking Techniques

## Cutting

Circular saws and jig saws cut wood as the blade passes up through the material, which can cause splintering or chipping on the top face of the wood. For this reason, always cut from the back (or unexposed) side of your workpiece.

To ensure a straight cut with a circular saw, clamp a straightedge to your workpiece to guide the foot of the saw as you cut **(photo A).**

To make an internal cutout in your workpiece, drill starter holes near cutting lines and use a jig saw to complete the cut **(photo B).**

A power miter saw is the best tool for making straight or angled cuts on narrow boards and trim pieces **(photo C).** This saw is especially helpful for cutting hardwood. An alternative is to use an inexpensive hand miter box fitted with a backsaw **(photo D).**

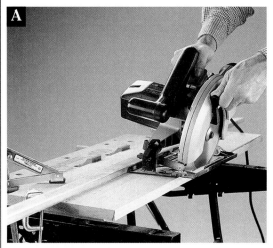

*The foot of the circular saw rides along the straightedge to make straight, smooth cuts.*

*Make contoured cutouts by drilling starter holes and cutting with a jig saw.*

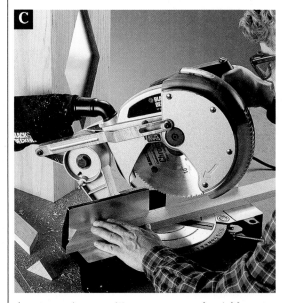

*A power miter saw is easy to use and quickly makes clean, accurate angle cuts in any wood.*

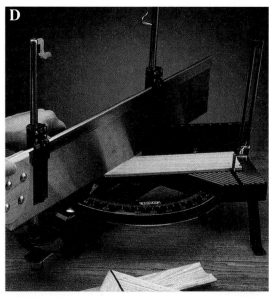

*A hand miter box keeps your backsaw in line for making a full range of angle cuts.*

# Shaping

Create detailed shapes by drawing a grid pattern on your workpiece. Use the grid to mark accurate centers and endpoints for the shapes you will cut. Make smooth roundovers and curves using a standard compass **(photo E).**

You can also create shapes by enlarging a drawing detail, using a photocopier and transferring the pattern to the workpiece.

A belt sander makes short work of sanding tasks and is also a powerful shaping tool. Mounting a belt sander to your workbench allows you to move and shape the workpiece freely—using both hands **(photo F).** Secure the sander by clamping the tool casing in a benchtop vise or with large handscrew or C-clamps. Clamp a scrap board to your bench to use as a platform, keeping the workpiece square and level with the sanding belt.

To ensure that matching pieces, such as armrests, have an identical shape, clamp them together before shaping **(photo G).** This technique is known as gang-sanding.

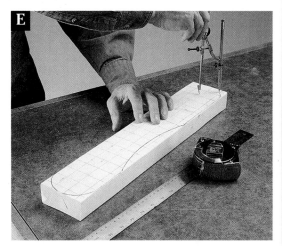

*Use a square grid pattern and a compass to draw patterns on your workpiece.*

*Gang-sanding is an easy method for creating two or more identical parts.*

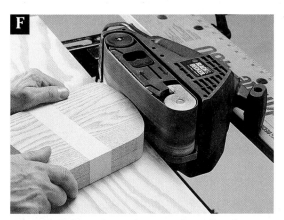

*Clamp a belt sander and a scrap board to the workbench to create a stationary shaping tool.*

# Squaring a Frame

Squaring is an important technique in furniture construction. A frame or assembly that is not square will result in a piece that teeters on two legs or won't stand up straight. Always check an assembly for square before fastening the parts together.

To square a frame, measure diagonally from corner to corner **(photo H).** When the measurements are equal, the frame is square. Adjust the frame by applying inward pressure to diagonally opposite corners. A framing square or a combination square can also be used to see if two pieces form a right angle.

*Clamp frame parts together. Then, measure the diagonals to check for square before fastening.*

# Piloting and Drilling

Pilot holes make it easier to drive screws or nails into a workpiece, and they remove some material to prevent the fastener from splitting the wood. If you find that your screws are difficult to drive or that the wood splits, switch to a larger piloting bit. If the screws are not holding well or are stripping the pilot holes, use a smaller bit to pilot subsequent holes. When drilling pilot holes for finish nails, use a standard straight bit.

A combination pilot bit drills pilot holes for the threaded and unthreaded sections of the screw shank, as well as a counterbore recess that allows the screw to seat below the surface of the workpiece **(photo A)**. The counterbore portion of the bit drills a ⅜"-dia. hole to accept a standard wood plug. A bit stop with a setscrew allows you to adjust the drilling depth.

When drilling a hole through a workpiece, clamp a scrap board to the piece on the side where the drill bit will exit **(photo B)**. This "backer board" will prevent the bit from splintering the wood and is especially important when drilling large holes with a spade bit.

To make perfectly straight or uniform holes, mount your drill to a portable drill stand **(photo C)**. The stand can be adjusted for drilling to a specific depth and angle.

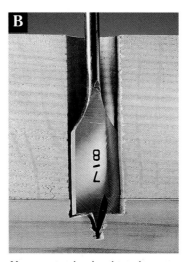

*A combination pilot bit drills pilot holes and counterbores for wood screws in one step.*

*Use a scrap backer board to prevent tearout when drilling through a workpiece.*

*A portable drill stand helps you drill straight or angled holes.*

# Gluing

A gluing surface should be smooth and free of dust but not sanded. Glue and fasten boards soon after they are cut—machined surfaces dry out over time and bond best when they are freshly cut.

Before gluing, test-fit the pieces to ensure a proper fit. Then, clean the mating edges with a clean, dry cloth to remove dust **(photo D)**.

Apply glue to both surfaces and spread it evenly, using a stick or your finger **(photo E)**. Use enough glue to cover the area, with a small amount of excess.

Promptly assemble and clamp the pieces with enough clamps to apply even pressure to the joint. Watch the glue oozing from the joint to gauge the distribution of pressure. Excessive "squeeze-out" indicates that the clamps are too tight or that there is too much glue. Wipe up excess glue with a damp—not wet—cloth.

*Clean the mating surfaces with a cloth to remove dust.*

*Spread glue evenly over the entire mating surface of both pieces.*

# Prepping Wood for Finishing Touches

Most projects require that nail heads be set below the surface of the wood, using a nail set **(photo F).** Choose a nail set with a point slightly smaller than the nail head.

Screws that have been driven well below the surface (about ¼") can be hidden by filling the counterbores with glued wood plugs **(photo G).** Tap the plug into place with a wood mallet or a hammer and scrap block, leaving the plug just above the surface. Then, sand the plug smooth with the surrounding surface.

Fill nail holes and small defects with wood putty **(photo H).** When applying a stain or clear finish to a project, use a tinted putty to match the wood, and avoid smearing it outside the nail holes. Use putty to fill screw holes on painted projects.

A power drill with a sanding drum attachment helps you sand contoured surfaces smooth **(photo I).**

Use a palm sander to finish-sand flat surfaces. To avoid sanding through thin veneers, draw light pencil marks on the surface and sand just until the marks disappear **(photo J).**

To finish-sand your projects, start with medium sandpaper (100- or 120-grit) and switch to increasingly finer papers (150- to 220-grit).

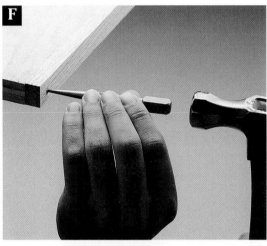

*Set finish nails below the surface, using a nail set slightly smaller than the head of the nail.*

*Apply glue to wood plugs and insert them into screw counterbores to hide the screws.*

*Fill holes and wood defects with plain or tinted wood putty.*

*Smooth curves and hard-to-reach surfaces with a drum attachment on your power drill.*

*Draw pencil marks on veneered surfaces to prevent oversanding.*

# Umbrella Stand

*Keep your umbrellas, canes and walking sticks within easy reach with this classic umbrella stand.*

PROJECT
POWER TOOLS

## CONSTRUCTION MATERIALS

| Quantity | Lumber |
|----------|--------|
| 2 | 1 × 10" × 6' oak |
| 1 | ¾ × ¾" × 4' oak cove molding |
| 2 | 8 × 22" tin |

This umbrella stand is the perfect rainy-day project. It easily holds up to six umbrellas, canes or walking sticks, so you'll never again have to search for these items on the way out the door. The umbrella stand is a natural in a hallway, entryway or foyer and a classy alternative to storing umbrellas in your closet.

Built from solid oak for sturdiness and good looks, the umbrella stand has miter-cut top trim and cove molding, and decorative diamond cutouts backed with tin panels. This project can be painted or finished with natural stain. Use an oak finish on the feet and trim, and your umbrella stand will blend in nicely with wood staircases and doors.

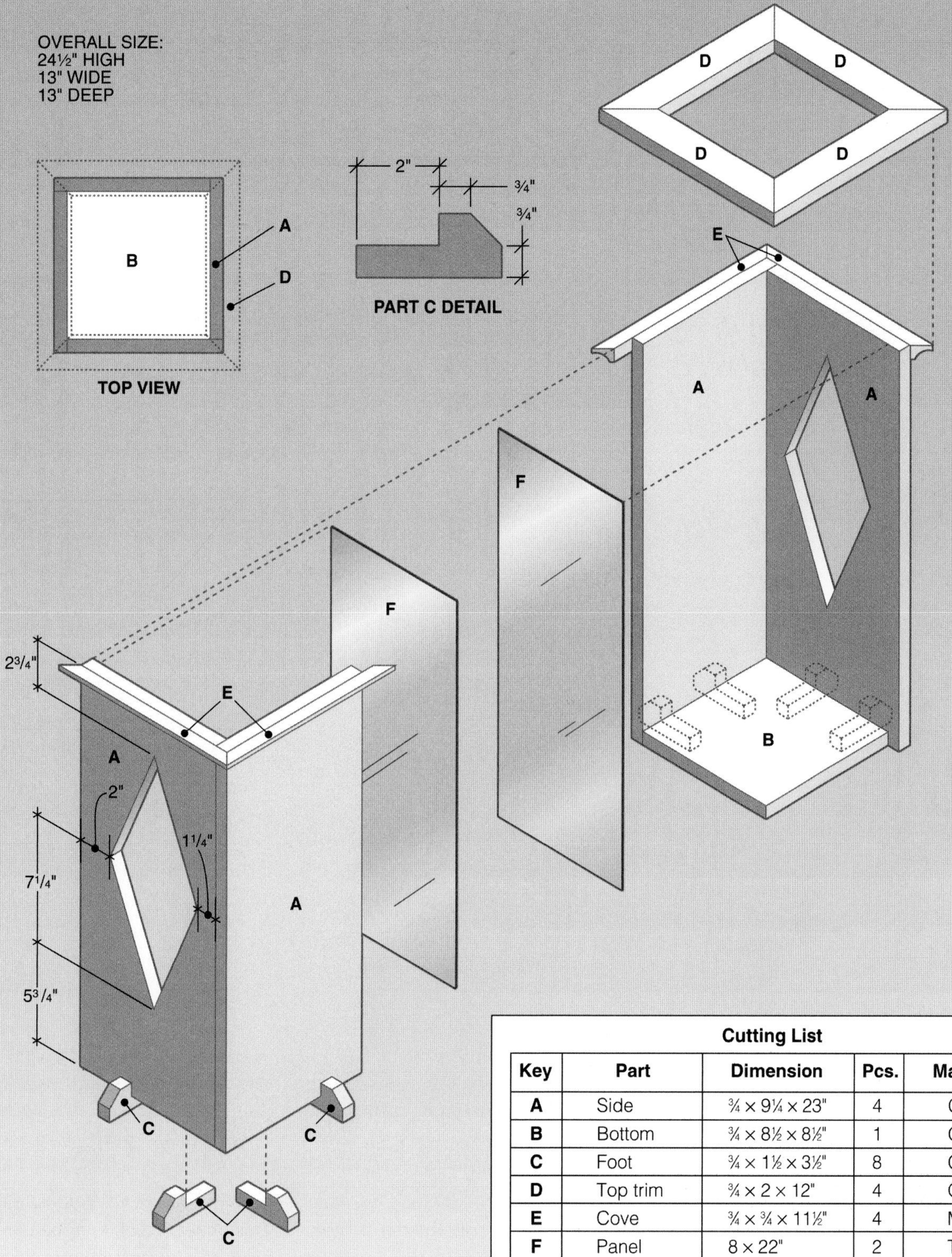

OVERALL SIZE:
24½" HIGH
13" WIDE
13" DEEP
B
A
D
TOP VIEW
2"
¾"
¾"
PART C DETAIL
D
D
D
D
E
A
A
B
F
F
2¾"
E
A
2"
7¼"
1¼"
A
5¾"
C
C
C


**Cutting List**

| Key | Part | Dimension | Pcs. | Material |
|---|---|---|---|---|
| A | Side | ¾ × 9¼ × 23" | 4 | Oak |
| B | Bottom | ¾ × 8½ × 8½" | 1 | Oak |
| C | Foot | ¾ × 1½ × 3½" | 8 | Oak |
| D | Top trim | ¾ × 2 × 12" | 4 | Oak |
| E | Cove | ¾ × ¾ × 11½" | 4 | Molding |
| F | Panel | 8 × 22" | 2 | Tin |

**Materials:** #6 × 1¼" wood screws, #6 × ½" panhead screws, 2d and 4d finish nails, 16-ga. × 1" brads, wood glue, finishing materials.

**Specialty tools:** Aviation snips.

**Note:** Measurements reflect the actual size of dimension lumber.

Drill starter holes. Then, cut out the diamond shapes with a jig saw.

Use the diamond cutout as a guide when attaching the tin panel around the cutout.

## Directions: Umbrella Stand

### CUT THE SIDES AND BOTTOM.

**1.** Cut the sides (A) and bottom (B) to size. Sand the cuts smooth with medium-grit sandpaper.

**2.** Draw the diamond on two sides (for measurements, see *Diagram*, page 11). NOTE: When the box is assembled, the diamonds will be centered side to side. Drill starter holes, using a backer board to prevent splintering. Cut out the diamond shapes with a jig saw **(photo A).** Sand the cutouts smooth.

**3.** Cut the tin panels (F) to size with aviation snips. Position the tin panels on the inside face of each cutout side, leaving a ¾" space at the bottom and along the right edge for the bottom piece and adjoining side. Drill ³⁄₃₂" pilot holes, and attach the tin panel with ½" panhead screws. Drive screws at the cor-

Attach the cove molding to the sides with glue and 1" brads.

ners and along the edges of the cutout. Use a cutout diamond section as a guide to position the screws **(photo B).**

### ASSEMBLE THE BOX.

**1.** Lay one of the plain sides on your worksurface. Butt a cutout side upright at a 90° angle against the left edge (make sure the tin panel is not covered). Drill pilot holes through the cutout side and into the edge of the plain side.

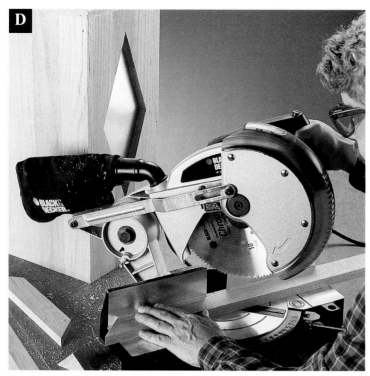

*Use a miter saw to cut 45° angles on the top trim.*

*Attach the feet with 1¼" wood screws.*

Counterbore the holes ⅛" deep, using a ⅜" counterbore bit. Join the pieces with glue and 1¼" wood screws.

**2.** Rotate the assembly so the cutout is facedown. Butt the other plain side against the left edge. Drill pilot holes through the plain side and into the edge of the cutout side. Counterbore the holes. Attach the piece with glue and 1¼" wood screws.

**3.** Position the bottom piece inside the assembly, flush with the bottom edges. Drill pilot holes through the sides and into the bottom. Counterbore the holes. Attach the bottom with glue and 1¼" wood screws.

**4.** Rotate the assembly, and attach the remaining cutout side.

## ATTACH THE COVE MOLDING AND TOP TRIM.

Miter the cove molding on the ends, and lock-nail the joints together to prevent separation (see *Tip*).

**1.** Cut the cove molding (E) to length, mitering the ends at 45° angles.

**2.** Position the molding so the top edges are flush with the tops of the sides. Drill ¹⁄₁₆" pilot holes through the molding, and attach the molding with glue and 1" brads **(photo C).**

**3.** Cut the top trim (D) to size, mitering the ends at 45° angles **(photo D).**

**4.** Position the trim so it overhangs the outer edges of the cove by ¼". Drill ¹⁄₁₆" pilot holes through the trim pieces. Attach them with glue and 4d finish nails. Lock-nail the mitered ends with 2d finish nails. Set all nails with a nail set.

## CUT THE FEET.

**1.** Cut blanks for the feet (C).

**2.** With a jig saw, trim off the corners, and make the notches (see *Diagram*). Sand the cut edges smooth.

## APPLY FINISHING TOUCHES.

**1.** Fill all nail and screw holes with wood putty. Sand the wood, and finish as desired.

**2.** To paint the sides, mask the cove and trim, and cover the tin panel with contact paper. When the paint dries, remove the paper and apply amber shellac to the tin.

**3.** Apply finish to the cove, trim and feet. Position two feet at the bottom of each side, 2⅛" in from the outside edges. Drill pilot holes and counterbore the holes. Attach the feet with 1¼" wood screws **(photo E).**

> ### TIP
>
> *Lock-nailing is a technique used to reinforce mitered joints. The idea is to drive finish nails through both mating surfaces at the joint. Start by drilling pilot holes all the way through one board (to avoid splitting the wood) and partway into the other mating surface. Drive a small finish nail (2d or 4d) or a brad through each pilot hole to complete the lock-nailing operation.*

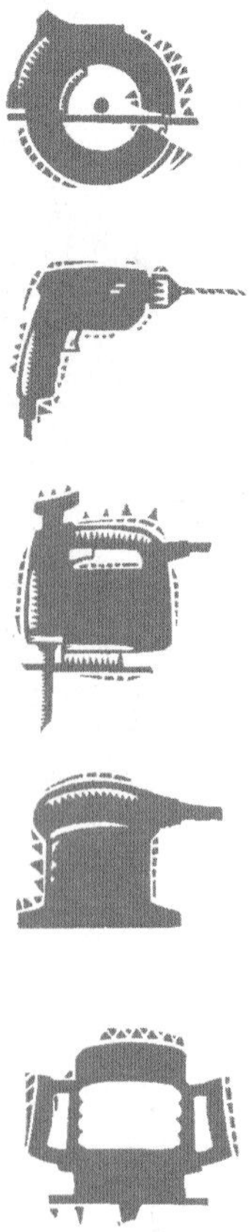

# Mirrored Coat Rack

*Nothing welcomes visitors to your home like an elegant,
finely crafted mirrored coat rack.*

CONSTRUCTION MATERIALS

| Quantity | Lumber |
| --- | --- |
| 1 | 1 × 2" × 3' oak |
| 1 | 1 × 3" × 4' oak |
| 1 | 1 × 4" × 6' oak |
| 1 | ½ × ¾" × 4' molding |
| 1 | ¼" × 2 × 4' hardboard |
| 1 | ⅛ × 15¾ × 24¾" mirrored glass |

An entryway or foyer seems naked without a coat rack and a mirror, and this simple oak project gives you both features in one striking package. The egg-and-dart beading at the top and the decorative porcelain and brass coat hooks provide just enough design interest to make the project elegant without overwhelm-

ing the essential simplicity of the look.

You can use inexpensive red oak to build your mirrored coat rack. Or, if you are willing to invest a little more money, use quarter-sawn white oak to create an item with the look of a true antique. For a special touch, have the edges of the mirror beveled.

OVERALL SIZE:
22¾" HIGH
32" WIDE
1½" DEEP

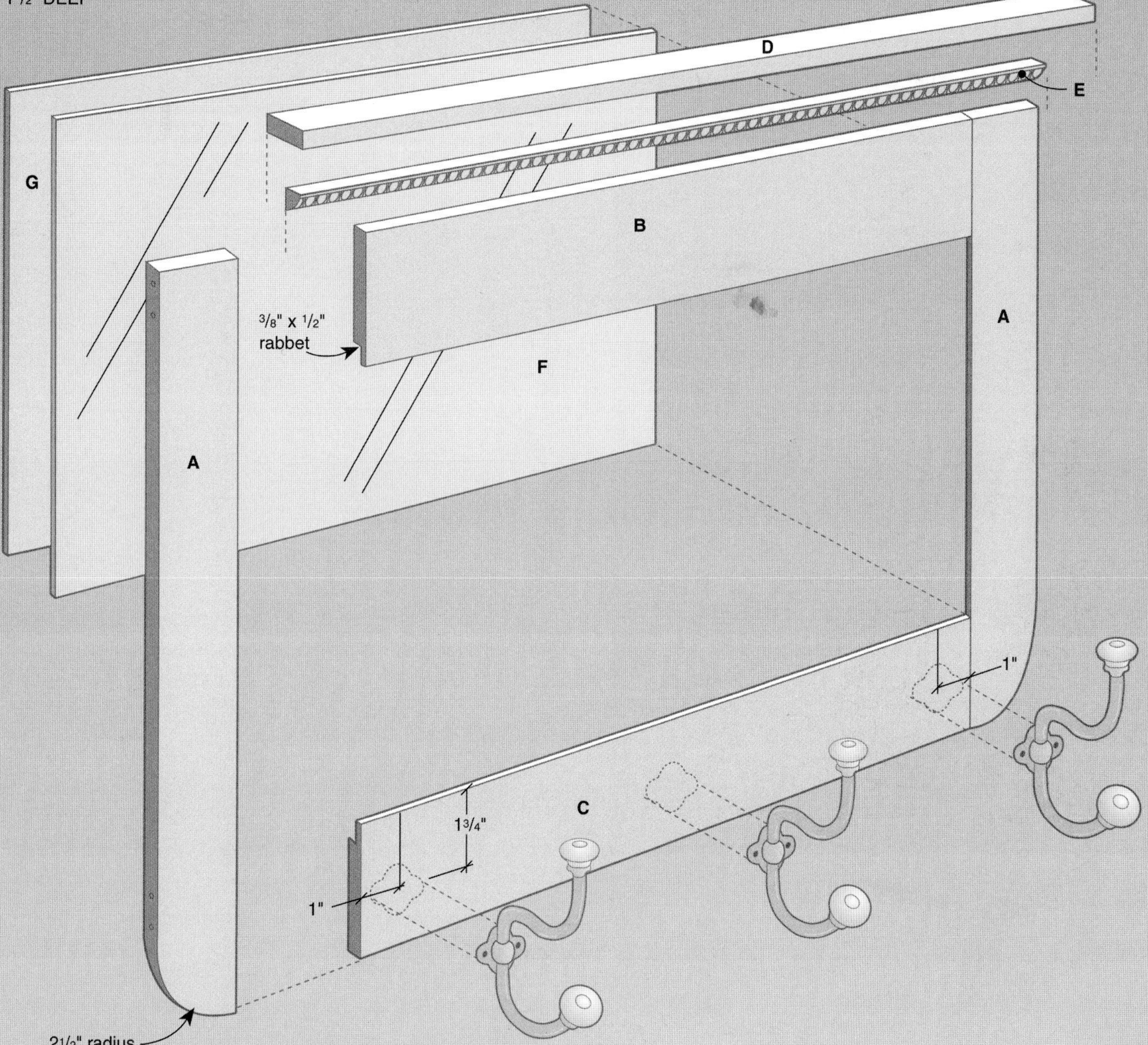

D
E
G
B
A
F
3/8" x 1/2" rabbet
A
1"
C
1 3/4"
1"
2 1/2" radius roundover


**Cutting List**

| Key | Part | Dimension | Pcs. | Material |
|---|---|---|---|---|
| **A** | Stile | ¾ × 2½ × 22" | 2 | Oak |
| **B** | Top rail | ¾ × 3½ × 24" | 1 | Oak |
| **C** | Bottom rail | ¾ × 3½ × 24" | 1 | Oak |
| **D** | Cap | ¾ × 1½ × 32" | 1 | Oak |
| **E** | Molding | ½ × ¾ × 29" | 1 | Oak |
| **F** | Mirror | ⅛ × 15¾ × 24¾" | 1 | Mirror |
| **G** | Mirror back | ¼ × 15¾ × 24¾" | 1 | Hardboard |

**Materials:** #6 × 1½" wood screws, 16-ga. × 1" brads, coat hooks with screws (3), ¼ × 36" oak dowel, wood glue, finishing materials.

**Note:** Measurements reflect the actual size of dimension lumber.

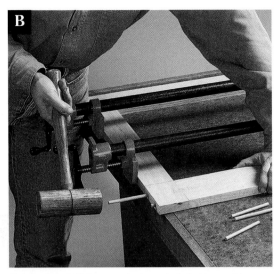

*Clamp the frame components together. Then, drill 3½"-deep guide holes for the through-dowel joints.*

*Drive glued 4"-long oak dowels into the guide holes to make the dowel joints.*

*Mount a belt sander to your worksurface, and use it to smooth the roundover cuts on the frame.*

### Directions:
### Mirrored Coat Rack

MAKE THE MIRROR FRAME.
**1.** Cut the stiles (A) to length. Cut the top rail (B) and bottom rail (C) to length.

**TIP**

*Through-dowel joints are the easiest dowel joints to make—all you need are a good bar or pipe clamp and the ability to drill a reasonably straight guide hole. The visible dowel ends at the joints contribute to the traditional design of the project.*

**2.** Lay the rails between the stiles on your worksurface to form a frame. Square the frame. Then, use a bar or pipe clamp to hold it together.
**3.** Through-dowel joints hold the frame together. To make them, drill two evenly spaced ¼"-dia. × 3½"-deep guide holes at each joint, drilling through the stiles and into the rails **(photo A).** Cut eight ¼"-dia. × 4"-long oak dowels. Unclamp the frame assembly, and squirt a little glue into each guide hole. Coat each dowel with a

light layer of glue. Drive a dowel into each guide hole, using a wood mallet so you don't break the dowels **(photo B).**
**4.** When all joints are made, clamp the frame assembly together. Once the glue has dried, remove the clamps, and trim off the ends of the dowels with a backsaw. Sand them flush with the surface, and scrape off excess glue.

ROUND OVER THE
FRAME ENDS.
**1.** On the bottom end of each stile, draw an arc with a 2½" radius to mark the decorative roundovers. Cut along the arc line, using a jig saw.
**2.** Smooth the cut with a belt sander mounted to your worksurface **(photo C).**

DRILL MOUNTING HOLES
AND CUT THE MIRROR
RECESS.
**1.** Drill ¹¹⁄₆₄" holes through the fronts of the stiles, 6" down from the top, so you can attach the rack to a wall. With a counterbore bit, drill ⅜"-dia. × ¼"-deep counterbores for oak plugs to cover the screw heads after you

Use a router with a ⅜" rabbeting bit to cut a recess for the mirror in the frame back.

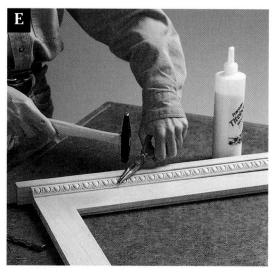

Center egg-and-dart trim molding under the cap, and attach it with glue and brads.

Install the mirror and mirror back. Then, secure them to the frame with brads, using a brad pusher.

hang the coat rack.

**2.** Cut a groove around the back inside edges of the frame to make a recess for the mirror and back. The easiest way to cut this kind of groove (called a rabbet) is with a router and a ⅜" rabbeting bit. Set the cutting depth of the router to ⅜", then trim around the back inside edges of the frame **(photo D).** Reset the router depth to ½", and make another pass around the edges to complete the rabbet. Square the grooves at the corners with a wood chisel.

### INSTALL THE CAP AND MOLDING.

**1.** Cut the cap (D) to length.
**2.** Drill 3/32" pilot holes through the cap and into the top rail. Counterbore the holes ¼" deep, using a ⅜" counterbore bit. Attach the cap flush with the back edge of the rail, using glue and 1½" wood screws. The cap overhangs the stiles 1½" on each end.
**3.** Cut a piece of egg-and-dart style molding (E) to length. Sand a slight bevel at each end.
**4.** Attach the molding flush against the underside of the

cap, centered side to side, using glue and 1" brads driven with a tack hammer **(photo E).** Drill 1/16" pilot holes through the molding to prevent splitting. Set the nail heads, using a nail set.

### APPLY FINISHING TOUCHES AND INSTALL THE MIRROR.

**1.** Sand all sharp edges on the frame. Fill the screw holes with oak plugs, and sand them flush with the surface. Apply a finish. When it's dry, install the coat hooks (see *Diagram*, page 15).
**2.** Have the mirrored glass cut to size at a glass store. Set the glass into the rabbet in the frame. Cut ¼"-thick hardboard to make the mirror back (G), and install it behind the mirror. Secure the mirror and mirror back by driving 1" brads into the edges of the frame with a brad pusher **(photo F).**
**3.** Hang the coat rack (see *Tip*, above). Fill the mounting screw holes with oak plugs. Sand them flush with the surface and touch up the area with finish.

> **TIP**
>
> *Try to hit a wall stud with the mounting screws when hanging heavy objects on a wall. Use toggle bolts to mount where no studs are present.*

# Mitten Chest

*This convenient mitten chest keeps your entryway clutter-free
and stores hats and mittens right where you need them.*

## CONSTRUCTION MATERIALS

| Quantity | Lumber |
|---|---|
| 1 | ¾" × 4 × 8' plywood |
| 2 | ½ × 1⅜" × 7' stop molding |
| 1 | ¼ × 1⁵⁄₁₆" × 7' corner molding |
| 2 | ¾ × 1⅜" × 7' cap molding |

This roomy mitten chest makes the most of valuable floor space in your entryway. It's large enough to hold all your family's mittens, hats and scarves. Move it to your den or family room and this chest also makes a fine coffee table.

The mitten chest is a very simple project, made from four plywood panels, top and bottom panels and some decorative trim molding.

For a nice, contemporary appearance, paint your mitten chest in soft pastel tones. Be sure to use glossy enamel paint—enamel paint finishes are easiest to clean.

Another finishing option for the mitten chest is to line the interior with aromatic cedar liners to ward off moths and give your hand and head gear a fresh scent. Aromatic cedar liners are sold in 4 × 8 sheets and self-adhesive strips.

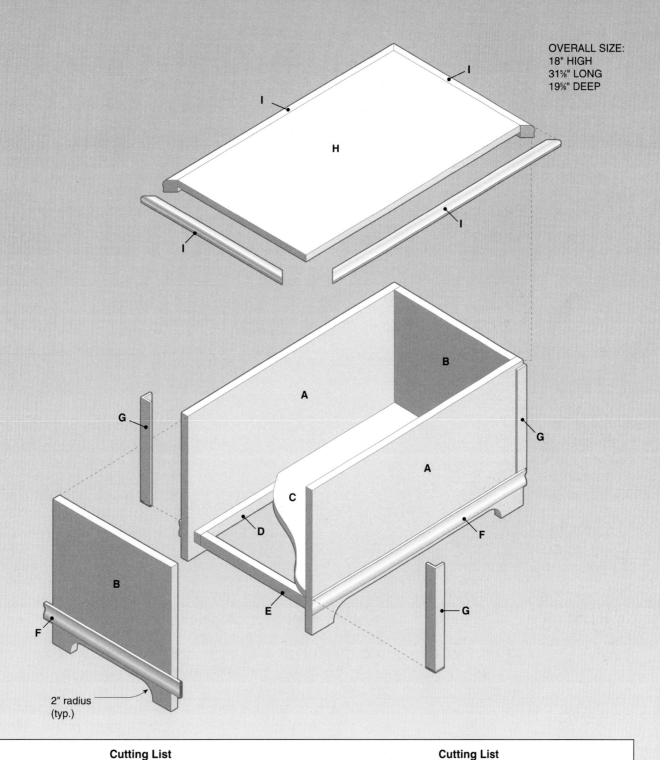

OVERALL SIZE:
18" HIGH
31⅝" LONG
19⅝" DEEP

2" radius
(typ.)

## Cutting List

| Key | Part | Dimension | Pcs. | Material |
|-----|------|-----------|------|----------|
| **A** | Side panel | ¾ × 17¼ × 30" | 2 | Plywood |
| **B** | End panel | ¾ × 17¼ × 16½" | 2 | Plywood |
| **C** | Bottom panel | ¾ × 16½ × 28½" | 1 | Plywood |
| **D** | Side cleat | ¾ × 1½ × 28½" | 2 | Plywood |
| **E** | End cleat | ¾ × 1½ × 15" | 2 | Plywood |

## Cutting List

| Key | Part | Dimension | Pcs. | Material |
|-----|------|-----------|------|----------|
| **F** | Bottom molding | ½ × 1⅜ × *" | 4 | Stop molding |
| **G** | Corner molding | ¼ × 1⁵⁄₁₆ × 12" | 4 | Corner molding |
| **H** | Lid | ¾ × 18⅛ × 30⅛" | 1 | Plywood |
| **I** | Top cap | ¾ × 1⅜ × *" | 4 | Cap molding |

**Materials:** #6 × 1¼" and 2" wood screws, 16-ga. × ¾" and 1¼" brads, 2d and 4d finish nails, wood glue, finishing materials.

**Note:** Measurements reflect the actual size of dimension lumber.

*Cut to fit.

Use a jig saw and a straightedge as a guide to make the "kick space" cuts in the end and side panels.

using a straightedge to guide the long, straight portion of the cut. Sand the edges to smooth any rough spots.

**3.** To draw the cutting lines for the kick spaces on the end panels, first draw cutting lines 2" up from one short edge. Set the compass to draw a 2"-radius semicircle, and position the point of the compass as close as possible to the bottom edge, 4¼" in from the ends of the end panels. Draw the curved semicircles, and make the cutouts with a jig saw. Sand the edges to smooth any rough spots.

### Directions: Mitten Chest

#### MAKE THE SIDES AND ENDS.

**1.** Cut the side panels (A) and end panels (B) to size.

**2.** To make the cutouts, or "kick spaces," on the bottom edges of the sides, draw cutting lines on the sides, 2" in from one long edge. Use a compass to draw the curved cutting lines at the ends of each kick space. Set the compass to draw a 2"-radius semicircle, and position the point of the compass as close as possible to the bottom edge, 5" in from the ends of the side panels. Draw the semicircles. Clamp the sides to your worksurface, and make the cutouts with a jig saw **(photo A),**

#### ASSEMBLE THE CHEST.

Attach cleats to the inside faces of the side and end panels. The cleats support the bottom panel of the chest, so it is important to attach them with their top edges aligned.

**1.** Cut the side cleats (D) and end cleats (E) to size.

**2.** To help you position the cleats, draw reference lines on

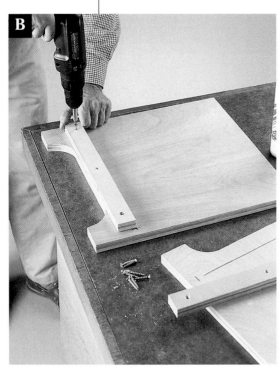

Center the end cleats over the kick spaces, leaving ¾" at each end where the side cleats will fit.

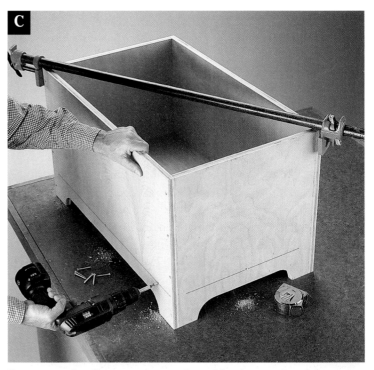

Draw opposite chest corners together with a bar or pipe clamp to keep the chest square.

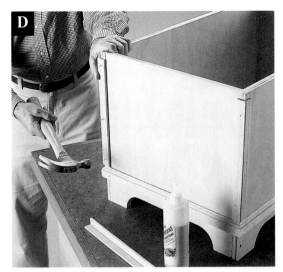

Fasten the corner molding over the corners to conceal the joints and screw heads.

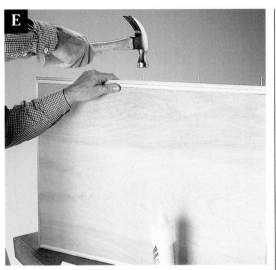

Attach the top cap around the perimeter of the lid. Drive nails in partially before positioning the strips.

the side and end panels, 3½" up from the bottom edges and ¾" in from the side edges. Position the cleats so their top edges are flush with the reference lines. Drill ⁵⁄₆₄" pilot holes through the cleats and into the panels. Counterbore the holes ⅛" deep, using a ⅜" counterbore bit. Fasten with glue and 1¼" wood screws **(photo B)**.

**3.** With the cleats facing in, position the end panels between the side panels. Drill pilot holes through the side panels and into the end panels. Counterbore the holes. Fasten with glue and evenly spaced 2" wood screws. Make sure the top and bottom edges are flush and the outside faces of the ends are flush with the side edges.

**4.** Cut the bottom panel (C) to size, and sand it smooth. Test-fit the bottom panel by setting it on top of the cleats. Remove the panel. Apply glue to the top edges of the cleats and along the underside edges of the panel, and reposition the panel inside the chest. Clamp diagonal chest corners with a bar or pipe clamp to hold the piece

square while you fasten the bottom panel **(photo C)**. To make sure you drive the screws directly into the bottom, mark the screw centerpoints 3⅞" up from the bottoms of the sides and ends. Drill pilot holes through the sides and ends and into the edges of the bottom panel. Counterbore the holes. Attach with 2" wood screws.

ATTACH THE MOLDING.
**1.** Cut the bottom molding (F) to fit around the chest, miter-cutting the ends at 45° angles so they will fit together at the corners.
**2.** Position the molding so the top edges are 4⅜" up from the bottom edges of the sides and ends. Fasten it with glue and 4d finish nails, driven through ¹⁄₁₆" pilot holes. Apply glue, and drive 2d nails through the joints where the molding pieces meet to lock-nail the pieces (see *Tip*, page 13).
**3.** Cut the corner molding (G) to length. Use glue and ¾" brads to fasten the corner molding over the joints between the end and side panels

**(photo D)**. Make sure the bottom edges of the corner molding butt against the top edges of the bottom molding. Sand the bottom edges of the corner molding to meet the bottom molding. Sand the top edges of the ends and sides to smooth the edges and corners.

MAKE THE LID.
**1.** Cut the lid (H) to size, and sand it smooth.
**2.** Cut four pieces of top cap (I) to fit around the perimeter of the lid.
**3.** Drill ¹⁄₁₆" pilot holes. Use glue and 4d finish nails to attach the top cap pieces, keeping the top edges flush with the top face of the lid **(photo E)**. Glue and lock-nail the mitered corner joints. Set the lid into the top opening—no hinges are used.

APPLY FINISHING TOUCHES.
Use a nail set to set all nails and brads on the chest. Fill all visible nail holes with wood putty. Sand any rough spots smooth. Finish as desired.

# Entry Valet

*The friendly face of this valet hides the fact that it's a functional
storage unit, with a drop-down bin and a covered scarf box.*

## CONSTRUCTION MATERIALS

| Quantity | Lumber |
|----------|--------|
| 1 | 1 × 12" × 6' pine |
| 2 | 1 × 10" × 8' pine |
| 1 | 1 × 6" × 6' pine |
| 1 | 1 × 4" × 6' pine |
| 1 | 1 × 3" × 6' pine |
| 1 | ¾ × ¾" × 6' pine stop molding |
| 1 | ¼" × 4 × 4' plywood |

This entry valet is designed to provide handy storage in one of the busiest areas of your house—the entryway. It is equipped with a spacious pivoting bin at the top, and a scarf storage box with a hinged lid that also functions as a shelf and a stretcher to give the valet added strength.

Because the entry is the first part of your house that most visitors will see, it is important that entry furnishings be pleasing to look at, as well as functional. For that reason, we used simple construction that is reminiscent of popular Shaker styling, and added decorative contours that give the valet a touch of Colonial style as well.

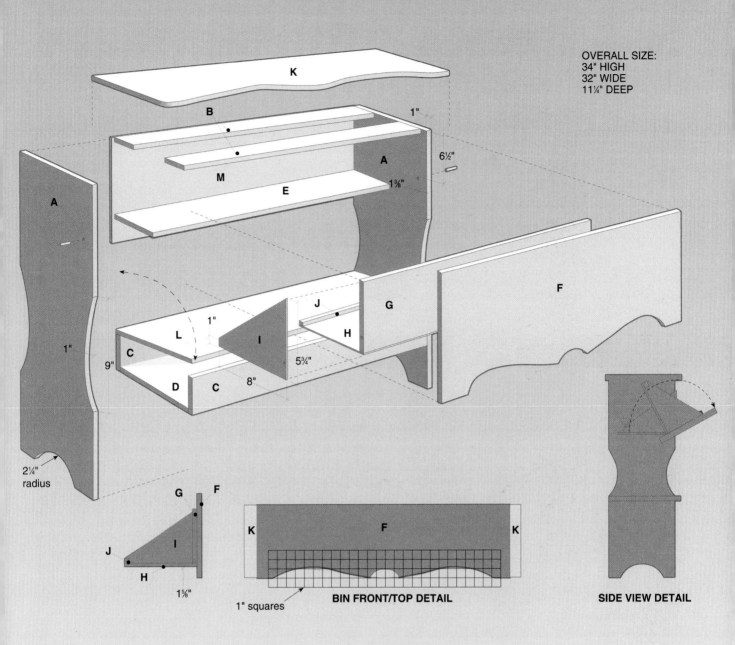

OVERALL SIZE:
34" HIGH
32" WIDE
11¼" DEEP

**BIN FRONT/TOP DETAIL**

1" squares

**SIDE VIEW DETAIL**

| Key | Part | Dimension | Pcs. | Material |
|-----|------|-----------|------|----------|
| **A** | End | ¾ × 9¼ × 33¼" | 2 | Pine |
| **B** | Top stretcher | ¾ × 2½ × 28½" | 2 | Pine |
| **C** | Box side | ¾ × 3½ × 28½" | 2 | Pine |
| **D** | Box bottom | ¾ × 7¾ × 28½" | 1 | Pine |
| **E** | Bin stop | ¾ × 5½ × 28½" | 1 | Pine |
| **F** | False front | ¾ × 9¼ × 28¼" | 1 | Pine |
| **G** | Bin front | ¾ × 5½ × 27⅝" | 1 | Pine |

| Key | Part | Dimension | Pcs. | Material |
|-----|------|-----------|------|----------|
| **H** | Bin bottom | ¼ × 8 × 27⅝" | 1 | Plywood |
| **I** | Bin side | ¼ × 5¾ × 8" | 2 | Plywood |
| **J** | Bin back lip | ¾ × ¾ × 27⅝" | 1 | Stop molding |
| **K** | Top | ¾ × 11¼ × 32" | 1 | Pine |
| **L** | Lid | ¾ × 9½ × 28¼" | 1 | Pine |
| **M** | Valet back | ¼ × 8⅜ × 29½" | 1 | Plywood |
| | | | | |

**Materials:** #6 × 1¼" wood screws, 16-ga. × 1" wire nails, 2" butt hinges with ½" wood screws (2), ⅜"-dia. × 4" wood dowel, ⅜"-dia. wood plugs, wood glue, finishing materials.

**Note:** Measurements reflect the actual size of dimension lumber.

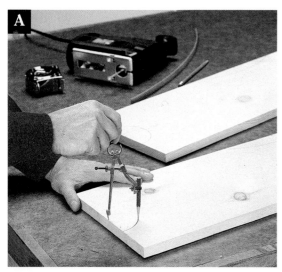

Use a compass to draw 2¼"-radius semicircles on the bottoms of the end pieces.

Fasten the bin stop board between the end panels to complete the assembly of the valet framework.

Fasten the bin sides with glue and wire nails.

## Directions: Entry Valet

### CUT AND CONTOUR THE END PIECES.

**1.** Cut the end panels (A) to length.

**2.** To make the side cutouts, mark points at each side edge, 17⅜" from the bottom edges. At the points, measure in 1" from the side edge to mark the deepest point of the cutout. Mark points 4½" above and below each mark at the side edges to mark endpoints. Draw curved lines from endpoint to endpoint, through the centerpoint. To help you draw the lines, flex a ruler between endpoints as a guide. Make the cutouts with a jig saw and sand smooth.

**3.** To make the bottom cutouts, mark the center of each end panel on the bottom edge. Set a compass to 2¼" radius, and set the tip on the centerpoint. Draw a semicircular cutting line at the bottom of each panel **(photo A).** Make the cutouts and sand smooth.

### ASSEMBLE THE FRAMEWORK.

**1.** Cut the scarf box sides (C), box bottom (D), top stretchers (B) and bin stop (E) to size.

**2.** Position the box pieces, and drill ⁵⁄₆₄" pilot holes through the box sides and into the edges of the box bottom. Counterbore the holes ¼" deep, using a ⅜" counterbore bit. Attach the pieces with glue and three or four evenly spaced, 1¼" wood screws.

**3.** Attach the box assembly to the inside faces of the end panels so the box sides are flush with the front and back edges of the end panels. The box bottom should be 7¼" up from the bottoms of the end panels.

**4.** Position the top stretchers between the end panels, face up. One stretcher should be flush with the back and top edges of the end panels, and the other should be flush with the tops, but recessed 1" from the front edges (see *Diagram*, page 23). Drill pilot holes through the end panels and into the stretchers. Counterbore the holes. Attach with glue and 1¼" wood screws.

**5.** Install the bin stop between the end panels so its top face is 7⅞" down from the tops of the panels, and its back is flush with the back edges **(photo B).**

### BUILD THE BIN.

**1.** Cut the bin front (G) and the bin bottom (H). Attach the bin bottom to the bin front with glue and 1" wire nails driven up through the bottom and into the front piece.

**2.** Cut the triangular bin sides (I) (see *Diagram*). Attach the sides to the bottom/front assembly with glue and 1" wire nails **(photo C).**

**3.** Cut the bin back lip (J) to length. Glue the lip to the top face of the bin bottom so the ends fit between the bin sides.

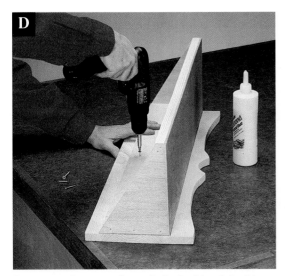

*Drive wood screws through the inside of the bin and into the back of the false front.*

*Clamp the bin to the valet framework. Then, drill dowel holes through the sides and into the bin.*

## CUT AND ATTACH THE FALSE FRONT FOR THE BIN.

**1.** Cut the false front (F) to length. Plot a grid with 1" squares on the face of it. Use the pattern on page 23 as a guide to draw the cutout shape onto the false front. Make the cutout with a jig saw, and sand the edges smooth.

**2.** Draw a reference line on the inside face of the false front, 1⅝" up from the bottom edge. Attach the false front to the bin front so the bin rides on the reference line. Use glue, and drive 1¼" wood screws through the bin and into the false front **(photo D).**

## INSTALL THE BIN.

**1.** Set the bin onto the bin stop board so it is flush against the front top stretcher and the bin stop. Use spacer blocks and C-clamps to hold the bin in place. Mount a portable drill stand to your portable drill, and drill a ⅜"-dia. × 1⅝"-deep hole through each end panel and into the sides of the bin **(photo E).** The centerpoints of the holes should be 6½" down from the tops of the end panels, and 1¾"

in from the front edges. Remove the C-clamps and the bin.

**2.** Cut the valet top (K) to size. Make the decorative cutout on the front edge using the same pattern and techniques used for the bin false front. (The valet top does not have the small scallop in the center that is cut into the false front.)

**3.** Drill pilot holes through the valet top and into the end panels. Counterbore the holes. Attach the top with glue and 1¼" wood screws. The top overhangs the outside faces of the end panels by 1" and the front edges of the panels by 1¼".

**4.** Cut the scarf box lid (L) to size from the 1 × 12 stock.

## APPLY FINISHING TOUCHES.

**1.** Fill screw holes in the end panels, the box sides and the top with ⅜" wood plugs. Sand flush with the surface. Finish-sand all pieces and apply finish.

**2.** Attach the lid to the box with 2" butt hinges at the back of the lid. Attach one leaf of the hinges to the bottom face of the lid and the other leaf to the back face of the rear box side.

**3.** Cut two 1½" pieces from

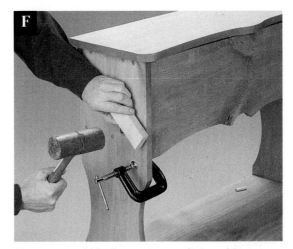

*Using a wood block to prevent splitting, drive dowels into the dowel holes to serve as pivots.*

⅜"-dia. dowel. Squirt a small amount of wood glue into the dowel holes in the bin. Position the bin. Drive the dowels into the holes, using a wood block to prevent splitting **(photo F).** After the glue sets, sand the dowels flush and refinish.

**4.** Cut the valet back (M) to size. Position it so its top edge butts against the bottom of the valet top. Center it side to side. Drive 1" wire nails through the valet back and into the back edges of the top stretcher, bin stop and end panels.

# Mission Window Seat

*Curl up with a good book,
or just enjoy the view from this cozy window seat.*

## CONSTRUCTION MATERIALS

| Quantity | Lumber |
|----------|--------|
| 3 | 1 × 2" × 8' oak |
| 1 | 1 × 2" × 6' oak |
| 1 | 1 × 3" × 6' oak |
| 4 | 1 × 4" × 6' oak |
| 9 | ½ × 1¾" × 4' oak* |
| 1 | ½ × 2¾" × 2' oak* |
| 8 | ½ × 2¾" × 3' oak* |
| 2 | ½ × 2¾" × 4' oak* |
| 1 | ½ × 2¾" × 5' oak* |
| 6 | ½ × 3¾" × 5' oak* |
| 1 | ¾" × 2 × 6' oak plywood |

*Stock sizes commonly available at most wood-
working supply stores.

**Y**ou'll find this Mission-style window seat to be an excellent place to spend an afternoon. Though it fits nicely under a window, the frame is wide enough so you won't ever feel cramped. The length is perfect for taking a nap, enjoying a sunset or watching children playing in the yard. Or perhaps you'd prefer to sit elsewhere to simply admire your craftsmanship from a distance.

The window seat uses oak for its strength and warm texture, and includes a frame face and nosing trim for a more elegant appearance. The rails are capped to make comfortable armrests, and the back is set lower than the sides so it won't block your window view. Though this project has many parts, it requires few tools and is remarkably easy to build. A few hours of labor will reward you with a delightful place to enjoy many hours of relaxation.

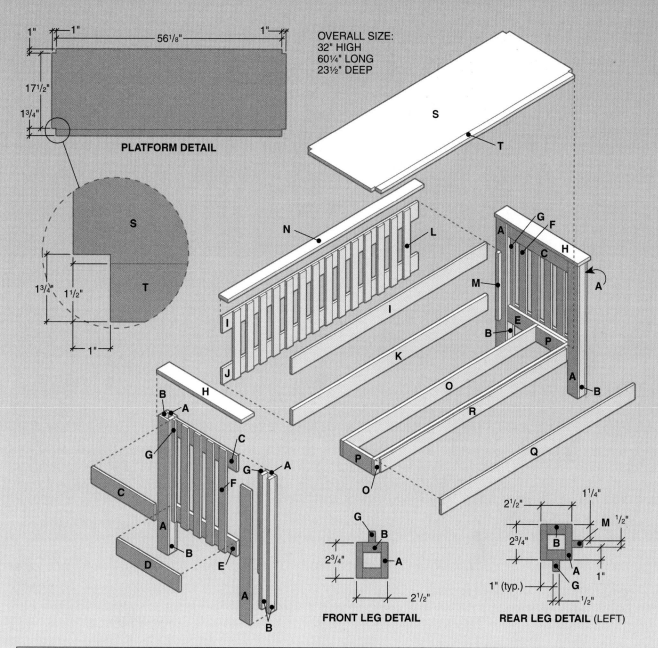

**PLATFORM DETAIL**

OVERALL SIZE:
32" HIGH
60¼" LONG
23½" DEEP

**FRONT LEG DETAIL**

**REAR LEG DETAIL** (LEFT)

**Cutting List**

| Key | Part | Dimension | Pcs. | Material | Key | Part | Dimension | Pcs. | Material |
|-----|------|-----------|------|----------|-----|------|-----------|------|----------|
| **A** | Wide leg piece | ½ × 2¾ × 31¼" | 8 | Oak | **K** | Inner bottom rail | ¾ × 3½ × 54¼" | 1 | Oak |
| **B** | Narrow leg piece | ¾ × 1½ × 31¼" | 8 | Oak | **L** | Back slat | ½ × 1¾ × 15¾" | 14 | Oak |
| **C** | End top rail | ½ × 3¾ × 17½" | 4 | Oak | **M** | Back half slat | ½ × ⅞ × 15¾" | 2 | Oak |
| **D** | Outer bottom rail | ½ × 3¾ × 17½" | 2 | Oak | **N** | Back cap | ¾ × 2½ × 54¼" | 1 | Oak |
| **E** | Inner bottom rail | ¾ × 3½ × 17½" | 2 | Oak | **O** | Support side | ¾ × 3½ × 54¾" | 2 | Oak |
| **F** | End slat | ½ × 1¾ × 23¾" | 8 | Oak | **P** | Support end | ¾ × 3½ × 8" | 2 | Oak |
| **G** | End half slat | ½ × ⅞ × 23¾" | 4 | Oak | **Q** | Frame face | ½ × 3¾ × 54¼" | 1 | Oak |
| **H** | End cap | ¾ × 3½ × 23½" | 2 | Oak | **R** | Spacer | ½ × 2¾ × 52" | 1 | Oak |
| **I** | Back top rail | ½ × 3¾ × 54¼" | 2 | Oak | **S** | Platform | ¾ × 18¾ × 56⅛" | 1 | Plywood |
| **J** | Outer bottom rail | ½ × 3¾ × 54¼" | 1 | Oak | **T** | Platform nosing | ¾ × 1½ × 54⅛" | 1 | Oak |

**Materials:** #6 × ⅝", 1¼" and 1½" wood screws, 16-ga. × 1" brads, 3d finish nails, ¾" oak veneer edge tape (8'), ⅜"-dia. oak plugs, wood glue, finishing materials.

**Note:** Measurements reflect the actual size of dimension lumber.

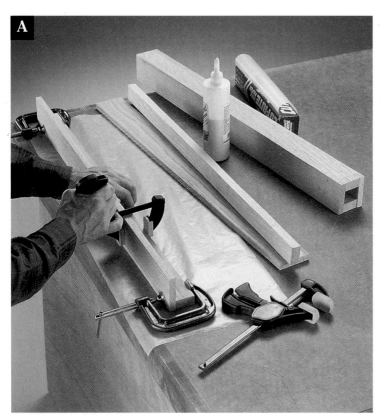

*Assemble the legs with glue and clamps, using wax paper to protect your worksurface.*

*Attach the end slats to the outer rails with glue and wood screws, using a spacer as a guide.*

### Directions:
### Mission Window Seat

For all screws used in this project, drill ³⁄₃₂" pilot holes. Counterbore the holes ¼" deep, using a ⅜" counterbore bit.

ASSEMBLE THE LEGS.
**1.** Cut the wide leg pieces (A) and narrow leg pieces (B) to length.
**2.** For each leg, lay a narrow leg piece on your worksurface. Butt a wide leg piece against an edge to form an "L." Apply wood glue, and clamp the pieces together **(photo A).**
**3.** Assemble and glue together another "L" in the same fashion. Glue the two L-assemblies together to form a leg. Repeat to make the other legs.

BUILD THE END ASSEMBLIES.
To ensure that the end rails and slats remain square during the assembly process, build a simple jig by attaching two 2 × 2 boards at a 90° angle along adjacent edges of a 24 × 48" piece of plywood.
**1.** Cut the end top rails (C), outer bottom rails (D), inner bottom rails (E) and end slats (F) to length. Sand the pieces smooth.
**2.** Place a top rail and an outer bottom rail in the jig. Position two slats over the rails, 2⅝" in

> **T**IP
>
> *Take care to counterbore for all screw heads when building furniture that will be used as seating.*

from each end. Adjust the pieces so the ends of the slats are flush with the edges of the rails, and keep the entire assembly tight against the jig. Attach with glue, and drive ⅝" wood screws through the slats and into the rails.
**3.** Using a 1¾"-wide spacer, attach the remaining end slats with glue and ⅝" wood screws **(photo B).** NOTE: Make sure to test-fit all of the slats for uniform spacing before attaching them to the rails.
**4.** Position an inner bottom rail over the slats, ¼" up from the

Attach the end half slats to the legs with glue and wood screws.

Attach the lower inner rail with glue and screws and the upper inner rail with glue and finish nails.

bottom edges of the slats. Attach it with glue, and drive 1¼" wood screws through the inner bottom rail and the slats.

**5.** Place a top rail over the slats, and attach it with glue and 1" brads.

**6.** Repeat the process to build the other end assembly.

## BUILD THE BACK ASSEMBLY.

**1.** Cut the back top rails (I), the outer bottom rail (J), the inner bottom rail (K) and the back slats (L) to length. Sand the pieces smooth.

**2.** Place a top rail and the inner bottom rail in the jig. Place two back slats on the rails, 2¾" in from each end. Adjust the pieces so the ends of the slats are flush with the edge of the top rail and overhang the edge of the bottom rail by ¼". Attach

the pieces with glue, and drive ⅝" wood screws through the slats and into the rails. Test-fit the remaining slats, spacing them about 1⅞" apart. Attach them with glue and screws.

**3.** Position the outer bottom rail so the edge is flush with the bottom edges of the slats. Attach the bottom rail with glue and 1" brads.

**4.** Place the remaining top rail over the slats. Attach it with glue and 1" brads.

## JOIN THE LEGS TO THE END ASSEMBLIES.

Half slats attached to the legs serve as cleats for attaching the end assembly.

**1.** Cut the end half slats (G) to size from ½ × 2¾" × 4' stock.

**2.** Place each leg on your work-surface with a narrow leg piece

facing up. Center the half slat on the face of the leg (see *Diagram,* page 27), with the top ends flush. Attach the half slats to the legs with glue. Drive 1¼" wood screws, locating them so the screw heads will be hidden by the rails when the seat is completed **(photo C).**

**3.** Position an end assembly between a front and rear leg so the half slats fit between the rails and the top edges are flush. Attach the parts with glue. Drive 1¼" wood screws through the inner bottom rail and into the half slats, taking care to avoid other screws.

**4.** Attach the top rail to the half slats with glue and 3d finish nails driven through ¹⁄₁₆" pilot holes **(photo D).**

**5.** Repeat this process for the other end assembly.

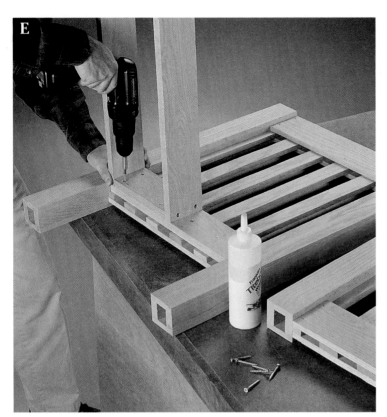

*Attach the support frame with glue, and drive screws through the support end and into the inner bottom rail.*

*Glue the platform nosing to the platform and hold it in place with bar clamps.*

### MAKE THE SUPPORT FRAME.

The support frame attaches to the inner bottom rails on the end assemblies and supports the seat.

**1.** Cut the support sides (O) and ends (P) to length.

**2.** Position the ends between the sides. Join the pieces with glue and 1¼" wood screws.

**3.** Lay one end assembly on your worksurface. Position the support frame upright so the front corner of the frame is tight against the front leg and the edges of the frame are flush with the edges of the bottom rail. Attach the support frame to the end assembly with glue and 1¼" wood screws **(photo E).**

**4.** Stand the window seat upright, and clamp the other end in position. Attach it with glue and 1¼" wood screws.

### ATTACH THE BACK.

Like the end assemblies, the back assembly attaches to the legs with half slats.

**1.** Cut the back half slats (M) to size from ½ × 2¾" × 2' stock.

**2.** On the inside face of each rear leg, measure 7½" up from the bottom, and draw a horizontal line. Measure in 1¼" from the back edge of the leg along this line, and draw a vertical line upward.

**3.** Position a half slat against the leg so its rear edge is on the vertical line and its bottom edge is on the horizontal line. Attach the half slat to the leg with glue and 1¼" wood screws. Repeat this step with the other rear leg.

**4.** With the half slats attached to the rear legs, slide the back assembly over the half slats so the top edges are flush. Attach with glue, and drive 1¼" wood

screws through the inner bottom rail and into the half slats.

**5.** Drill ⅟₁₆" pilot holes, and join the top rail to the back half slats with glue and 3d finish nails.

### ATTACH THE CAPS.

Caps attach to the ends and back of the window seat to create armrests and a backrest.

**1.** Cut the end caps (H) and back cap (N) to length.

**2.** Center the end caps over the end assemblies, with the back edges flush. Attach the pieces with glue, and drive 1½" wood screws through the end caps and into the legs.

**3.** Position the back cap over the back assembly so the front edge is flush with the front edges of the legs. Attach with glue, and drive 1½" wood screws through the back cap and into the top rails.

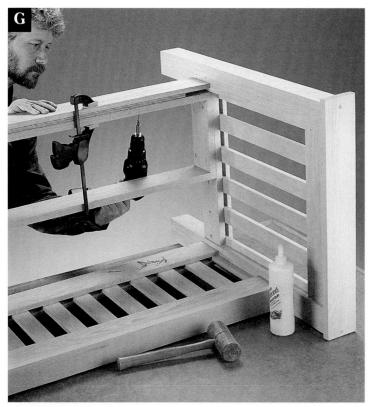

Clamp the spacer and frame face to the support frame. Attach them with glue, and drive screws through the inside of the support frame.

Attach the platform to the rails, frame face and support frame with glue and wood screws.

## MAKE THE PLATFORM.

The oak nosing and edge tape create the appearance of solid wood.

**1.** Cut the platform (S) and platform nosing (T) to size. Sand the top face of the platform smooth.

**2.** Glue the nosing to the front edge of the platform, leaving 1" exposed on each end. Clamp the nosing in place until the glue dries **(photo F)**.

**3.** To accommodate the legs, use a jig saw to cut a 1 × 1" notch in each back corner of the platform and a 1 × 1¾" notch in each front corner (see *Diagram*). Apply self-adhesive oak veneer edge tape to the side and back edges of the platform. (Don't apply tape to the notches.) Lightly sand the edges of the tape.

## ATTACH THE FRAME FACE.

**1.** Cut the frame face (Q) and spacer (R) to length.

**2.** Glue the pieces together, centering the spacer on the frame face. Clamp the pieces together until the glue dries.

**3.** Position the frame face assembly against the front of the support frame so the top edges of the face and support frame are flush. Attach with glue, and drive 1¼" wood screws from inside the support frame **(photo G)**.

## ATTACH THE PLATFORM.

Attach the platform to the support frame, frame face and bottom rails with glue and 1½" wood screws **(photo H)**.

## APPLY FINISHING TOUCHES.

**1.** Fill the screw holes with glued oak plugs. Sand them flush with the surface. Set all nails with a nail set, and fill the nail holes with wood putty. Scrape off any excess glue, and finish-sand the window seat. Apply the stain of your choice and a coat of polyurethane.

**2.** Add seat cushions that complement the wood tones of the window seat and the decorating scheme of your room.

### TIP

*If you find nail holes that were not filled before you applied stain and finish, you can go back and fill the holes with a putty stick that closely matches the color of the wood stain.*

# Behind-the-sofa Bookshelf

*This efficient bookshelf fits right behind your sofa or up against a
wall to provide display space and a useful table surface.*

CONSTRUCTION MATERIALS

| Quantity | Lumber |
|----------|--------|
| 2 | 1 × 10" × 8' aspen |
| 1 | 1 × 8" × 8' aspen |
| 3 | 1 × 4" × 8' aspen |
| 2 | 1 × 2" × 8' aspen |
| 2 | ¾ × 2½" × 8' casing molding |

The space behind your
sofa may not be the first
area that comes to mind
when you're searching for
extra storage, but it does hold
many possibilities for the
space-starved home. This
clever behind-the-sofa bookcase has display space below
and a spacious top that combine to make one slick wood

project. The top is high enough
so it can be used as an auxiliary coffee table, if you don't
mind reaching up for your bev-
erage or snack.

We used aspen to build this
table, then stained it for a natural appearance. If you prefer,
you can build it from pine and
paint it to match or complement your sofa.

OVERALL SIZE:
34" HIGH
59" LONG
9¼" DEEP

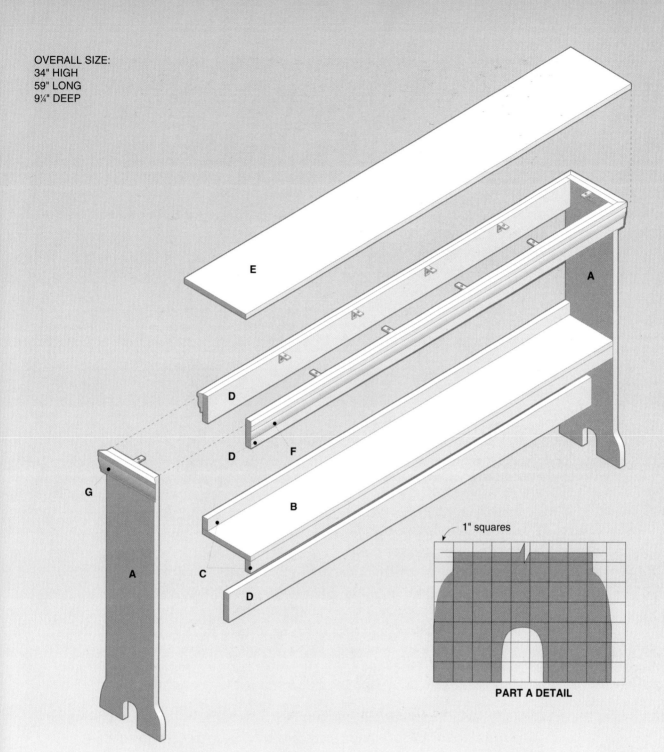

1" squares

PART A DETAIL

### Cutting List

| Key | Part | Dimension | Pcs. | Material |
|-----|------|-----------|------|----------|
| **A** | Leg | ¾ × 9¼ × 33¼" | 2 | Aspen |
| **B** | Shelf | ¾ × 7¼ × 55½" | 1 | Aspen |
| **C** | Shelf rail | ¾ × 1½ × 55½" | 2 | Aspen |
| **D** | Stretcher | ¾ × 3½ × 55½" | 3 | Aspen |

### Cutting List

| Key | Part | Dimension | Pcs. | Material |
|-----|------|-----------|------|----------|
| **E** | Top | ¾ × 9¼ × 59" | 1 | Aspen |
| **F** | Face trim | ¾ × 2½ × *" | 2 | Molding |
| **G** | End trim | ¾ × 2½ × *" | 2 | Molding |

**Materials:** #6 × 1¼" and 2" wood screws, #8 × ½" wood screws, 16-ga. × 1¼" brads, 1½" brass corner braces (10), ⅜"-dia. wood plugs, wood glue, finishing materials.

**Note:** Measurements reflect the actual size of dimension lumber.
**\*Cut to fit**

## Directions:
## Behind-the-sofa Bookshelf

### MAKE THE LEGS.

The decorative cutouts at the bottoms of the legs add style and create feet that add stability.

**1.** Cut the legs (A) to the full size listed in the *Cutting List,* page 33.

**2.** Use the *Part A Detail* pattern as a reference for laying out the cutting lines to form the feet at the bottoms of the legs. You may want to draw a 1"-square grid pattern at the bottom of one of the legs first. Lay out the leg shape on one leg, using a straightedge to make sure the 1" relief cuts that run all the way up the edges of the legs are straight.

**3.** Cut the straight section of one leg with a circular saw and a straightedge guide, and cut the patterned bottom with a jig saw. Sand the edges smooth.

**4.** Trace the profile onto the second leg and cut the shape to match **(photo A).**

### ATTACH THE
### SHELF AND RAILS.

The rails attach to the front and back of the shelf to add strength and to create a lip in back so display items don't fall between the bookcase and the sofa. The front rail fits up against the bottom of the shelf, flush with the front edge. The rear rail fits on the top of the shelf, flush with the back edge.

**1.** Cut the shelf (B) and shelf rails (C) to length.

**2.** Drill rows of ³⁄₃₂" pilot holes for #6 × 1¼" wood screws, ⅜" in from the front and back edges of the shelf, for attaching the rails. Locate the pilot holes at 8" intervals. Using a counterbore bit, counterbore each hole ¼" deep to accept a ⅜"-dia. wood

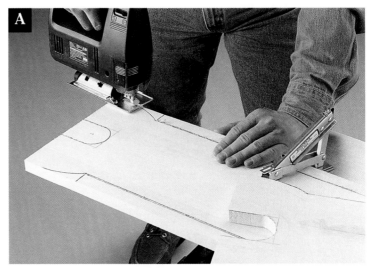

*Draw the shapes for the legs onto pieces of 1 × 10, then cut out the legs with a jig saw. Make the long, straight cuts with a circular saw.*

*Attach the shelf by driving wood screws through counterbored pilot holes in the legs.*

plug. Make sure to drill the rows of counterbores on opposite faces of the shelf.

**3.** Apply glue to the top edge of one rail, and clamp it to the shelf, making sure the front of the rail is flush with the edge of the shelf. Drive 1¼" wood screws through the counterbored pilot holes to secure the rail. Then, attach the other rail to the opposite face of the shelf.

**4.** To attach the shelf and rails to the legs, use a combination square to mark reference lines across one face of each leg, 16"

up from the bottom. Drill pilot holes ⅜" down from the guidelines and counterbore the holes.

**5.** Apply glue to the ends of the shelf and rails, and position them between the legs so the top of the shelf is flush with the reference lines. Drive 2" screws through the legs and into the shelf ends **(photo B).**

Use 1½" corner braces and ½" wood screws to attach the top to the stretchers and the insides of the legs.

## ATTACH THE STRETCHERS.

Three stretchers fit between the legs at the bottom and top to add stability. The top stretchers anchor the top.

**1.** Cut the stretchers (D) to length and sand them smooth.

**2.** Before attaching the stretchers, carefully mark their positions on the inside faces of the legs. Center one stretcher 6" up from the bottoms of the legs. Drill pilot holes through the legs and into the ends of the stretcher. Counterbore the holes. Attach the stretcher with glue and 2" wood screws.

**3.** Attach the remaining two stretchers at the tops of the legs, flush with the front, top and back edges.

## ATTACH THE TOP.

Attach the top to the leg assembly with 1½" brass corner braces. Once the top is fastened, cut the molding to fit, and attach it to the top stretchers and legs to complete the bookshelf.

**1.** Cut the top (E) to length. Sand the top with medium-grit sandpaper to smooth out all of the edges.

**2.** Turn the leg assembly upside down, and position it on the underside of the top. Center the legs to create a 1" overhang on all sides. Clamp the legs to the top. Use #8 × ½" wood screws and corner braces (four per side, one per end) to secure the top to the legs and stretchers **(photo C).**

## INSTALL THE TRIM.

**1.** Cut a piece of 2½" casing molding to about 64" in length to use for one face trim (F) piece.

**2.** Place the molding against a top stringer and mark the ends of the bookcase onto the molding. Make 45° miter cuts away from the marks. Tack the piece in place with a 1¼" brad. Mark and cut the other long trim piece the same way, and tack it in place.

**3.** Use the face trim pieces as references for cutting the end trim (G) pieces to fit.

**4.** Remove the trim pieces, then refasten them with glue, and drive 1¼" brads at regular intervals **(photo D).**

**5.** Drive two brads through each joint to lock-nail the mating trim pieces together. Set all nails with a nail set.

## APPLY FINISHING TOUCHES.

**1.** Glue ⅜"-dia. wood plugs into all screw holes, and sand them flush with the surface. Fill all nail holes with wood putty.

**2.** Finish-sand the bookcase with 180- or 220-grit sandpaper. Apply the finish of your choice. We used mahogany-tone stain and two coats of polyurethane.

Wrap the bookcase with trim pieces made from 2½" casing molding.

# Two-tier Bookshelf

*Here's a smart-looking, easy-to-build project
that requires no glue, screws or nails!*

## CONSTRUCTION MATERIALS

| Quantity | Lumber |
|----------|--------|
| 1 | ¾" × 4 × 8' Baltic birch plywood |
| 1 | 1" × 2' birch dowel |

This two-tier bookshelf provides ample room for encyclopedias, dictionaries and other useful references. Its distinctive profile complements many decorating motifs, and with the right finish, this project can become a vibrant accent piece. The bookshelf uses an unusual joinery method, known as *pinned mortise-and-tenon*, that requires no glue, screws or nails. Instead, wedges hold the joints together. When moving or storing the unit, you can simply remove the wedges.

With the included plan for a mortising jig, you can easily make several of these bookshelves to give as gifts.

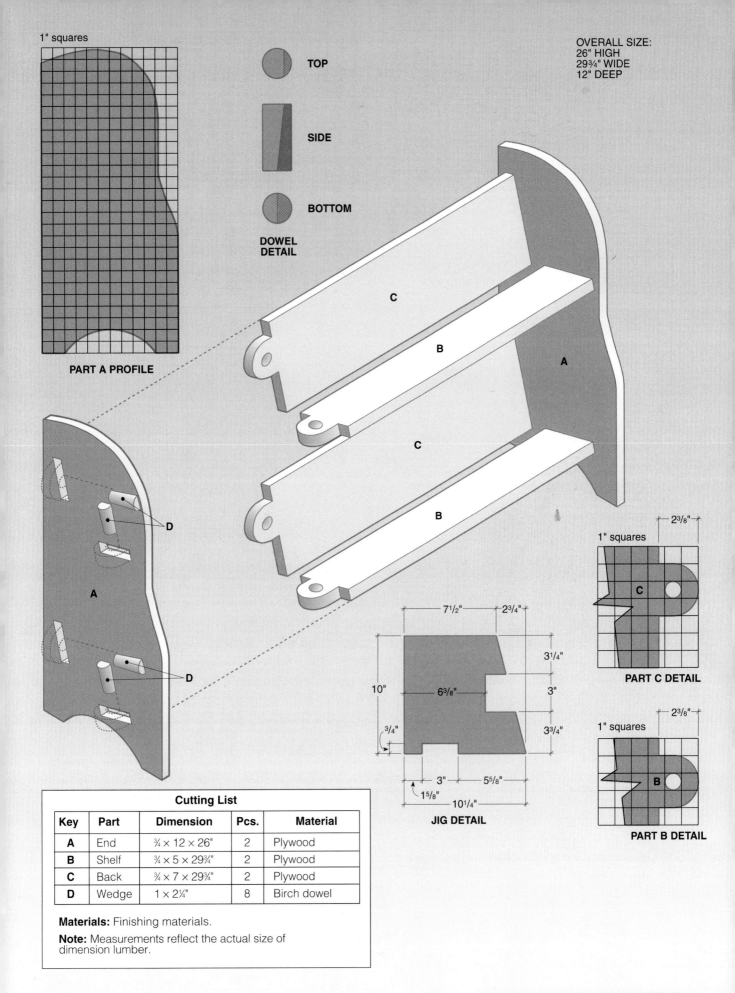

**1" squares**

**PART A PROFILE**

TOP

SIDE

BOTTOM

**DOWEL DETAIL**

C

B

A

C

B

D

A

D

**1" squares**

2³/₈"

C

**PART C DETAIL**

**1" squares**

2³/₈"

B

**PART B DETAIL**

**JIG DETAIL**

7½"    2¾"

3¼"

10"     6³/₈"     3"

¾"

3³/₄"

3"    5⁵/₈"

1⁵/₈"

10¼"

### Cutting List

| Key | Part | Dimension | Pcs. | Material |
|-----|------|-----------|------|----------|
| **A** | End | ¾ × 12 × 26" | 2 | Plywood |
| **B** | Shelf | ¾ × 5 × 29¾" | 2 | Plywood |
| **C** | Back | ¾ × 7 × 29¾" | 2 | Plywood |
| **D** | Wedge | 1 × 2¼" | 8 | Birch dowel |

**Materials:** Finishing materials.

**Note:** Measurements reflect the actual size of dimension lumber.

## Directions:
## Two-tier Bookshelf

### MAKE THE JIG.
A jig will help you accurately mark the location of mortises.
**1.** Cut a 10 × 10¼" blank from ¼" scrap material.
**2.** Measure and mark the diagonal line and the locations for the mortise guides (see *Diagram*, page 37). Use a jig saw to cut out the jig **(photo A)**.

### CUT THE ENDS.
**1.** Cut the end blanks (A) to size.
**2.** Transfer the pattern (see *Diagram*), and cut with a jig saw.
**3.** Lay both ends on your workbench with the back edges together, forming a mirror image. Measure from the bottom back corners and mark reference points at ⅞" and 14¾" **(photo B).**

> **TIP**
>
> *To yield an opening large enough to accommodate the tenons, make sure the mortises on your pattern are slightly oversized.*

**4.** Lay out the mortises by positioning the bottom back corner of the jig at the first reference point, keeping the back edges flush. Outline the two lower mortises. Slide the jig up to the second reference point, and mark the two higher mortises **(photo C).**
**5.** Remove the jig, and draw lines to close the ¾ × 3" rectangles. Drill starter holes, using a backer board. Cut the mortises with a jig saw **(photo D).**

### CUT THE SHELVES AND BACKS.
**1.** Cut the shelves (B) and backs (C) to size.
**2.** Lay out the profile for the tenons (see *Diagram*), and cut them out with a jig saw. Sand the edges smooth.

*Use a piece of ¼" scrap plywood and your jig saw to create the mortising jig.*

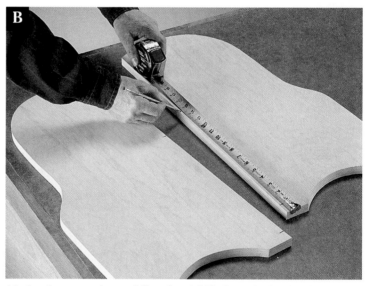

*Mark reference points at ⅞" and at 14¾" along the backs of both sides as guides for positioning the mortising jig.*

**3.** Drill wedge holes with a backer board and a 1" spade bit. Test-fit the tenons in the mortises. Adjust them if necessary.

### MAKE THE WEDGES.
**1.** Create wedges (D) by cutting 1"-dia. dowels to 2¼" lengths.
**2.** Measure from the edge, and mark reference lines across the top of the dowel at ¼" and across the bottom at ½". Connect the lines. Sand the dowels down to this line, using a belt

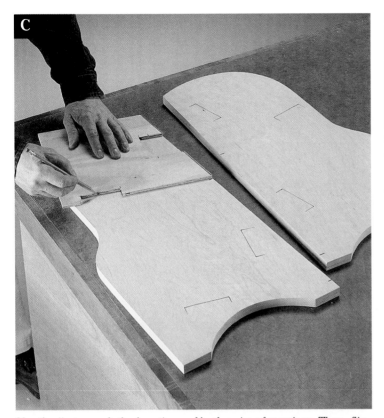

*Use the jig to mark the locations of both pairs of mortises. Then, flip the jig and mark corresponding mortises on the other end piece.*

*Drill pilot holes, using a backer board to prevent splintering, and cut the mortises with a jig saw.*

sander clamped horizontally to your worksurface **(photo E)**.

**3.** Assemble the shelves and backs between the ends, and test-fit the wedges. Disassemble the bookshelf for finishing.

APPLY FINISHING TOUCHES. Finish-sand the entire project. Then, paint or finish the bookshelf as desired. A light oil finish or bold aniline dye are both suitable. When the finish dries, assemble the pieces.

*Sand the wedges to the lines, using a belt sander clamped to your worksurface.*

# Liquor Locker

*Store spirits of all varieties safely under lock and key in this beautiful oak cabinet.*

Compact and elegant, this liquor locker provides protected storage for liquor or cordials, without looking like a bank safe. Made from oak and oak plywood, this functional furnishing has a formal style that features arched cabinet doors. A simple cylinder lock installed in one of the door frames keeps your alcohol products away from curious young hands.

The main compartment in the liquor locker is sized to hold several full-size bottles of your favorite liquors, cordials and aperitifs. A narrow shelf in the back of the compartment is perfect for storing mixers that usually come in smaller bottles, like bitters, vermouth or lime juice. Or, you can stow glassware on the shelf. The top of the cabinet is made from oak plywood. It is large enough to provide ample surface area for preparing or serving after-dinner drinks in your den.

To accentuate the natural tones of the red oak, we did not stain the wood but applied a clear topcoat of water-based polyurethane. When choosing a topcoat product, note that alcohol will dissolve products like shellac and paste wax.

## CONSTRUCTION MATERIALS

| Quantity | Lumber |
|---|---|
| 1 | ¾" × 4 × 8' oak plywood |
| 1 | ½" × 2 × 4' oak plywood |
| 1 | 1 × 2" × 8' oak |
| 1 | 1 × 4" × 6' oak |
| 2 | 2 × 2" × 8' oak |
| 1 | ¾ × ¾" × 6' cove molding |
| 2 | ¾ × ¾" × 8' base shoe molding |

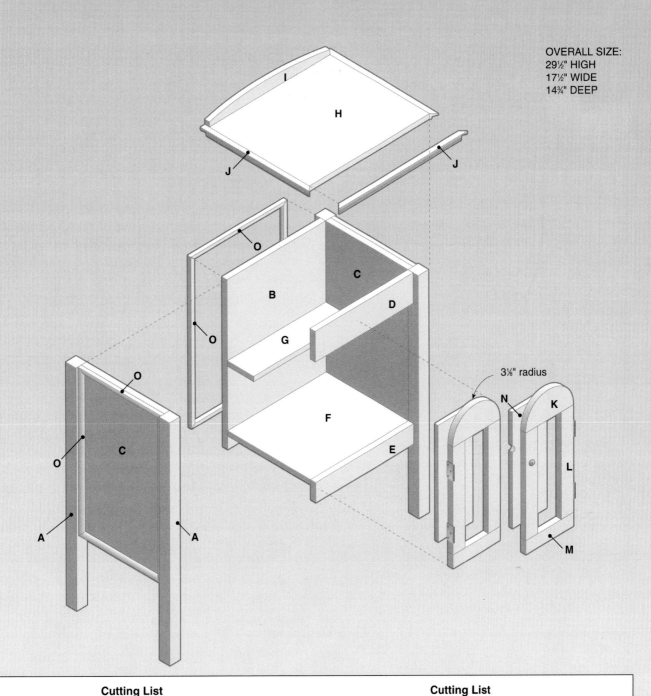

OVERALL SIZE:
29½" HIGH
17½" WIDE
14¾" DEEP

3⅛" radius

| Cutting List | | | | | | Cutting List | | | |
|---|---|---|---|---|---|---|---|---|---|
| **Key** | **Part** | **Dimension** | **Pcs.** | **Material** | | **Key** | **Part** | **Dimension** | **Pcs.** | **Material** |
| **A** | Leg | 1½ × 1½ × 27¼" | 4 | Oak | | **I** | Backsplash | ¾ × 1½ × 16" | 1 | Oak |
| **B** | Back panel | ¾ × 13 × 19¼" | 1 | Plywood | | **J** | Top molding | ¾ × ¾ × *" | 3 | Cove molding |
| **C** | Side panel | ¾ × 11 × 19¼" | 2 | Plywood | | **K** | Top door rail | ¾ × 3½ × 6¼" | 2 | Oak |
| **D** | Top rail | ¾ × 3½ × 13" | 1 | Oak | | **L** | Door stile | ¾ × 1½ × 12" | 4 | Oak |
| **E** | Bottom rail | ¾ × 2 × 13" | 1 | Oak | | **M** | Lower door rail | ¾ × 1½ × 6¼" | 2 | Oak |
| **F** | Bottom panel | ¾ × 11 × 13" | 1 | Plywood | | **N** | Door panel | ½ × 4¼ × 13" | 2 | Plywood |
| **G** | Shelf | ¾ × 3½ × 13" | 1 | Oak | | **O** | Side trim | ⅜ × ¾ × *" | 12 | Base shoe molding |
| **H** | Top panel | ¾ × 14 × 16" | 1 | Plywood | | | | | | |

**Materials:** #6 × 1¼", 2" and 2½" brass wood screws, 8d finish nails, 16-ga. × ¾" and 1¼" brass brads, 16-ga. × 1" wire nails, 2" brass corner braces (6), 1½ × 3" brass hinges (4), cylinder lock hardware, elbow catches (2), ⅜"-dia. oak plugs, wood glue, finishing materials.

**Note:** Measurements reflect the actual size of dimension lumber.
*Cut to fit.

## Directions:
## Liquor Locker

Oak plugs will conceal the screw holes, so counterbore all visible pilot holes ¼" deep, using a ⅜" counterbore bit.

### MAKE THE CABINET SECTION.

**1.** Cut the legs (A), back panel (B) and side panels (C) to size.
**2.** Arrange the legs in pairs. Position a side panel between the legs in each pair. One short edge of each side panel should be flush with the tops of the legs. The inside face of the panel should be flush with the inside edges of the legs. Drill ³⁄₃₂" pilot holes through the legs and into the edges of the side panels. Attach the sides between the legs with glue and 2½" wood screws.
**3.** Set the back panel on your worksurface, supported by ¾"-thick scraps. Butt the leg pairs against the edges of the back panel, making sure the tops are flush. Apply glue, and clamp the leg pairs to the back panel with bar or pipe clamps. Attach the legs to the back with 2½" wood screws **(photo A).**
**4.** Cut the top rail (D), bottom rail (E) and bottom panel (F) to size.
**5.** Fasten the top rail between the legs with glue and 2½" wood screws, with the top and inside edges flush.
**6.** Attach the bottom rail to the front edge of the bottom panel with glue and 2" wood screws, keeping the tops flush.
**7.** Apply glue to the edges of the bottom panel and bottom rail. Insert them into the cabinet. The top edge of the bottom rail should be 10¼" up from the bottoms of the legs. Drill pilot holes, and fasten the bottom panel and bottom rail with 2" wood screws. Like the sides, back and top rail, the front face of the bottom rail should be ¾" back from the outsides of the legs. Measure diagonally from corner to corner to make sure the cabinet is square **(photo B).**
**8.** Cut the shelf (G) to length.
**9.** Position the shelf so the bottom face is 7" up from the bottom panel. Attach the shelf with glue, and drive 1¼" wood screws through the back and side panels.

### MAKE THE TOP.

**1.** Cut the top panel (H) and backsplash (I) to size.
**2.** The peak of the curved backsplash, located at the midpoint, should be 1½" up from the bottom edge. To draw a smooth curve onto the backsplash, drive a finish nail partway into the board at the peak of the curve, then drive nails at the starting points of the curve, ½" up from the bottom edge of

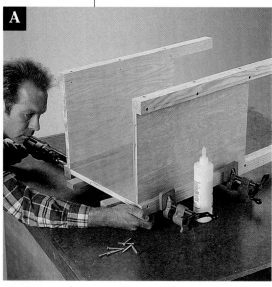

*Set the back panel on spacers, clamp it between the rear legs and fasten it with glue and wood screws.*

*Measure from corner to corner to check for square. If the project isn't square, apply pressure to one side or the other until it is square.*

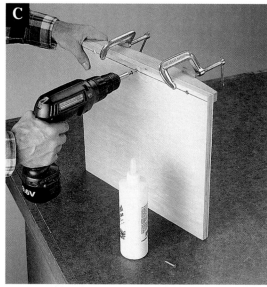

*Apply glue, clamp the backsplash in place and attach it to the top.*

the backsplash. Slip a flexible straightedge behind the nails at the starting points and in front of the nail at the peak to create a smooth curve. Trace along the inside of the straightedge. Cut the curve with a jig saw, and sand it smooth.

**3.** Clamp the backsplash to the top panel so the ends and back edges are flush. Drill pilot holes, apply glue, and fasten the backsplash to the top with 1¼" wood screws **(photo C).**

**4.** Cut the top molding (J) to length, miter-cutting the front ends of the side pieces and both ends of the front piece.

**5.** Apply glue to the top molding and attach it with 1¼" brads, forming miter joints at the front corners. Drill ⅟₁₆" pilot holes through the molding to prevent splitting.

**6.** Center the top panel over the cabinet, with the back edges flush. Clamp the top in place, and secure it with six 2" brass corner braces, spaced evenly on the inside faces of the side and back panels.

## MAKE THE DOORS.

**1.** Cut the top door rails (K) to length.

**2.** Use a compass to draw a 3⅛"-radius semicircle on each rail, centered ⅜" up from the bottom edge of the rail. The tops of the semicircles should just touch the top edges of the boards. Cut along the semicircles with a jig saw. Gang-sand both arches smooth with a belt sander to remove saw marks.

**3.** Cut the door stiles (L) and lower door rails (M) to length.

**4.** Drill pilot holes through the bottom edges of the door rails and into the door stiles. Counterbore the holes. Attach the lower door rails to the bottoms

of the door stiles with glue and 2" wood screws.

**5.** Position the semicompleted frame on your worksurface. Butt the arched rails against the free ends of the door stiles. Apply glue, and clamp the frame together with bar clamps. Check to make sure it is square. Drill ⁵⁄₆₄" pilot holes, and attach the arched top rails to the door stiles by driving 8d finish nails through the tops of the rails and into the door stiles **(photo D).**

**6.** When the glue has dried, drill a hole for a cylinder lock through the front face of one door stile, using a backer board to prevent splintering when the bit exits the stile on the other side. The lock hardware we used required a ⅞"-dia. hole, 3½" below the bottom of the arched rail.

**7.** Cut the door panels (N) to size and sand them smooth.

**8.** Draw reference lines on the back face of each door frame, ½" in from the inside edges. Position the panels within these lines. To accommodate the lock hole on one frame, cut a notch in the panel with a jig saw. Attach the panels with glue and 1" wire nails.

## APPLY FINISHING TOUCHES.

**1.** Cut the side trim (O) pieces to length from ¾" base shoe molding. Miter-cut the ends at 45° angles to make miter joints at the corners.

**2.** Drill ⅟₁₆" pilot holes through the molding pieces to prevent splitting. Attach the trim with glue and ¾" brads so it butts against the sides and legs and runs along the bottom and top edges of each side. Also frame the back panel with base shoe molding. Set all nails with a nail set, and fill the nail holes with

wood putty. Fill all screw holes with ⅜" oak plugs, and sand the plugs flush with the surface. Finish-sand the project.

**3.** Install two brass 1½ × 3" hinges on each door, 1" in from the ends of the stiles. Fasten the hinges to the legs, making sure the doors overlap the bottom rail by ¾". Install the lock. Fasten elbow catches at the top and bottom to secure the door without the lock **(photo E).**

**4.** Cover the hardware with masking tape and apply the finish of your choice.

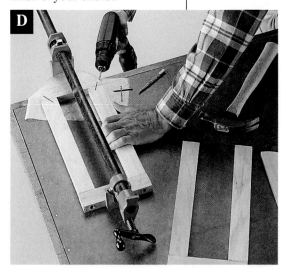

*Drill pilot holes, and drive 8d finish nails through the joint between the arch and stiles.*

*Attach elbow catches to the door that does not contain the lock.*

# Humidor Cabinet

*Keep cigars and pipe tobacco fresh inside this attractive humidor cabinet.*

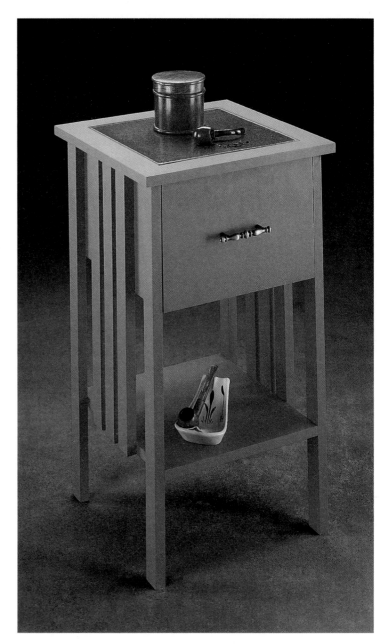

Increasing numbers of people today are allowing themselves the simple luxury of a fine cigar after a meal or a bowl of pipe tobacco enjoyed with a snifter of cognac or sherry. The social ritual of the after-dinner cigar in the living room or study is a large part of the appeal for today's casual smokers. With that appeal in mind (as well as the desire to keep tobacco products fresh), we've designed this humidor cabinet.

The humidor is a traditional home furnishing. Its distinguishing characteristics are a lined compartment that traps moist air—preventing tobacco from becoming dry and stale—as well as a heat-resistant top for holding ashtrays.

This humidor cabinet differs from most in that the tobacco compartment is removable. Creating a sealable compartment with a hinged door is difficult unless you want to use complex woodworking joinery. Instead, we built a separate, simple compartment that seals in moisture, and is then inserted into the cabinet.

## CONSTRUCTION MATERIALS

| Quantity | Lumber |
|----------|--------|
| 1 | ¾" × 4 × 4' plywood |
| 4 | 1 × 2" × 6' aspen |
| 1 | ½ × 7" × 3' aspen panel |

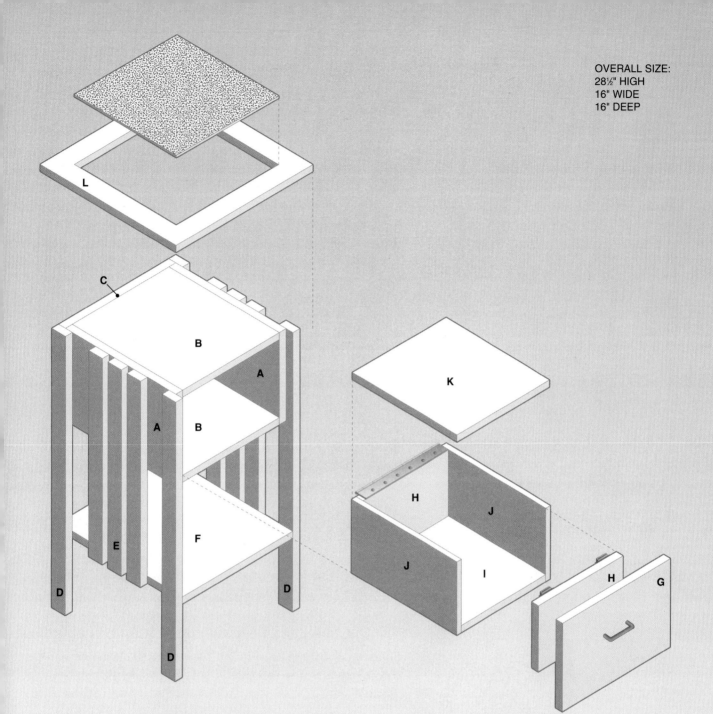

## Cutting List

| Key | Part | Dimension | Pcs. | Material |
|-----|------|-----------|------|----------|
| A | Side panel | ¾ × 9 × 13" | 2 | Plywood |
| B | Cabinet panel | ¾ × 11½ × 13" | 2 | Plywood |
| C | Back panel | ¾ × 9 × 13" | 1 | Plywood |
| D | Leg | ¾ × 1½ × 27¾" | 4 | Aspen |
| E | Slat | ¾ × 1½ × 20½" | 6 | Aspen |
| F | Shelf | ¾ × 13 × 14½" | 1 | Plywood |

## Cutting List

| Key | Part | Dimension | Pcs. | Material |
|-----|------|-----------|------|----------|
| G | Box front | ¾ × 8¾ × 12¾" | 1 | Plywood |
| H | Box end | ¾ × 5⅝ × 10" | 2 | Plywood |
| I | Box bottom | ¾ × 10 × 12½" | 1 | Plywood |
| J | Box side | ½ × 6⅜ × 12½" | 2 | Aspen |
| K | Box lid | ¾ × 11 × 12⅜" | 1 | Plywood |
| L | Top frame | ¾ × 16 × 16" | 1 | Plywood |

**Materials:** #6 × 1", 1¼" and 2" wood screws, 3d finish nails, chest handle, drawer pull, light-duty brass piano hinge (10"), tack-on drawer glides, magnetic catches (2), ¾" paintable edge tape (10'), wood glue, finishing materials, 12 × 12" ceramic floor tile, tinted grout, multipurpose thin-set mortar.
**Specialty tools:** V-notch adhesive trowel, grout float.
**Note:** Measurements reflect the actual size of dimension lumber.

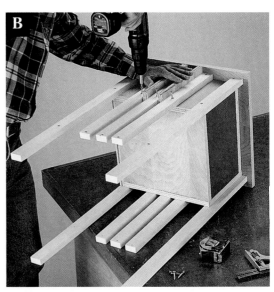

*Fasten the back panel to the side and end panels with glue and wood screws.*

*Use scrap spacers to maintain consistent gaps between the slats.*

## Directions:
## Humidor Cabinet

### MAKE THE CASE.
For all screws used in this project, drill ⁵⁄₆₄" pilot holes. Counterbore the holes ⅛" deep, using a ⅜" counterbore bit.

**1.** Cut the side panels (A), cabinet panels (B), back panel (C) and top frame (L) to size.

**2.** Use a household iron to apply self-adhesive edge tape to one short edge of each side and cabinet panel, and all four edges of the top frame. Trim and sand the taped edges smooth.

**3.** The top frame holds a piece of ceramic tile. Before marking the cutout on the top frame, measure the tile, and add ¼" to each dimension for the cutout. Use a combination square to draw cutting lines across the top frame, an equal distance in from each edge. Drill a starter hole inside the cutting lines, and make the cutout with a jig saw.

**4.** Draw reference lines on the top frame, 1½" in from the front and back edges, to help you position a cabinet panel beneath it. Apply glue, and position a cabi-

net panel against the top frame inside the reference lines and centered side to side. Drive 3d finish nails through the cabinet panel and into the top frame. Set the nails with a nail set.

**5.** Position the remaining cabinet panel between the side panels so the edges are flush. Attach with glue and drive 2" wood screws through the side panels and into the edges of the cabinet panel. NOTE: Arrange the screws so the heads will be covered by the legs and slats later in the assembly process (see *Diagram*, page 45).

**6.** Position the top frame onto the sides, and drive 2" wood screws through the side panels and into the edges of the cabinet panel.

**7.** Fasten the back panel to the side and cabinet panels with glue and 2" wood screws **(photo A).**

### BUILD THE STAND.
A shelf fastened between the legs helps stabilize the cabinet and adds a small storage space.

**1.** Cut the legs (D), slats (E)

and shelf (F) to size.

**2.** Apply edge tape to all of the shelf edges. Trim and sand the taped edges smooth.

**3.** Designate a top and bottom end on each leg. Draw a reference line across each leg 7¼" up from the bottom end.

**4.** Attach the legs and slats to the side panels with glue and 1¼" wood screws. Make sure the front legs overhang the front edges of the side panels by ¾". The back legs must be flush with the back face of the case. The legs and slats should butt up against the underside of the top. Center the slats between the legs, and use ¾"-thick scrap spacers to maintain even gaps between the slats as you attach them **(photo B).**

**5.** Position the shelf between the legs so its bottom face is flush with the reference lines. Attach it with 2" wood screws.

### MAKE THE HUMIDOR BOX.
The humidor box is enclosed and has a hinged top. To gain access to its contents, just pull the humidor box out of the case, and open the top.

A 10"-long piano hinge joins the box lid to the box end.

**TIP**

*Maintain the humidity in your humidor by keeping a damp sponge or a dish of water inside. If you want to monitor the humidity level closely, gauges for humidors are available at specialty stores.*

**1.** Cut the box front (G), box ends (H), box bottom (I), box sides (J) and box lid (K) to size.
**2.** Apply edge tape to all of the box front edges, box lid edges and one box bottom edge.
**3.** Position a box end face to face against the box front. Make sure the box end is centered on the box front. Fasten it with glue, and drive 1" wood screws through the box end and into the box front.
**4.** Set the box bottom on your worksurface. Position a box side squarely against one long edge with the ends flush. Fasten the box side with glue, and drive 1¼" wood screws through the box side and into the edge of the box bottom.
**5.** Attach the remaining box side, using the same method.
**6.** Set the remaining box end between the box sides. The outside face of the box end should be flush with the ends of the box sides and box bottom. Fasten the box end with glue and 1¼" wood screws.
**7.** Position the box sides against the box front. The front box end should fit between the box sides

and butt against the face of the box bottom. Apply glue, and fasten the front in place by driving 1¼" wood screws through the sides and into the box end.
**8.** Center a 10"-long piano hinge at the end of the box lid. The barrel of the hinge should be aligned with one short edge of the box lid. Fasten the hinge to the box lid, and attach the box lid to the rear box end **(photo C).**

APPLY FINISHING TOUCHES.
**1.** Fill all nail holes and screw holes with wood putty. Sand the surfaces smooth, and apply the finish of your choice.
**2.** Mount magnetic catches on the inside of the front box end and corresponding plates on the box lid. Attach a drawer-pull handle to the front of the humidor box and a chest handle to the rear end. Install drawer glides inside the cabinet to allow the humidor box to slide easily **(photo D).**
**3.** If you want the tile top to be flush with the frame, attach a piece of ¼"-thick plywood to the top cabinet panel. Mix thin-

set mortar, and apply a ⅜"-thick layer with a V-notch trowel. Set the tile into the mortar bed. Let the mortar dry overnight. Fill the gaps between the tile and top frame with tinted grout. Mask the frame before applying the grout.
**4.** To contain moisture effectively inside the humidor, line the box with light-gauge copper or tileboard, fastened to the inside walls of the box with construction adhesive.

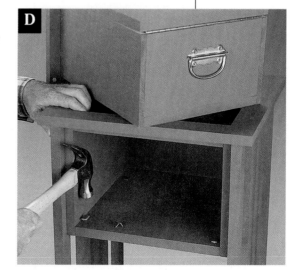

*Tack the drawer glides in place inside the case, allowing the humidor box to slide in and out easily.*

# Tile-top Coffee Table

*The dramatic, contrasting textures of floor tiles and warm red oak
will make you forget that this table is designed to create storage.*

## CONSTRUCTION MATERIALS

| Quantity | Lumber |
| --- | --- |
| 1 | ¾" × 4 × 8' oak plywood |
| 2 | 1 × 2" × 8' oak |
| 2 | 1 × 4" × 8' oak |
| 1 | ⅛ × ⅞" × 8' oak corner molding |

Functionally, the trim size and the amply proportioned storage shelf are the two most important features of this tile-top coffee table. But most people won't notice that. They'll be too busy admiring the striking tile tabletop and the clean oak lines of the table base.

Measuring a convenient 45" long × 20¼" wide, this coffee table will fit nicely even in smaller rooms. The shelf below is ideal for storing books,

magazines, newspapers, photo albums or anything else you want to keep within arm's reach when sitting on your sofa.

We used 6 × 6" ceramic floor tiles for our coffee table, but you can use just about any type or size of floor tile you want— just be sure to use floor tile, not wall tile, which is thinner and can fracture more easily.

After you've built this tile-top coffee table, you may like it so much that you'll want to build a tile-top end table to match.

OVERALL SIZE:
16" HIGH
20¼" WIDE
45" LONG

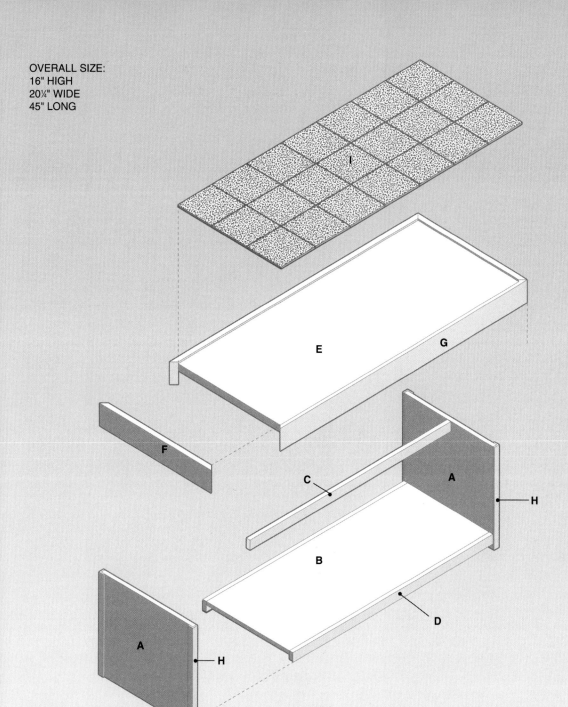

## Cutting List

| Key | Part | Dimension | Pcs. | Material |
|-----|------|-----------|------|----------|
| **A** | Side panel | ¾ × 16 × 15" | 2 | Plywood |
| **B** | Shelf panel | ¾ × 14½ × 35" | 1 | Plywood |
| **C** | Stringer | ¾ × 1½ × 35" | 1 | Oak |
| **D** | Shelf edge | ¾ × 1½ × 35" | 2 | Oak |
| **E** | Top panel | ¾ × 18¾ × 43½" | 1 | Plywood |

## Cutting List

| Key | Part | Dimension | Pcs. | Material |
|-----|------|-----------|------|----------|
| **F** | End skirt | ¾ × 3½ × 20¼" | 2 | Oak |
| **G** | Side skirt | ¾ × 3½ × 45" | 2 | Oak |
| **H** | Corner trim | ⅞ × ⅞ × 15" | 4 | Corner molding |
| **I** | Table tiles | ¼ × 6 × 6" | 21 | Ceramic |
|  |  |  |  |  |

**Materials:** #6 × 1½" wood screws, 3d and 6d finish nails, ⅜"-dia. oak plugs, wood glue, finishing materials, ceramic floor tiles (21), ceramic tile adhesive, tinted grout, ³⁄₁₆" plastic tile spacers, silicone grout sealer.

**Specialty tools:** V-notch adhesive trowel, rubber mallet, grout float.

**Note:** Measurements reflect the actual size of dimension lumber.

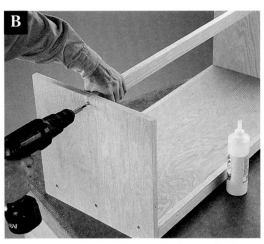

Fasten the shelf edges to the shelf panel with glue and 6d finish nails.

Secure the stringer in place with glue and screws.

## Directions:
## Tile-top Coffee Table

ASSEMBLE THE
TABLE BASE.

**1.** Cut the side panels (A) and shelf panel (B) to size using a circular saw and a straightedge as a cutting guide. Sand the faces of the plywood smooth with medium-grit sandpaper.
**2.** Cut the shelf edges (D) to length.
**3.** Fasten the shelf edges to the shelf panel with glue and 6d finish nails **(photo A).** Be sure to drill ³⁄₃₂" pilot holes through the edge pieces so you don't split them. Keep the top surfaces of the shelf edges and shelf panel flush when fastening.
**4.** Position the shelf upright, and set the shelf edging on ¾"-thick spacers. Stand a side panel upright on its bottom edge, against the end of the shelf panel. Keep

Miter-cut and attach one skirt board at a time to ensure a proper fit.

the edges of the side panel flush with the outside surfaces of the shelf edging. Drill ⁵⁄₆₄" pilot holes through the side panels and into the edges of the shelf panel. Counterbore the holes ¼" deep, using a ⅜" counterbore bit. Fasten the side panel to the shelf panel with glue and 1½" wood screws. Fasten the other side panel to the shelf panel.
**5.** Cut the stringer (C) to length.
**6.** Position the stringer between the side panels, flush with the top edges and centered midway across the side panels. Clamp it in place with a bar or pipe clamp. Drill pilot holes through the side panels and into the stringer. Counterbore the holes.

Remove the clamps and secure the stringer with glue and 1½" wood screws **(photo B).**

MAKE THE
TABLETOP FRAME.

The tabletop frame is a plywood panel framed with 1 × 4 oak. The joints in the 1 × 4 frame are mitered—you can use most manual miter boxes to cut a 1 × 4 placed on edge, but a power miter box is ideal for the job.

**1.** Cut the top panel (E) to size, using a circular saw and a straightedge as a cutting guide.
**2.** Position the top panel on the side panels. Be sure to leave an equal overhang on the ends

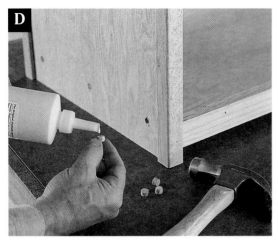
Fill all visible screw holes with oak plugs.

Tap the tiles lightly with a rubber mallet to set them firmly in the adhesive.

and sides. Drill pilot holes through the top panel and into the side panels and stringer. Counterbore the holes. Fasten with glue and 1½" wood screws.

**3.** Cut the end skirts (F) and side skirts (G) to length. Although the *Cutting List* on page 49 gives exact dimensions for these parts, your safest bet is to cut the first part slightly longer than specified. Then, custom-cut it to fit. Cut all the other skirt boards to length, using the first board as a guide **(photo C).**

**4.** Using a tile as a gauge, position the skirt pieces to create a lip slightly higher than the top of the tile. Drill pilot holes through the skirt boards, and fasten the boards to the edges of the top panel with glue and 6d finish nails.

## FASTEN THE CORNER TRIM.

**1.** Cut the corner trim (H) pieces to length.

**2.** Fasten the corner trim to the side panel edges with glue and 3d finish nails—be sure to drill ⅟₁₆" pilot holes through the trim pieces to prevent splitting.

## FINISH THE WOOD.

For clean results, perform the finishing steps on the table be-

fore installing the tile.

**1.** Fill all visible screw holes with oak plugs, and sand them flush with the surface **(photo D).** Finish-sand the entire coffee table, and apply sanding sealer to all exposed surfaces, except the top panel. Let the sealer dry thoroughly. Then, lightly sand the sealed surfaces with 180- or 220-grit sandpaper.

**2.** Apply stain to the sealed oak surfaces, if desired. Then, apply two or three light coats of polyurethane.

## INSTALL THE CERAMIC TOP.

**1.** Once the finish has dried, mask off the top edges of the skirts to protect the finished surfaces.

**2.** Test-fit the table tiles (I). Apply a layer of tile adhesive over the entire table surface, using a V-notch adhesive trowel. Line the borders of the table surface with plastic spacers. (We used ³⁄₁₆" spacers with 6" ceramic floor tile to make a surface that fits inside the tabletop frame.)

**3.** Begin setting tiles into the adhesive, working in straight lines. Insert plastic spacers between tiles to maintain an even gap. Tap each tile lightly with a rubber mallet to set it into the

adhesive **(photo E).** Once the tiles have been set in place, remove the spacers, and let the adhesive set overnight.

**4.** Use a grout float to apply a layer of grout to the tile surface so it fills the gaps between tiles **(photo F).** Wipe excess grout from the tile faces. Let the grout dry for about 30 minutes (check manufacturer's directions). Wipe off the grout film from the tiles with a damp sponge, wiping diagonally across the grout joints. Let the grout set for at least a week. Then, apply silicone grout sealer to the grout joints, following manufacturer's directions.

Use a grout float to apply tile grout in the gaps between tiles in the tabletop.

# Plant Stand

*Our plant stand is a great way to display your favorite potted foliage. Build it for a corner in your sunniest room.*

This plant stand is a perfect platform on which to set your favorite indoor plants. The simple lines and ceramic tile surfaces help focus the attention on the plants themselves, rather than on the stand. Make no mistake, however—our plant stand has a sleek design that fits almost any

environment or decor. Once you paint it, you can position it almost anywhere to showcase your plants. It's lightweight, so you can move it easily from place to place. But it's strong enough to support heavy pots without fear of a shattering experience.

The leg assemblies provide a sturdy base, while ceramic tile inserts on the shelf and top give

our plant stand some weight and stability. It's perfect for a corner nook in a sun room or kitchen, and the tile pieces make cleaning up spills an easy task. What's more, the ceramic tile will not fall apart or rot due to moisture and aging. So, you are sure to enjoy this original and practical plant stand for many years.

## CONSTRUCTION MATERIALS

| Quantity | Lumber |
|----------|--------|
| 1 | 1 × 8" × 4' pine |
| 2 | 1 × 3" × 10' pine |
| 1 | ¼ × 1" × 8' pine stop molding |
| 1 | ½" × 2 × 2' plywood |

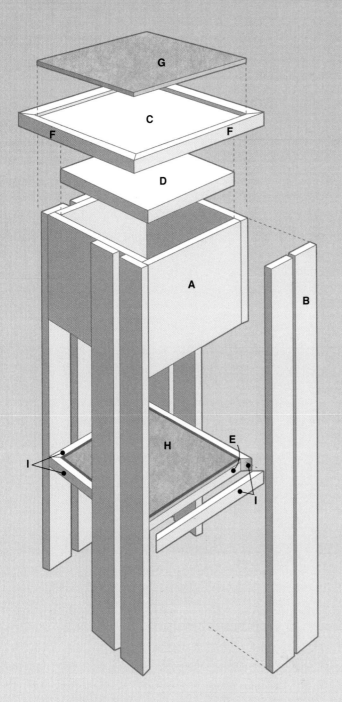

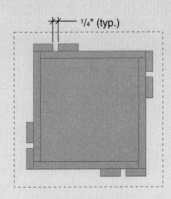

¼" (typ.)

**LEG LAYOUT DETAIL**

| | Cutting List | | | |
|---|---|---|---|---|
| **Key** | **Part** | **Dimension** | **Pcs.** | **Material** |
| **A** | Box side | ¾ × 7¼ × 8" | 4 | Pine |
| **B** | Leg | ¾ × 2½ × 29½" | 8 | Pine |
| **C** | Top tile base | ½ × 12¼ × 12¼" | 1 | Plywood |
| **D** | Box top | ¾ × 7¼ × 7¼" | 1 | Pine |
| **E** | Shelf | ½ × 7¾ × 7¾" | 1 | Plywood |

| | Cutting List | | | |
|---|---|---|---|---|
| **Key** | **Part** | **Dimension** | **Pcs.** | **Material** |
| **F** | Top frame | ½ × 1 × 13¼" | 4 | Molding |
| **G** | Top tile | 12 × 12" | 1 | Ceramic |
| **H** | Shelf tile | 7½ × 7½" | 1 | Ceramic |
| **I** | Shelf frame | ½ × 1 × 8¾" | 4 | Molding |
| | | | | |

**Materials:** 1", 1¼" and 1½" deck screws, 3d and 4d finish nails, wood glue, finishing materials, ceramic tile, ceramic tile adhesive, tinted grout.

**Specialty tools:** V-notch adhesive trowel, grout float.

**Note:** Measurements reflect the actual size of dimension lumber.

Assemble the box using simple butt joints.

Place the top tile base and box top onto the box, and fasten them with screws.

Attach the leg pairs with glue and screws, obscuring the visible joints on the box.

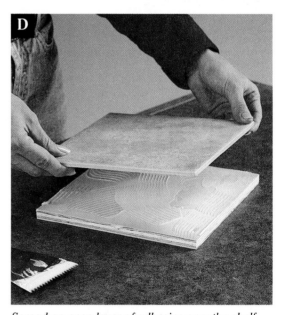

Spread an even layer of adhesive over the shelf, and attach the tile.

## Directions: Plant Stand

### BUILD THE BOX.

Tile size varies from piece to piece, so measure your tile before cutting the top tile base (C). Allow a ⅛" gap for the grout joint between the tile and the top frame.

**1.** Cut the box sides (A), top tile base (C) and box top (D) to size. Sand with 150-grit sandpaper.
**2.** Fasten the sides with simple butt joints, which will be obscured by the legs. Drill ⁵⁄₆₄" pilot holes. Counterbore the holes ⅛" deep, using a ⅜" counterbore bit. Use glue and 1½" deck screws to attach the sides together, making sure the edges are flush **(photo A).**
**3.** Center the box top on the bottom face of the top tile base.

Fasten the pieces by driving 1" deck screws through the top tile base and into the box top.
**4.** Place the top tile base and box top onto the box **(photo B).** Drill pilot holes through the box sides and into the box top. Counterbore the holes. Attach the box top with 1½" deck screws.

### ATTACH THE LEGS.

**1.** Cut the legs (B) to length.
**2.** Drill pilot holes through the legs and into the box sides.

Counterbore the holes. Fasten the legs to the sides with glue and 1¼" deck screws. Make sure each outside leg is flush with the side edge **(photo C).** Maintain a ¼"-wide space between the pieces of each leg pair.

## ATTACH THE SHELF

**1.** Cut the shelf (E) to size.
**2.** Miter-cut the shelf frame (I) pieces to length.
**3.** Attach the shelf tile (H) to the shelf with tile adhesive **(photo D).** Spread the adhesive on the shelf, using a V-notch trowel. Press the tile into place, centered on the shelf, and allow the adhesive to dry.
**4.** Fasten the shelf frame to the shelf with 3d finish nails. Make sure the top frame edges are flush with the top face of the tile.
**5.** Attach the shelf to the legs by driving 4d finish nails through the legs and into the frame and shelf **(photo E).** The lower edge of the shelf should be 10" from the legs' bottom edges.

## ATTACH THE TOP TILE.

**1.** Miter-cut the top frame (F) pieces to length.
**2.** Attach the top tile (G) to the top tile base with adhesive. Nail the top frame in place against the top tile base, keeping the top edges flush with the tile face **(photo F).** When driving the nails, be sure they line up with the top tile base, not the tile.

## APPLY FINISHING TOUCHES.

**1.** Set all nails with a nail set. Fill the nail and screw holes with wood putty. Finish-sand the surfaces with fine-grit sandpaper, and smooth the edges on the bottom of the legs.
**2.** Prime and paint the plant stand as desired. Coat it with two coats of satin-gloss polyurethane finish.
**3.** When the finish is dry, mask the frame pieces with masking tape. Fill the gaps between the tiles and frames with tinted grout. Use a small grout float to pack the grout into the gaps. Smooth the joints with a damp sponge to remove excess grout.

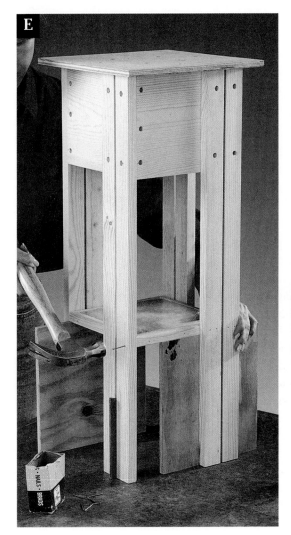

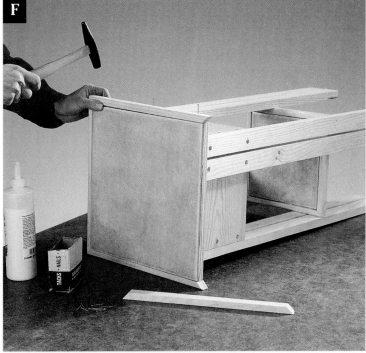

*(above) Install the top frame around the top tile base, using a lightweight tack hammer and 3d finish nails.*

*(left) Use pieces of scrap wood as spacers, and attach the shelf with 4d finish nails.*

# Bookcase

*A simple, functional bookcase on which to set your picture frames, books and decorations, this project is as useful as it is attractive.*

An attractive bookcase adds just the right decorative and functional touch to a family room or den. And you don't need to shell out large amounts of cash for a

high-end bookcase or settle for a cheap, throw-together particleboard unit—this sturdy bookcase looks great and will last for many years.

Four roomy shelf areas let you display and store everything from framed pictures to reference manuals. The decorative trim on the outside of the bookcase spices up the overall appearance of the project, while panel molding along the front edges of the shelves soft-

ens the corners and adds structural stability. With a few coats of enamel paint, this bookcase takes on a smooth, polished look.

Although the project is constructed mostly of plywood, the molding that fits around the top, bottom and shelves allows the bookcase to fit in almost anywhere in the house. This bookcase is a great-looking, useful addition to just about any room.

## CONSTRUCTION MATERIALS

| Quantity | Lumber |
| --- | --- |
| 1 | ¾" × 4 × 8' birch plywood |
| 1 | ¼" × 4 × 8' birch plywood |
| 2 | ¾ × 1⅝" × 8' panel molding |
| 1 | ¾ × ¾" × 6' cove molding |
| 2 | ¾ × ¾" × 8' quarter-round molding |
| 1 | ¾ × 2⅝" × 6' chair-rail molding |

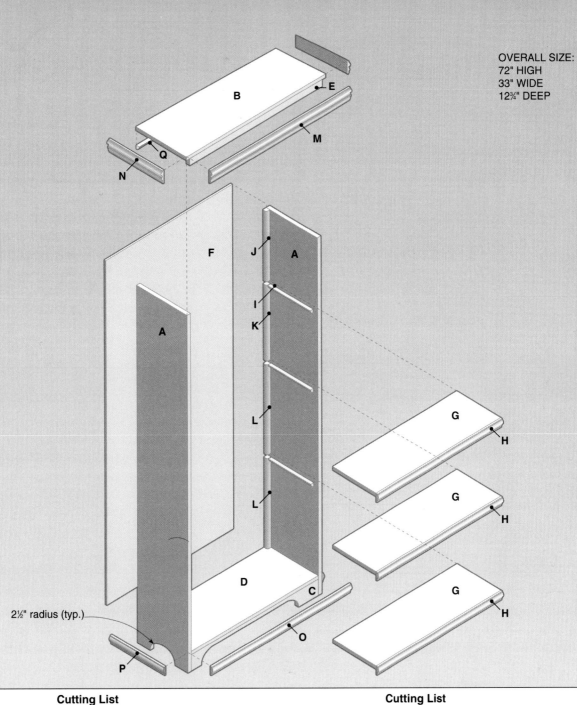

OVERALL SIZE:
72" HIGH
33" WIDE
12¾" DEEP

2½" radius (typ.)

| Key | Part | Dimension | Pcs. | Material |
|-----|------|-----------|------|----------|
| **A** | Side | ¾ × 12 × 71¼" | 2 | Plywood |
| **B** | Top | ¾ × 11¾ × 31½" | 1 | Plywood |
| **C** | Front rail | ¾ × 3¼ × 30" | 1 | Plywood |
| **D** | Bottom | ¾ × 11¾ × 30" | 1 | Plywood |
| **E** | Top rail | ¾ × 1½ × 30" | 1 | Plywood |
| **F** | Back | ¼ × 30 × 68¾" | 1 | Plywood |
| **G** | Shelf | ¾ × 10½ × 30" | 3 | Plywood |
| **H** | Shelf nosing | ¾ × 1⅝ × 30" | 3 | Panel molding |
| **I** | Shelf cleat | ¾ × ¾ × 9¾" | 6 | Cove molding |

| Key | Part | Dimension | Pcs. | Material |
|-----|------|-----------|------|----------|
| **J** | Back brace | ¾ × ¾ × 14" | 2 | Quarter-round |
| **K** | Back brace | ¾ × ¾ × 15" | 2 | Quarter-round |
| **L** | Back brace | ¾ × ¾ × 18" | 4 | Quarter-round |
| **M** | Top facing | ¾ × 2⅝ × 33" | 1 | Chair-rail molding |
| **N** | Top side molding | ¾ × 2⅝ × 12¾" | 2 | Chair-rail molding |
| **O** | Bottom facing | ¾ × 1⅝ × 33" | 1 | Panel molding |
| **P** | Bottom side molding | ¾ × 1⅝ × 12¾" | 2 | Panel molding |
| **Q** | Back brace | ¾ × ¾ × 28½" | 1 | Quarter-round |

**Materials:** #6 × 2" wood screws, 4d and 6d finish nails, 16-ga. × 1" and 1¼" brads, 16-ga. × ¾" wire nails, ¾" birch veneer edge tape (25'), wood glue, finishing materials.

**Note:** Measurements reflect the actual size of dimension lumber.

## Directions: Bookcase

### MAKE THE SIDES AND FRONT RAIL.

**1.** Cut the sides (A) and front rail (C) to size from ¾"-thick plywood. Sand the parts smooth and clean the edges thoroughly.

**2.** Cut two strips of self-adhesive edge tape slightly longer than the long edge of the side piece. Attach the tape to one long edge of each side piece by pressing it onto the wood with a household iron set at a medium-low setting. The heat will activate the adhesive. Trim and sand the edges of the tape.

**3.** To make the arches in the sides, designate a top and bottom to each side. Draw a cutting line across each side, 2½" up from the bottom edge. Draw marks on the bottom edges of the sides, 5½" in from the front and rear edges. Set a compass to draw a 2½"-radius arc, using the marks on the bottom edges as centerpoints. Set the point of the compass as close as possible to the bottom edges of the sides, and draw the arcs. Use a jig saw to cut the arch.

**4.** Repeat these steps to make the arch in the front rail, but place the point of the compass 4¾" in from each end of the front rail. Cut the front rail to shape with a jig saw **(photo A).**

### BUILD THE CARCASE.

The top, bottom and sides of the bookcase form the basic cabinet—called the carcase.

**1.** Cut the top (B), bottom (D) and top rail (E) to size. Sand the parts smooth.

**2.** Draw reference lines across the faces of the sides, 3¼" up from the bottom edges. Set the sides on edge, and position the bottom between them, just above the reference lines. Attach the bottom to the sides with glue and 2" wood screws, keeping the front edges flush. Drill ⁵⁄₆₄" pilot holes for the screws. Counterbore the holes ⅛" deep, using a ⅜" counterbore bit.

**3.** Set the sides upright, and position the front rail between the sides, flush with the side and bottom edges. Glue the rail edges. Then, clamp it to the bottom board. Drill ¹⁄₁₆" pilot holes, and secure the front rail with 6d finish nails driven through the sides, and 1¼" brads driven through the bottom **(photo B).** Set all nails with a nail set.

**4.** Use glue and 6d finish nails to attach the top to the top ends of the sides, keeping the side and front edges flush.

**5.** Fasten the top rail between the sides, flush with the front edges of the sides and top. Use glue and 6d finish nails to secure the top rail in place.

### MAKE THE BACK.

**1.** Cut the back braces (J, K, L, Q) to length.

**2.** Set the carcase on its side.

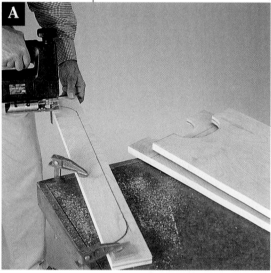

*Cut arches along the bottoms of the side panels and front rail to create the bookcase "feet."*

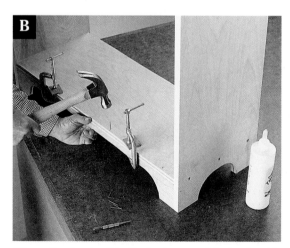

*Clamp the front rail to the bottom, and fasten it with glue, finish nails and brads.*

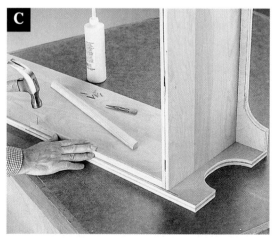

*Attach the back braces to the sides, creating a ¼" recess for the back panel.*

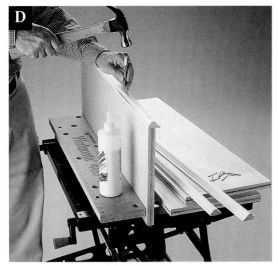

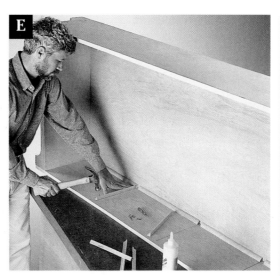

*Attach strips of panel molding to the front edges of the shelves.*

*Attach the shelf cleats with glue and brads.*

Starting at the bottom, use glue and 1¼" brads to fasten the back braces to the sides and top, ¼" in from the back edges **(photo C)**. Use a ¾"-thick spacer to create gaps for the shelves between the strips. Install the top back brace (Q) flush with the back edge of the top. Place the carcase on its front edges.

**3.** Cut the back (F) to size.

**4.** Set the back in place so it rests on the back braces. Check for square by measuring diagonally from corner to corner across the back. When the measurements are the same, the carcase is square. Drive ¾" wire nails through the back and into the back braces. Do not glue the back in place.

### MAKE THE SHELVES.

**1.** Cut the shelves (G) and shelf nosing (H) to size.

**2.** Drill ¹⁄₁₆" pilot holes through the nosing pieces. Use glue and 4d finish nails to attach the nosing to the shelves, keeping the top edges flush **(photo D)**. Set the nails with a nail set.

**3.** Cut the shelf cleats (I) to length.

**4.** To help you position the shelf cleats, use a combination square to draw reference lines perpendicular to the front edges of each side. Start the lines at the top of the lower back braces (K, L ), and extend them to within 1" of the front edges of the sides. Apply glue to the cleats, and position them on the reference lines. Attach the shelf cleats to the inside faces of the sides with 1" brads **(photo E)**.

**5.** Apply glue to the top edges of the shelf cleats. Then, set the shelves onto the cleats. Drive 6d finish nails through the sides and into the ends of the shelves.

**6.** Drive ¾" wire nails through the back panel and into the rear edges of the shelves.

### APPLY FINISHING TOUCHES.

**1.** Cut the top facing (M), top side molding (N), bottom facing (O) and bottom side molding (P) to length. Miter-cut both ends of the top facing and bottom facing and the front ends of the side moldings at a 45° angle so the molding pieces will fit together at the corners.

**2.** Fasten the top molding with glue and 4d finish nails, keeping the top edges flush with the top face of the top piece.

**3.** Attach the bottom facing, keeping the top edges flush with the top face of the bottom.

**4.** To help you align the bottom side molding, draw reference lines on the sides before attaching the pieces. The reference lines should be flush with the top of the bottom facing **(photo F)**. Attach the bottom side molding.

**5.** Set all nails with a nail set, and fill the nail holes with wood putty. Finish-sand the project and apply the finish of your choice—we used primer and two coats of enamel paint.

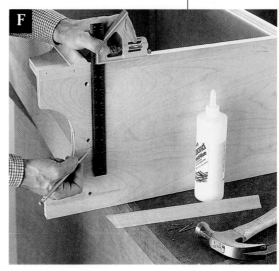

*Using a combination square, draw lines on the sides, aligned with the top of the bottom facing.*

PROJECT
POWER TOOLS

# Library Table

*This oak library table features a clean, sophisticated appearance that suits any family room or study.*

## CONSTRUCTION MATERIALS

| Quantity | Lumber |
|----------|--------|
| 1 | ¾" × 4 × 8' oak plywood |
| 1 | ½" × 2 × 4' oak plywood |
| 2 | 1 × 2" × 8' oak |
| 3 | 1 × 4" × 8' oak |
| 2 | 1 × 6" × 6' oak |
| 2 | 2 × 2" × 8' oak |

High-quality, stylish furniture doesn't need to be overly expensive or difficult to make, and this library table is the proof. We used a traditional design for this old favorite. The simple drawer construction, beautiful oak materials and slender framework add up to one great-looking table.

Consider the possibilities for this table in your family room or study. These areas of the home call out for a simple yet elegant table to support a lamp or books, or just to add a decorative accent. We applied a two-tone finish. But no matter how you finish it, this library table serves many needs—and it looks great in the process.

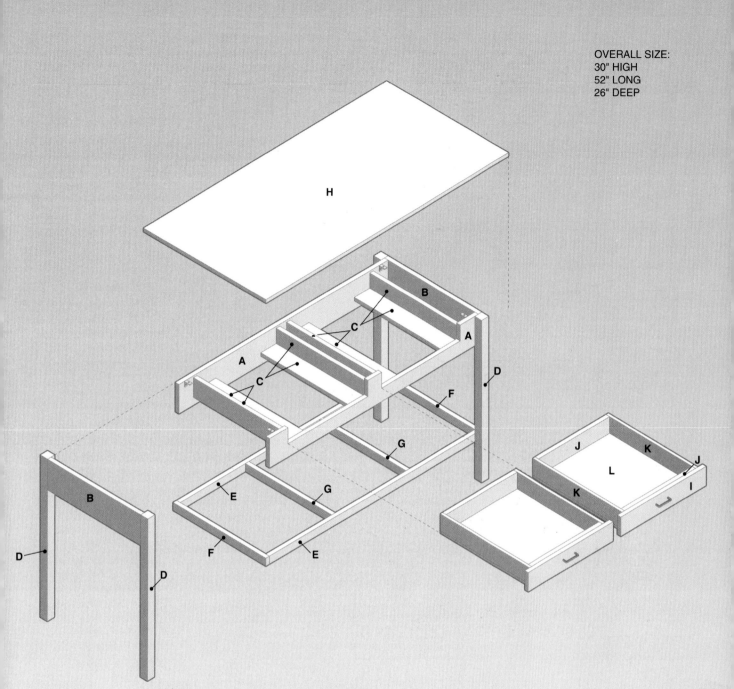

OVERALL SIZE:
30" HIGH
52" LONG
26" DEEP

## Cutting List

| Key | Part | Dimension | Pcs. | Material |
|-----|------|-----------|------|----------|
| A | Side | ¾ × 5½ × 44½" | 2 | Oak |
| B | End | ¾ × 5½ × 20" | 2 | Oak |
| C | Guide | ¾ × 3½ × 18½" | 8 | Oak |
| D | Leg | 1½ × 1½ × 29¼" | 4 | Oak |
| E | Side rail | ¾ × 1½ × 44½" | 2 | Oak |
| F | End rail | ¾ × 1½ × 20" | 2 | Oak |

## Cutting List

| Key | Part | Dimension | Pcs. | Material |
|-----|------|-----------|------|----------|
| G | Cross rail | ¾ × 1½ × 18½" | 2 | Oak |
| H | Top | ¾ × 26 × 52" | 1 | Plywood |
| I | Drawer front | ¾ × 3½ × 18" | 2 | Oak |
| J | Drawer end | ¾ × 2⅜ × 15⅞" | 4 | Oak |
| K | Drawer side | ½ × 2⅜ × 19" | 4 | Plywood |
| L | Drawer bottom | ½ × 16⅞ × 19" | 2 | Plywood |

**Materials:** #6 × 1", 1⅝" and 2" wood screws, 4d and 6d finish nails, 2" corner braces with ⅝" screws (4), 4" drawer pulls (2), ⅞"-dia. rubber feet (4), tack-on furniture glides (4), ¾" oak veneer edge tape (15'), ⅜"-dia. oak plugs, wood glue, finishing materials.

**Note:** Measurements reflect the actual size of dimension lumber.

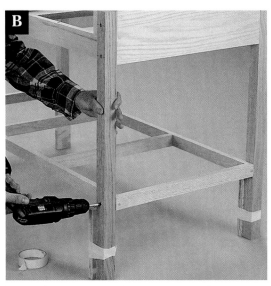

Measure the diagonals and adjust the apron frame as needed until it is square.

Tape 8"-long blocks of scrap wood to the legs to hold the rail assembly for installation.

## Directions: Library Table

For all screws used in this project, drill ³⁄₃₂" pilot holes. Counterbore the holes ¼" deep, using a ⅜" counterbore bit.

### MAKE THE APRON ASSEMBLY.

**1.** Cut the sides (A) and ends (B) to length and sand the pieces smooth.
**2.** Decide which side you want to be the front, and draw two 3"-deep × 17"-long rectangular outlines for the drawer cutouts on it. The outlines should start 3¾" in from each end of the front. Make cutouts with a jig saw, using a straightedge as a guide.
**3.** Attach the sides between the ends with glue, and drive 1⅝" wood screws through the ends and into the sides. The outside faces of the sides should be flush with the ends of the end pieces.
**4.** Cut the guides (C) to length.
**5.** The guides form supporting corners on either side of the drawer notches. Fasten the guides together in right-angle pairs by butting one guide's long edge against the face of

another guide, while keeping the ends flush. Attach the guides with glue and 1⅝" wood screws.
**6.** Position the guide pairs between the sides so the inside faces are flush with the bottom and sides of the rectangular cutouts. Make sure the vertical halves of the guides do not extend above the top edges of the sides. (Set the guide pairs on spacers to keep them aligned with the cutouts as you work.) Before fastening the guides, check the apron frame for

square by measuring from corner to corner **(photo A).** If the measurements are not the same, adjust as needed. Drill ¹⁄₁₆" pilot holes and drive 6d finish nails through the sides and into the guides to fasten them in place. Set the nails with a nail set.

### MAKE THE RAIL ASSEMBLY.

**1.** Cut the side rails (E), end rails (F) and cross rails (G) to length.
**2.** Position the side rails on edge. Attach the side rails be-

Support the drawer with ½"-thick scrap wood. Then, center the drawer front by measuring the overhang on both sides.

tween the end rails with glue and 1⅝" wood screws. The resulting frame should sit flat on your worksurface.

**3.** Attach the cross rails between the side rails, 14" in from the inside faces of the end rails.

**4.** Fill all screw holes with oak plugs, and sand them flush with the surface. Sand the rail assembly smooth.

## ASSEMBLE THE TABLE.

**1.** Cut the legs (D) to length, and sand them smooth.

**2.** Use glue and 2" wood screws to fasten the legs to the apron so the top edges and outside end faces are flush. Position the screws so they do not strike the screws joining the apron parts.

**3.** Stand the table up. Clamp or tape 8"-long scrap blocks to the inside edges of the legs, flush with the bottom leg ends. These blocks hold the rail assembly in place as you attach it. Fasten the rail assembly to the legs with glue and 2" wood screws. Make sure the end rails are flush with the outside edges of the legs **(photo B).**

**4.** Cut the top (H) to size. Clean the edges thoroughly.

**5.** Cut strips of self-adhesive edge tape slightly longer than all four edges of the top. Attach the tape by pressing it onto the edges with a household iron set at a medium-low setting. The heat will activate the adhesive. Trim the excess tape and sand the edges smooth.

**6.** Sand the top. Choose the smoothest, most attractive side to face up. Draw reference lines on the underside of the top, 3¾" in from the long edges. Fasten two 2" corner braces on each line, 5¼" in from the ends, using ⅝" screws. Center the apron assembly on the top and attach it to the braces.

## MAKE THE DRAWERS.

**1.** Cut the drawer ends (J) and drawer sides (K) to size. Sand the pieces smooth.

**2.** Fasten the drawer ends between the drawer sides, using glue and 4d finish nails. Drill 1/16" pilot holes through the sides to prevent splitting. Make sure the outside faces of the drawer ends are flush with the ends of the drawer sides.

**3.** Cut the drawer bottoms (L)

to size, and sand them smooth.

**4.** Center the bottoms over the drawer assemblies, and drill pilot holes for 4d finish nails. Attach the bottom to the drawer ends and sides, driving the nails through the bottom and into the edges. Do not use glue to attach the drawer bottoms.

**5.** Cut the drawer fronts (I) to length.

**6.** To attach the drawer fronts, set the drawers on a ½"-thick piece of scrap wood. This will ensure that the top-to-bottom spacing is correct when you attach the drawer fronts. Position the drawer fronts against the drawer ends, centering them from side to side **(photo C).** Clamp the drawer fronts in place. Drive 1" wood screws through the drawer ends and into the drawer fronts. Test-fit the drawers and adjust the fronts if they are uneven on the front of the apron.

## APPLY FINISHING TOUCHES.

**1.** Set all nails with a nail set, and fill the nail holes with wood putty. Fill all screw holes with oak plugs. Finish-sand the entire project. Apply the finish of your choice.

**2.** When the finish has dried, install the drawer pulls on the drawer fronts. Wax the top faces of the guides with paraffin. Insert the drawers, and set the table on its back edges. Attach ⅞"-dia. rubber feet to the bottoms of the drawers to prevent them from being pulled out of the table **(photo D).** Tack furniture glides to the leg bottoms.

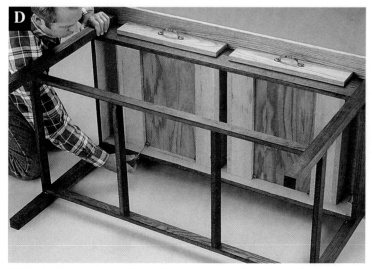

*Slide the drawers into place. Then, install rubber feet at the back corners to serve as drawer stops and keep the drawers centered.*

# Card Table

*This stylish table proves that card tables don't always
have to be flimsy and unappealing.*

## CONSTRUCTION MATERIALS

| Quantity | Lumber |
|----------|--------|
| 1 | ½" × 4 × 4' oak plywood |
| 2 | 2 × 2" × 8' pine |
| 2 | 1 × 3" × 8' pine |
| 4 | ¾ × ¾" × 8' oak edge molding |

The card table has always been thought of as overflow seating for those houseguests who are most lacking in seniority. But the diners assigned to this contemporary wood card table will feel more like they have favored status. The warm tones of the oak tabletop contrast vividly with the painted legs and apron for a lovely effect that will blend into just about any setting—from formal dining to a Friday night poker game.

The fold-up legs on this card table are attached with special fasteners designed just for card tables. You can find these fasteners, as well as the oak apron trim, at most hardware and woodworking supply stores.

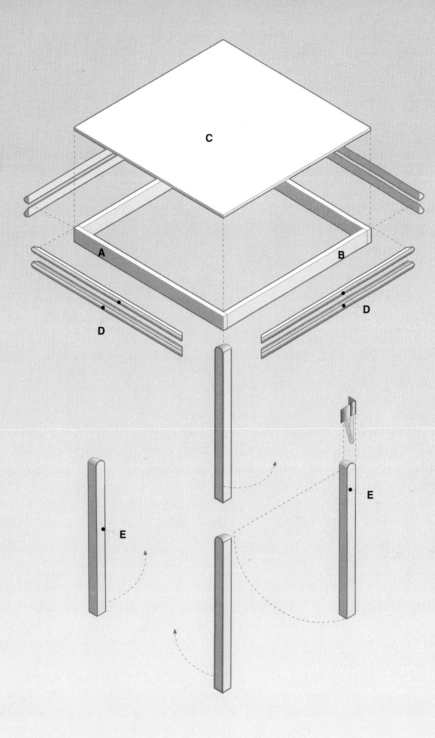

C

A

B

D

D

E

E

| Cutting List | | | | | | Cutting List | | | | |
|---|---|---|---|---|---|---|---|---|---|---|
| Key | Part | Dimension | Pcs. | Material | | Key | Part | Dimension | Pcs. | Material |
| A | Side apron | ¾ × 2½ × 32" | 2 | Pine | | D | Edge trim | ¾ × ¾ × *" | 8 | Edge molding |
| B | End apron | ¾ × 2½ × 30½" | 2 | Pine | | E | Leg | 1½ × 1½ × 28" | 4 | Pine |
| C | Tabletop | ½ × 32 × 32" | 1 | Plywood | | | | | | |

**Materials:** #6 × 1½" wood screws, 3d finish nails, ¼ × 2" machine bolts with locking nuts (4), card-table leg fasteners (4), oak-tinted wood putty, wood glue, finishing materials.

**Note:** Measurements reflect the actual size of dimension lumber.    * Cut to fit.

## Directions: Card Table

### BUILD THE TABLETOP.

The tabletop for this card table is a sheet of oak plywood framed with an apron made from 1 × 3 pine. Strips of oak molding attached around the top and bottom of the apron protect the edges of the table when it is being stored.

**1.** Cut the side aprons (A) and end aprons (B) to length.

**2.** Fasten the end aprons between the side aprons with glue and 1½" wood screws to form a square **(photo A).** Drill ⁵⁄₆₄" pilot holes for the screws. Counterbore the holes ⅛", using a ⅜" counterbore bit. Keep the outside edges and faces of the aprons flush.

**3.** Cut the tabletop (C) to size, using a circular saw and a straightedge as a cutting guide.

**4.** Position the tabletop on the frame, keeping the edges flush with the outer faces of the aprons. Fasten the tabletop to the top of the frame with glue and 3d finish nails **(photo B).**

### SHAPE THE LEGS.

**1.** Cut the legs (E) to length.

**2.** Round over one end of each leg so it will pivot smoothly inside the card-table leg fastener. Center the point of a compass ¾" in from the end of the leg, and draw a ¾"-radius curve. Cut the curves with a jig saw.

Fasten the end aprons between the side aprons with glue and wood screws to construct the apron frame.

### PAINT THE FRAME AND LEGS.

If you plan to apply a combination finish, paint the legs and frame before you assemble the table and attach the edge trim.

**1.** Finish-sand the pine surfaces and wipe them clean. Apply primer to the aprons and legs.

**2.** Apply several coats of enamel paint in the color of your choice.

### ATTACH THE EDGE TRIM.

When the paint has dried, attach the edge trim to the tabletop edges and the aprons. Use a plain or decorative molding, but be sure to use oak to match the tabletop.

**1.** Miter-cut the edge trim pieces (D) to length, using a power miter saw or hand miter box. The best method is to cut the 45° miter on one end of the first piece, and position the trim against the apron or tabletop edges. Mark the appropri-

ate length, and miter-cut the other end.

**2.** Fasten the edge trim to the aprons or the tabletop edge using wood glue and 3d finish nails. To prevent splitting, drill ¹⁄₁₆" pilot holes through the trim pieces before driving the nails. Continue this process, keeping the mitered ends tight when marking for length **(photo C).** Be sure to keep the tops of the upper trim pieces flush with the surface of the tabletop. Keep the bottoms of the lower trim pieces flush with the bottoms of the aprons.

### FASTEN THE LEGS AND HARDWARE.

The legs attach to the table with locking card-table leg fasteners.

**1.** Attach a leg fastener to the rounded end of each leg by drilling a ¼"-dia. hole through the leg then securing the fastener to the leg with a 2" machine bolt and a locking nut.

### TIP

*Use sanding sealer before you apply wood stain to create more even absorption that helps eliminate blotchy finishes. Sanding sealer is a clear product, usually applied with a brush. Check the product labels on all of the finishing products you plan to apply to make sure they are compatible. To be safe, choose either water-based or oil-based products for the whole project.*

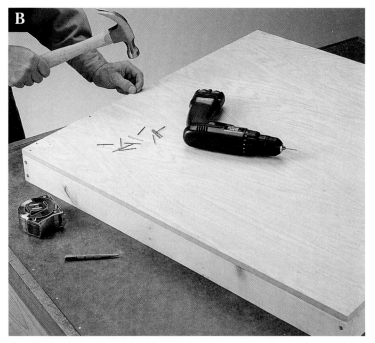

Fasten the oak plywood tabletop to the top of the apron frame with glue and finish nails.

Glue and nail oak trim around the tabletop and apron, making mitered joints at the corners.

Attach the card-table leg fasteners to the rounded ends of the legs. Then, attach them at the inside corners of the tabletop frame.

(The fastening method may vary, so be sure to read any manufacturer's directions that come with the hardware.) Attach the fasteners to the legs with the screws provided with the hardware. Do not tighten the screws completely yet.

**2.** Lay the tabletop upside down on a flat worksurface. Attach the leg fasteners to the insides of the aprons at each corner of the tabletop frame **(photo D).** Test the legs to make sure they fit properly when folded up and that the fasteners operate smoothly. Also, check to make sure the table is level and stable when resting on a flat surface. Make any needed adjustments to the positioning or length of the legs. Then, fully tighten all hardware screws.

APPLY FINISHING TOUCHES.
**1.** Set all nails with a nail set, and fill the nail holes with oak-tinted wood putty. Finish-sand the unfinished surfaces and wipe them clean.
**2.** Apply sanding sealer for an even finish (see *Tip*, opposite page). If desired, apply a wood stain to color the wood. If you are using medium to dark stain, mask the painted surfaces first. Apply two or three light coats of a protective topcoat to the entire table.

# Game Table

*Kids will appreciate the size of this table, but adults
will remember the craftsmanship.*

## CONSTRUCTION MATERIALS

| Quantity | Lumber |
|----------|--------|
| 3 | 1 × 2" × 8' oak |
| 4 | 1 × 3" × 8' oak |
| 1 | ¾" × 2 × 2' MDF* |
| 1 | ¼" × 2 × 4' hardboard |

\* Medium-density fiberboard

Our game table is a striking piece of furniture that can easily double as a decorative end table. Sturdy leg units and an internal cleat structure make this table durable and stable enough for constant use. A slim drawer underneath the game table is great for holding score pads,

cards or other game supplies.

The most notable feature of our game table is the veneered top. The pattern is accomplished with four panels of self-adhesive oak veneer applied in different directions for a striking appearance. Rabbet joints cut with a router join the oak border trim to the tabletop.

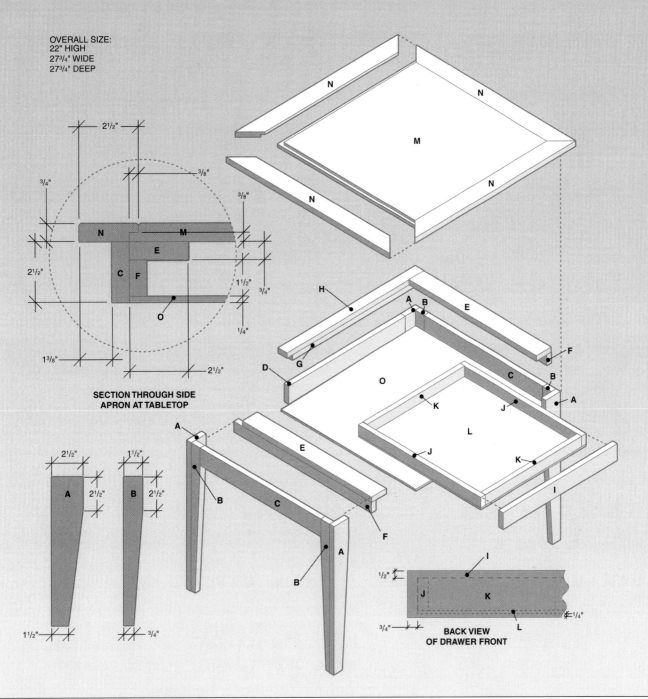

OVERALL SIZE:
22" HIGH
27¾" WIDE
27¾" DEEP

**SECTION THROUGH SIDE APRON AT TABLETOP**

**BACK VIEW OF DRAWER FRONT**

| Key | Part | Dimension | Pcs. | Material |
|-----|------|-----------|------|----------|
| **A** | Wide leg piece | ¾ × 2½ × 21¼" | 4 | Oak |
| **B** | Narrow leg piece | ¾ × 1½ × 21¼" | 4 | Oak |
| **C** | Side apron | ¾ × 2½ × 20½" | 2 | Oak |
| **D** | Back apron | ¾ × 2½ × 20" | 1 | Oak |
| **E** | Side stretcher | ¾ × 2½ × 22" | 2 | Oak |
| **F** | Side cleat | ¾ × 1½ × 23½" | 2 | Oak |
| **G** | Back cleat | ¾ × 1½ × 22" | 1 | Oak |
| **H** | Back stretcher | ¾ × 1½ × 23½" | 1 | Oak |

| Key | Part | Dimension | Pcs. | Material |
|-----|------|-----------|------|----------|
| **I** | Drawer front | ¾ × 2½ × 19¾" | 1 | Oak |
| **J** | Drawer side | ¾ × 1½ × 21" | 2 | Oak |
| **K** | Drawer end | ¾ × 1½ × 16¾" | 2 | Oak |
| **L** | Drawer bottom | ¼ × 18¼ × 21" | 1 | Hardboard |
| **M** | Top | ¾ × 23½ × 23½" | 1 | MDF |
| **N** | Trim | ¾ × 2½ × 27¾" | 4 | Oak |
| **O** | Bottom | ¼ × 23½ × 23½" | 1 | Hardboard |

**Cutting List** (×2, above each table)

**Materials:** #6 × 1¼" wood screws, 4d finish nails, 2 x 3' self-adhesive oak veneer (2), wood glue, finishing materials.

**Specialty tools:** J-roller.

**Note:** Measurements reflect the actual size of dimension lumber.

*Use a sharp blade to cut the veneer pieces along the template. Press firmly to prevent the veneer from sliding.*

*Clamp the top securely to your worksurface to keep it from slipping when rabbeting the edges.*

### Directions: Game Table

#### CUT AND ASSEMBLE THE VENEER.

The veneer top consists of four triangular quadrants. Cut two from each piece of veneer.

**1.** Make an 18"-square template from ¼" scrap hardboard. From one corner of the template, measure 17" along adjacent sides and mark points. Tape the opposite edges of the template to your cutting surface. Slide one sheet of veneer under the template until the sides meet the marks and the veneer is positioned at a 45° angle to the edges of the hardboard. Cut down to the marks with a utility knife **(photo A).** Remove the template and cut between the marks to complete the triangle.

**2.** Repeat to cut the three remaining veneer pieces. Keep the grain aligned as in photo A.

**3.** Tape the triangular veneer pieces together on their finished faces to form a square.

#### MAKE THE TOP.

**1.** Cut the top (M) from MDF. Draw diagonal reference lines connecting opposite corners.

**2.** Place the veneer on the top, aligning the seams with the diagonal reference lines. When the veneer is in position, clamp one side in place. Fold back the opposite half and peel away the backing. Lay the exposed veneer back onto the top. Press to bond. Remove the clamps, fold back the remaining half, peel the backing and apply the veneer. Press seams firmly in place with a J-roller. Trim the edges.

**3.** Rabbet the edges of the top, using your router and a ⅜" self-guiding rabbeting bit set to a depth of ⅜" **(photo B).** Also rabbet one edge of the 1 × 3 stock you will use for the trim pieces. First, use scrap wood to test-fit the depth of the cut against the rabbeted edges of the top to ensure the faces will be flush.

**4.** With a block plane or sander, make a ¹⁄₁₆" chamfer (bevel) on the perimeter of the top and along upper edges of the 1 × 3.

**5.** Cut the trim (N) pieces to length, mitering the ends at 45° angles.

**6.** Attach the trim pieces to the top with glue. Clamp in place. Drill pilot holes and use finish nails to lock-nail the trim pieces together at the joints. Set the nails with a nail set.

#### MAKE THE LEGS.

**1.** Cut the wide and narrow leg pieces (A, B) to length.

**2.** Glue and clamp the edge of each narrow leg piece to the face of a wide piece so edges and ends are flush **(photo C).**

**3.** Once dry, mark the diagonal taper on each leg (see *Diagram*, page 69). Cut with a jig saw or a circular saw and sand smooth.

#### BUILD THE CLEAT ASSEMBLIES.

For all screws used in this project, drill ³⁄₃₂" pilot holes. Counterbore the holes ⅛" deep, using a ⅜" counterbore bit.

**1.** Cut side stretchers (E), side cleats (F), back stretcher (H) and back cleat (G) to length.

**2.** Arrange the stretchers and cleats in pairs (see *Diagram*). Attach the stretchers to the cleats with glue and 1¼" wood screws. Make sure the back cleat is centered on its stretcher, with a ¾" space at each end. The front ends of the side stretchers should be flush with the front ends of the side cleats.

Join the wide and narrow leg pieces with glue; when this is done carefully no nails or screws are required.

**Cleat assembly**   **Apron**

Use glue and screws to join the leg pairs to the cleat assemblies and aprons.

Attach the top with glue and screws driven through the stretchers and into the top.

## ASSEMBLE THE TABLE FRAMEWORK.

**1.** Cut the side aprons (C) and back apron (D) to length.
**2.** Lay a side apron on your worksurface. Place the right cleat assembly over it so the side stretcher is standing on edge, flush with the top edge of the apron. Arrange the right front and back legs in their correct position, with the narrow leg pieces flat on the worksurface. The side cleat should butt against the wide leg pieces, and the side apron should butt against the narrow leg pieces. Make sure the parts are flush at the top edges.

Then, glue and clamp the parts together. Drive 1¼" wood screws through the side cleat into the apron and legs **(photo D).** Repeat to assemble the left leg pair.
**3.** Position the finished leg pairs upright with the back legs resting on the worksurface. Position the back apron and back cleat assembly between the back legs so the edges are flush. Fasten with glue and 1¼" wood screws.

## ATTACH THE TOP AND BOTTOM.

**1.** Place the top upside down on the worksurface. Set the leg/apron assembly over it. Align the

leg corners on the miter joints. Attach the top with glue and 1¼" wood screws **(photo E).**
**2.** Cut the bottom (O) to size.
**3.** Fasten the bottom to the bottom edges of the cleats, using glue and 1¼" wood screws.

## BUILD THE DRAWER.

**1.** Cut the drawer parts (I, J, K and L) to size.
**2.** Place the drawer ends between the drawer sides so the edges are flush. Attach with glue and 1¼" wood screws.
**3.** Position the drawer bottom on the drawer box. Attach with glue and 1¼" wood screws. Lay the drawer front facedown on your worksurface and position the drawer box on it (see *Diagram*). Fasten the parts with glue, and drive 1¼" wood screws through the end and into the front.

## APPLY FINISHING TOUCHES.

Fill all nail and screw holes with wood putty, and finish-sand the table. A water-based finish may loosen the veneer, so use alkyd-based polyurethane. The chamfered joint may be painted black after the finish has cured.

# Table/Chair

*Based on a design from Colonial America, this clever furnishing features a tabletop that can be raised to form a backrest for a sturdy armchair.*

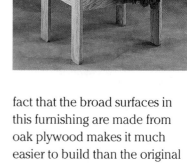

L iving space was a scarce commodity in the tiny cottages of Colonial America. One clever solution devised to solve the space crunch was the unique table/chair. With a tabletop that flipped up to do double duty as a backrest, the table/chair was a prime example of multifunctional design.

The updated version of the table/chair offered here has the same sturdy construction and multiple uses as the original, although there are a few notable differences. The tabletops on most of the original table/chairs were round. If your aim is to make an authentic reproduction, you can certainly build your own table/chair that way. But the difficulty of creating a perfectly round tabletop, together with the increased wall space covered by the tabletop when raised, makes the square version shown here a more appealing project for most people. This table/chair design has the added bonus of a generous storage compartment below the seat. And the

fact that the broad surfaces in this furnishing are made from oak plywood makes it much easier to build than the original Colonial version, which would likely require edge-gluing pine boards together.

## CONSTRUCTION MATERIALS

| Quantity | Lumber |
|----------|--------|
| 1 | 1 × 6" × 8' oak |
| 3 | 1 × 4" × 8' oak |
| 1 | ¾" × 4 × 4' oak plywood |
| 1 | ¾"-dia. × 12" oak dowel |
| 1 | ⅜"-dia. × 12" oak dowel |

OVERALL SIZE:
28¾" HIGH
26" WIDE
24" DEEP

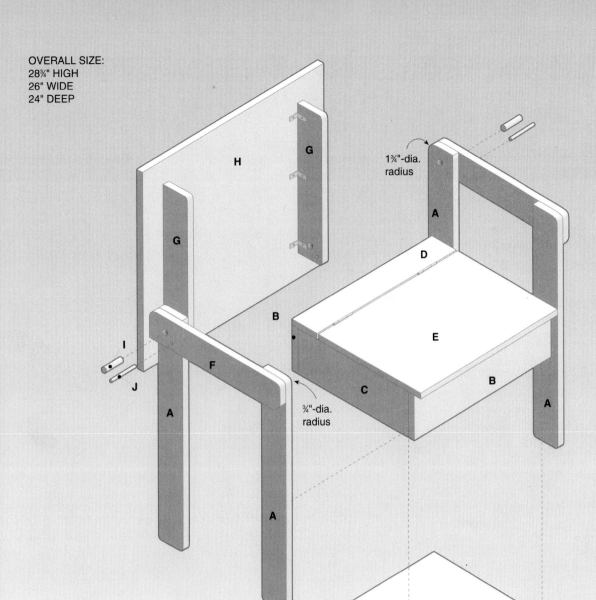

1¾"-dia. radius

¾"-dia. radius

| Cutting List | | | | |
|---|---|---|---|---|
| Key | Part | Dimension | Pcs. | Material |
| A | Leg | ¾ × 3½ × 28" | 4 | Oak |
| B | Box side | ¾ × 5½ × 20" | 2 | Oak |
| C | Box end | ¾ × 5½ × 15¾" | 2 | Oak |
| D | Hinge cleat | ¾ × 3½ × 20" | 1 | Oak |
| E | Seat | ¾ × 14½ × 19¾" | 1 | Plywood |
| F | Armrest | ¾ × 3½ × 18" | 2 | Oak |

| Cutting List | | | | |
|---|---|---|---|---|
| Key | Part | Dimension | Pcs. | Material |
| G | Table cleat | ¾ × 3½ × 18" | 2 | Oak |
| H | Tabletop | ¾ × 24 × 26" | 1 | Plywood |
| I | Pivot | ¾"-dia. × 2¼" | 2 | Oak dowel |
| J | Locking pin | ⅜"-dia. × 3½" | 2 | Oak dowel |
| K | Box bottom | ¾ × 15¾ × 18½" | 1 | Plywood |

**Materials:** #6 × 1", 1¼" and 2" wood screws, 4d finish nails, 1¼ × 1¼" brass corner braces with ⅝" screws (6), 1½ × 3" brass butt hinges (2), ¾" oak veneer edge tape (15'), ⅜"-dia. oak plugs, paste wax, wood glue, finishing materials.

**Note:** Measurements reflect the actual size of dimension lumber.

The 1¾"-radius roundovers at the ends of the armrests and two of the legs allow the tabletop to pivot. Cut them with a jig saw.

Make sure the legs are square to the box frame. Then, fasten them together with glue and screws.

## Directions: Table/Chair

### MAKE THE LEGS AND ARMRESTS.

For all screws used in this project, drill ³⁄₃₂" pilot holes. Counterbore the holes ¼" deep, using a ⅜" counterbore bit.

**1.** Cut the legs (A) and armrests (F) to length.

**2.** Use a compass to draw ¾"-radius curves on three corners of the front legs and on the two bottom corners of the back legs. Cut the curves with a jig saw and sand them smooth.

**3.** On one corner of an armrest, draw a 1¾"-radius roundover, and cut it with a jig saw. Use the cut piece to trace identical curves on a corner of the other armrest and on one square corner of the back legs. Make the 1¾"-radius cuts, and gang-sand the pieces to a uniform shape **(photo A).**

**4.** Cut ¾"-radius curves on the front corners of the armrests.

### BUILD THE BOX FRAME.

**1.** Cut the box sides (B), box ends (C) and box bottom (K) to size.

**2.** Position the ends between the sides. Attach the pieces with glue, and drive evenly spaced 1¼" wood screws through the sides and into the ends.

**3.** Use glue and 1¼" wood screws to attach the bottom inside the ends and sides, flush with the bottom edges.

### ATTACH THE BOX FRAME.

**1.** Draw a reference line on the inside face of each leg, 10¾" up from the bottom edge. Clamp the armrests to the outside faces of the legs with the rounded corners up, keeping the top edges and ends flush. Make sure the 1¾" roundovers on the armrests and the back legs are aligned.

**2.** Position the box between the legs, so the bottom is flush with the reference lines on the

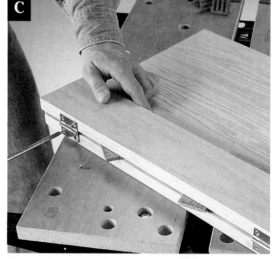

Fasten the seat to the hinge cleat with two brass butt hinges. Use spacers to align the hinges.

legs. The box should be flush with the back edges of the rear legs, and ¾" in from the front edges of the front legs. Fasten the box between the legs with glue and 1" wood screws **(photo B).**

**3.** Fasten the armrests to the outside faces of the legs with glue and 1" wood screws. Position the screws to avoid the dowel locations.

### ATTACH THE SEAT.

**1.** Cut the hinge cleat (D) and the seat (E) to size.

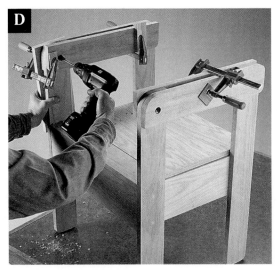

With a backer board clamped to the outside of the legs, drill guide holes for the dowel pivots.

Attach the tabletop to the table cleats with brass corner braces.

**2.** Cut strips of ¾" self-adhesive edge tape to fit all four edges of the seat. Press them in place with a household iron. Trim off any excess with a sharp utility knife. Sand the edges smooth.

**3.** Attach a pair of 1½ × 3" hinges to one long edge of the hinge cleat. Lay the cleat face-down on the seat top, using scrap wood spacers that match the width of the hinge barrels. Make sure the cleat overhangs the seat equally on both ends, and fasten the seat to the hinges **(photo C).**

**4.** Attach the hinge cleat so its back edge is flush with the back of the box frame, using glue and 2" wood screws.

## MAKE THE TABLETOP.

**1.** Cut the tabletop (H) and table cleats (G) to size.

**2.** Apply edge tape to all four edges of the tabletop.

**3.** Use a compass to draw a ¾"-radius curve on two of the corners of each cleat, aligned on the same long edge. Cut the curves with a jig saw.

**4.** To drill holes for the dowel pivots, clamp the table cleats to the inside faces of the legs, so

the top and front edges are flush. Clamp a backer board over the outside face of each armrest before drilling. Mark drilling points that are 1¾" down from the top and 1¾" in from the back end of each table cleat. Drill ¾"-dia. holes through the table cleats, legs and armrests, using a ¾" spade bit **(photo D).**

**5.** Mark drilling points for ⅜"-dia. holes for the lock pins ⅞" up from the bottom edges of the table cleats and ⅞" in from the inside edges of the back legs. With the backer board in place, drill the holes with a ⅜" spade bit.

**6.** Cut the pivots (I) and lock pins (J). Test-fit the pieces.

## APPLY THE FINISH.

Before attaching the tabletop, apply a finish to the parts. We used medium-oak wood stain with two coats of polyurethane. Glue oak plugs into all screw holes, and finish-sand the project thoroughly before applying the finish.

## ATTACH THE TABLETOP.

**1.** Replace the table cleats next

to the legs and clamp them in place with ⅛"-thick spacers between the cleats and the legs. Secure the pivots within the dowel holes in the legs and armrests but not within the holes of the table cleats. This allows for free pivotal movement of the tabletop. Apply glue to the insides of the dowel holes in the legs and armrests only. Drive the pivots through the holes in the table cleats and into the legs and armrests. Drill a 3/32" pilot hole through the back end of each armrest and into the pivot. Drive a 6d finish nail to secure each pivot.

**2.** Leaving the clamps in place, apply glue to the tops of the table cleats. Center the table-top over the cleats so it over-hangs the armrests by 3" at the front and back, and 1½" at the sides. Clamp the tabletop to the armrests. Fasten a 1¼ × 1¼" corner brace at each joint, about 1" in from the front of each table cleat. Unclamp the table-top, then tilt it up so you can attach the other braces **(photo E).**

**3.** Apply paste wax to the locking pins and insert the pins into their holes.

# Sideboard

*This elegant sideboard has plenty of room to hold everything from a meal with all the trimmings to stacks of important files.*

The sideboard is an attractive, multipurpose fixture that can be used as a food serving counter, file holder—anything that requires shelf or counter space. The sideboard is a traditional home fixture, adding low-profile storage to just about any area of the home. Positioned against a wall or behind a desk, the sideboard is out of the way, yet is perfect for storing games, photo albums and other items you want to keep close at hand.

We made the sideboard out of oak and oak plywood. The construction is simple and sturdy. Two long interior shelves span the length of the project, giving you a surprising amount of storage space for such a small unit. The top shelf is concealed by two plywood doors, while the bottom shelf is left open for easy access to stored items. Cove molding fastened around the edges of the top and the curved profiles of the legs add a touch of style to this simple project.

## CONSTRUCTION MATERIALS

| Quantity | Lumber |
|----------|--------|
| 1 | ¾" × 4 × 8' oak plywood |
| 2 | 1 × 4" × 8' oak |
| 2 | ¾ × ¾" × 8' oak cove molding |

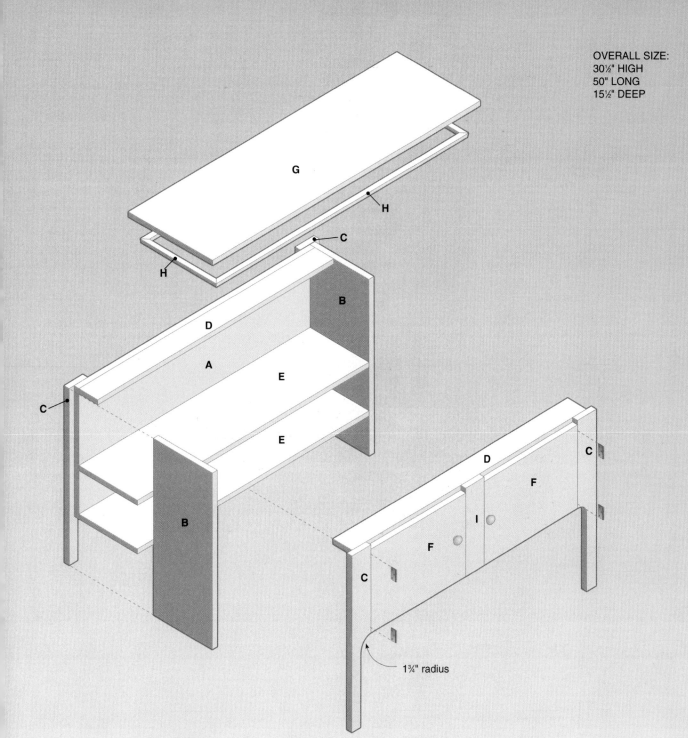

OVERALL SIZE:
30½" HIGH
50" LONG
15½" DEEP

1¾" radius

## Cutting List

| Key | Part | Dimension | Pcs. | Material |
|-----|------|-----------|------|----------|
| **A** | Back panel | ¾ × 20 × 44" | 1 | Plywood |
| **B** | End panel | ¾ × 11 × 29¾" | 2 | Plywood |
| **C** | Leg | ¾ × 3½ × 29¾" | 4 | Oak |
| **D** | Cleat | ¾ × 2½ × 44" | 2 | Plywood |
| **E** | Shelf | ¾ × 10¼ × 44" | 2 | Plywood |

## Cutting List

| Key | Part | Dimension | Pcs. | Material |
|-----|------|-----------|------|----------|
| **F** | Door | ¾ × 13⅛ × 17⅜" | 2 | Plywood |
| **G** | Top panel | ¾ × 15½ × 50" | 1 | Plywood |
| **H** | Top trim | ¾ × ¾ × *" | 4 | Cove molding |
| **I** | Stile | ¾ × 3½ × 14" | 1 | Oak |
| | | | | |

**Materials:** #6 × 1" and 2" wood screws, 16-ga. × 1¼" brads, 1½ × 3" brass butt hinges (4), ⅞"-dia. tack-on furniture glides (4), 1"-dia. brass knobs (2), roller catches (2), ¾" oak veneer edge tape (35'), ⅜"-dia. oak plugs, wood glue, finishing materials.

**Note:** Measurements reflect the actual size of dimension lumber.
*Cut to fit.

## Directions: Sideboard

### MAKE THE CARCASE.

For all screws used in this project, drill ³⁄₃₂" pilot holes. Counterbore the holes ¼" deep, using a ³⁄₈" counterbore bit.

**1.** Cut the back panel (A), end panels (B) and shelves (E) to size. Sand the shelf edges.

**2.** Use a household iron to apply self-adhesive edge tape to one long edge of each shelf. Trim the edges with a utility knife. Sand all parts smooth.

**3.** Set the back flat on your

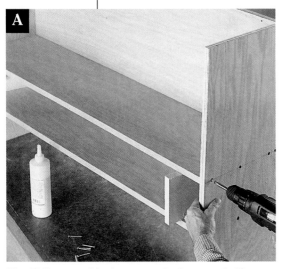

*Use 5¼" spacer blocks set on the bottom shelf to position the top shelf for fastening.*

worksurface. Position one face of an end panel against each short edge of the back panel, making sure the top edges are flush. Attach the panels with glue and drive 2" wood screws through the end panels and into the back. Be sure to keep the outside face of the back panel flush with the back edges of the end panels.

**4.** Position the bottom shelf between the end panels, making sure the edge with the veneer tape faces away from the back panel. The bottom face of the shelf should be flush with the bottom edge of the back. Attach the bottom shelf with glue and drive 2" wood screws through the end panels and back panels and into the shelf.

**5.** Set the carcase (or cabinet frame) upright. Position 5¼"-wide spacer blocks on the bottom shelf. Set the top shelf on the spacer blocks. Attach the top shelf with glue and 2" wood screws **(photo A).**

**6.** Cut the cleats (D) to size, and sand them smooth.

**7.** Use glue and 2" wood screws to fasten one cleat between the end panels so one

long edge is flush with the front edges of the end panels.

**8.** Attach the remaining cleat to the end and back panels so one long edge is butted against the back panel. Both cleats should be flush with the tops of the carcase.

### MAKE THE LEGS.

The sideboard legs have curves that taper them to 1¾" in width.

**1.** Cut the legs (C) to length.

**2.** Designate a top and bottom of each leg. Draw a centerline from top to bottom on each leg. Then, draw reference lines across the legs, 14" and 15¾" up from the bottom. Set a compass to draw a 1¾"-radius semicircle. Set the point of the compass on the lower reference line, as close as possible to one long edge. Draw the semicircle to complete the curved portion of the cutting line.

**3.** Clamp the legs to your worksurface, and use a jig saw to cut them to shape, starting at the bottom and following the centerline and semicircle all the way to the end of the top reference line **(photo B).** Sand the cutouts smooth.

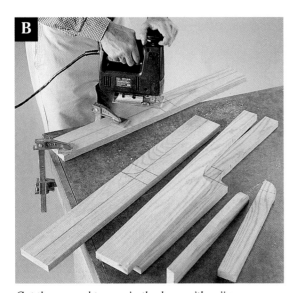

*Cut the curved tapers in the legs with a jig saw.*

*Fasten the legs to the front edges of the end panels. Make sure the outside edges of the legs overhang the end panels by ¼".*

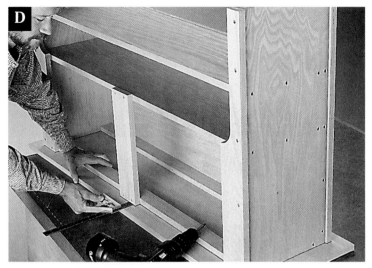

*Measure the front and back overhang to make sure the carcase is centered on the top panel.*

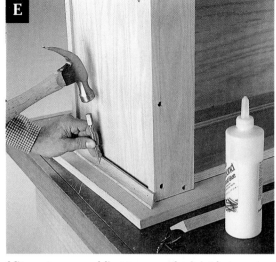

*Miter-cut cove molding to cover the joint between the top panel and the carcase.*

*Attach each door to a leg, using 1½ × 3" butt hinges.*

## ATTACH THE LEGS AND STILE.

**1.** Position two legs against the front edges of the end panels, with the cutout edges facing in. Make sure the legs are flush with the end panels at the top and bottom edges, and that they overhang the outside faces of the end panels by ¼". Attach the legs to the edges of the end panels with glue and 2" wood screws **(photo C).**
**2.** Cut the stile (I) to length.
**3.** Center the stile between the legs so it spans the gap between the cleat and top shelf. Make sure the bottom edge of the stile is flush with the bottom of the top shelf. Attach it with glue and 2" wood screws.
**4.** Turn the project over. Fasten the remaining legs to the back and ends. Maintain the ¼" overhang of the end panels, and keep the top edges flush.

## INSTALL THE TOP PANEL.

**1.** Cut the top panel (G) to size.
**2.** Apply edge tape to all four edges of the top. Sand the surfaces smooth.
**3.** Lay the top on your worksurface with its better face down.

Center the carcase over the top. The top should extend 1½" beyond the front and back of the legs, and 2¼" beyond the outside faces of the end panels **(photo D).** Drive 1" wood screws through the cleats and into the top.
**4.** Cut the top trim (H) to fit around the underside of the top, miter-cutting the ends at 45° angles so they fit together at the corners.
**5.** Drill ¹⁄₁₆" pilot holes through the trim pieces to prevent splitting. Apply glue and drive 1¼" brads through the top trim and into the top panel. Set the brads with a nail set **(photo E).**

## ATTACH THE DOORS.

**1.** Cut the doors (F) to size.
**2.** Apply edge tape to all four edges of each door.
**3.** Attach 1½ × 3" brass butt hinges to one short edge of each door, starting 2" in from the top and bottom. Mount the doors on the carcase by attaching the hinges to the legs **(photo F).** Make sure the bottom edges of the doors are flush with the bottom of the top shelf.

## APPLY FINISHING TOUCHES.

**1.** Fill all nail holes with stainable wood putty. Glue oak plugs into all screw holes. Finish-sand all of the surfaces. Remove the door hinges and apply the finish of your choice.
**2.** When the finish has dried, reattach the doors. Fasten 1"-dia. brass knobs to the door fronts, and mount roller catches on the doors and stile, 5" down from the top of the stile. Tack furniture glides to the bottom ends of the legs.

# Drafting Stool

*Simple and sturdy, this oak beauty keeps your posture perfect as you work at your drafting table or writing desk.*

## CONSTRUCTION MATERIALS

| Quantity | Lumber |
|----------|--------|
| 3 | 1 × 2" × 8' oak |
| 2 | 1 × 4" × 6' oak |
| 2 | 2 × 2" × 8' oak |

Proper seating is the key to comfort and productivity at a writing desk, drafting table or any workstation. An ultra-soft reclining or swiveling chair can sometimes make you drowsy, resulting in poor sitting posture and sore muscles. On the other hand, an unsupportive, rigid chair with a low backrest can make working at your desk uncomfortable and unpleasant. This drafting stool offers firm support without lulling you to sleep.

We designed this solid oak stool for use with the writing desk (page 84). The style and scale of the stool match those of the writing table, but you'll find there are many additional uses for this versatile project. You may want to use it as a bar stool in your den, or place it in the kitchen to provide seating at your breakfast counter.

We used oak lumber, but you can select building materials to match your desk or room decor. For a finished look, we filled the screw holes in our chair with oak plugs, but contrasting plugs would provide an interesting design element. There certainly are many options for building and using this drafting stool. Best of all, this piece is much easier to build than its appearance suggests.

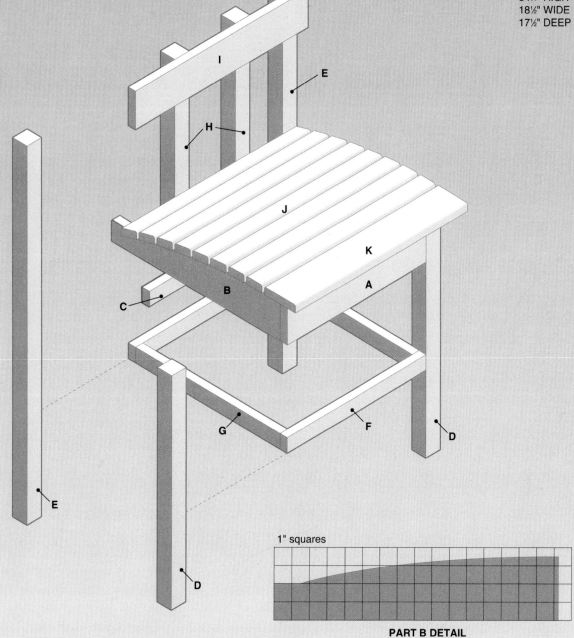

1" squares

**PART B DETAIL**

| Key | Part | Dimension | Pcs. | Material |
|-----|------|-----------|------|----------|
| **A** | Front | ¾ × 3½ × 15" | 1 | Oak |
| **B** | Side | ¾ × 3½ × 16¼" | 2 | Oak |
| **C** | Back | ¾ × 2 × 13½" | 1 | Oak |
| **D** | Front leg | 1½ × 1½ × 21¼" | 2 | Oak |
| **E** | Rear leg | 1½ × 1½ × 34¼" | 2 | Oak |
| **F** | End rail | ¾ × 1½ × 15" | 2 | Oak |

**Cutting List**

| Key | Part | Dimension | Pcs. | Material |
|-----|------|-----------|------|----------|
| **G** | Side rail | ¾ × 1½ × 15½" | 2 | Oak |
| **H** | Back brace | 1½ × 1½ × 16½" | 2 | Oak |
| **I** | Backrest | ¾ × 3½ × 18½" | 1 | Oak |
| **J** | Slat | ¾ × 1½ × 18½" | 8 | Oak |
| **K** | Front slat | ¾ × 3½ × 18½" | 1 | Oak |

**Cutting List**

**Materials:** #6 × 1⅝" wood screws, 10d finish nails, ⅜"-dia. oak plugs, wood glue, finishing materials.

**Note:** Measurements reflect the actual size of dimension lumber.

*Gang-sand the sides with a belt sander, making sure their profiles are identical.*

*Align the seat frame on the top reference lines, and fasten it to the legs.*

### Directions: Drafting Stool

MAKE THE SEAT FRAME.
For all screws used in this project, drill $3/32$" pilot holes. Counterbore the holes $1/4$" deep, using a $3/8$" counterbore bit. The seat frame is sloped from front to back, forming the seat shape. Make this slope by cutting the side pieces, following the grid pattern on page 81.
**1.** Cut the front (A), sides (B) and back (C) to length.
**2.** Draw a grid with 1" squares onto a face of a side piece. (Use the *Part B Detail* from page 81 as a guide for drawing the side contour.) Cut the side to shape with a jig saw, and sand the cut edges.
**3.** Trace the outline of the finished side onto the other side piece, and cut it to shape. Clamp the sides together, and gang-sand them with a belt sander to make sure their profiles are identical **(photo A).**
**4.** Position the front against the front ends of the sides. Fasten the front to the sides with glue,

and drive 1⅝" wood screws through the front piece and into the ends of the sides.
**5.** Position the back (C) between the sides so the rear face is 1½" in from the ends of the sides. Make sure the bottom edges of the parts are flush. Fas-

ten the back with glue, and drive 1⅝" wood screws through the sides and into the back.

ATTACH THE LEGS.
Before attaching the frame and legs, draw reference lines to mark the positions for the legs.

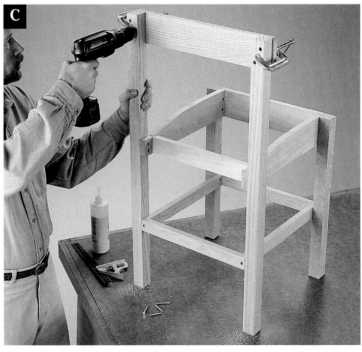

*Clamp the backrest in place at the tops of the rear legs. Then, fasten it with glue and wood screws.*

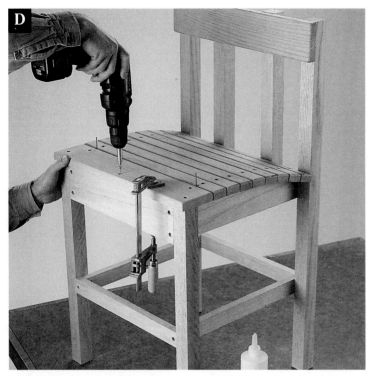

D

*Using 10d nails as spacers, fasten the seat slats to the top of the seat frame, finishing with the front slat.*

**1.** Cut the front legs (D) and rear legs (E) to length. Sand the parts smooth. Draw reference lines on the inside face of each leg, 8" and 17¾" up from the bottom end.
**2.** Position one front leg and one rear leg on your worksurface. Set the seat frame on the legs so the bottom edge is flush with the top reference lines. Apply glue and fasten the seat frame to the rear leg, keeping the ends flush and the frame square to the leg. Drive 1⅝" wood screws through the seat side and into the leg.
**3.** Make sure the seat frame is flush with the front edge of the front leg and with the top reference line. Fasten the frame to the front leg with glue and 1⅝" wood screws **(photo B).**
**4.** Turn the assembly over. Attach the remaining front leg and rear leg, using the same methods.

## ATTACH THE RAILS.
**1.** Cut the end rails (F) and side rails (G) to length.
**2.** Position the side rails between the end rails so their top edges are flush and the outside faces of the side rails are flush with the ends of the end rails. Fasten the pieces with glue and 1⅝" wood screws.
**3.** Position the rail assembly between the legs so its bottom edges are flush with the bottom reference lines. Attach the assembly with glue, and drive 1⅝" wood screws through the side rails and into the legs. To avoid hitting the screws in the rail assembly, these screws must be slightly off center. The front and rear edges of the rail assembly should be flush with the front and rear leg edges.

## ATTACH THE BACK BRACES AND BACKREST.
**1.** Cut the back braces (H) and backrest (I) to length.

**2.** Clamp the backrest to the fronts of the rear legs so the top edges are flush. The backrest should extend ¼" past the rear legs on both sides. Check the back legs for square, and drill staggered pilot holes with ⅜"-deep counterbores through the legs. Apply glue and fasten the backrest to the rear legs with 1⅝" wood screws **(photo C).**
**3.** Drill ⅜"-deep counterbores into the braces. Attach the back braces to the back and backrest with glue and 1⅝" wood screws. Use a piece of 1 × 4 scrap as a spacer to maintain an equal distance between the rear legs and back braces.

## ATTACH THE SLATS.
**1.** Cut the slats (J) and the front slat (K) to length. Sand the slats, slightly rounding over the top edges.
**2.** Starting at the rear of the seat, with the first slat flush against the legs and back braces, attach the slats with glue and 1⅝" wood screws. Maintain a ⅛"-wide gap between slats—10d finish nails make good spacers. The slats should overhang both sides of the seat frame by ¼".
**3.** Test-fit the front slat, and trim it, if necessary, so it overhangs the front piece by ½". Clamp the front slat to the seat frame, and attach it with glue and 1⅝" wood screws **(photo D).**

## APPLY FINISHING TOUCHES.
Insert glued oak plugs into all screw holes, and sand the plugs flush with the surface. Finish-sand all surfaces with 180-grit sandpaper. Apply the finish of your choice. We used three coats of tung oil.

PROJECT
POWER TOOLS

# Writing Desk

*Build this practical, attractive writing desk for a fraction of the cost of manufactured models.*

## CONSTRUCTION MATERIALS

| Quantity | Lumber |
|----------|--------|
| 1 | ¾" × 4 × 8' oak plywood |
| 2 | 1 × 2" × 6' oak |
| 2 | 1 × 4" × 6' oak |
| 1 | 1 × 6" × 8' oak |
| 1 | 1 × 10" × 6' oak |
| 2 | 2 × 2" × 8' oak |
| 1 | ¼" × 2 × 4' acrylic sheet |
| 2 | ¾ × 1⁵⁄₁₆" × 6' oak panel molding |
| 2 | ⅜ × 1¹⁄₁₆" × 6' oak stop molding |

A beautiful piece of furniture, this writing desk is based loosely on popular Shaker styling. With its hinged top, you have access to a storage area for keeping important papers organized and out of the way. We built the writing desk out of red oak, an attractive and durable hardwood, so the project would to look great for a long time. Designed to match the drafting stool and secretary topper (pages 80, 90), the writing desk also works well as a stand-alone piece. And, it can be built for a fraction of the cost of similar furnishings, even those sold by catalog. The worksurface is covered with a sheet of clear acrylic, giving you a hard, smooth surface for writing. When the acrylic gets scratched or worn, just slip it out of the top frame and turn it over.

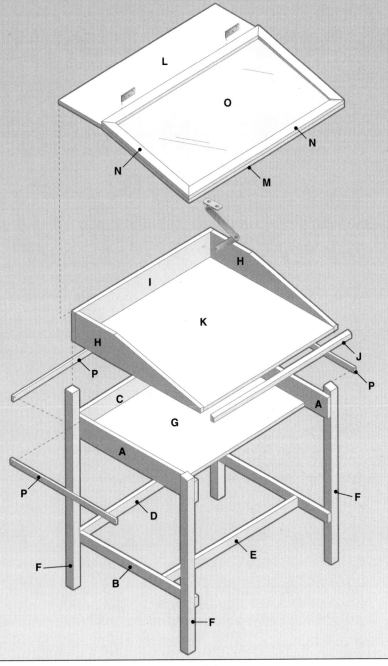

## Cutting List

| Key | Part | Dimension | Pcs. | Material |
|-----|------|-----------|------|----------|
| **A** | Apron side | ¾ × 3½ × 24¾" | 2 | Oak |
| **B** | Side rail | ¾ × 1½ × 24¾" | 2 | Oak |
| **C** | Apron back | ¾ × 3½ × 30" | 1 | Oak |
| **D** | Back rail | ¾ × 1½ × 30" | 1 | Oak |
| **E** | Kick rail | ¾ × 1½ × 28½" | 1 | Oak |
| **F** | Leg | 1½ × 1½ × 35¾" | 4 | Oak |
| **G** | Shelf | ¾ × 20 × 28½" | 1 | Plywood |
| **H** | Desk side | ¾ × 5½ × 26½" | 2 | Oak |

## Cutting List

| Key | Part | Dimension | Pcs. | Material |
|-----|------|-----------|------|----------|
| **I** | Desk back | ¾ × 5½ × 30" | 1 | Oak |
| **J** | Desk front | ¾ × 1 × 30" | 1 | Oak |
| **K** | Desk bottom | ¾ × 26½ × 28½" | 1 | Plywood |
| **L** | Desk top | ¾ × 9¼ × 34" | 1 | Oak |
| **M** | Worksurface | ¾ × 21 × 34" | 1 | Plywood |
| **N** | Top molding | ¾ × 1⁵⁄₁₆ × *" | 4 | Panel molding |
| **O** | Top protector | ¼ × 19⅛ × 32⅛" | 1 | Acrylic |
| **P** | Side trim | ⅜ × 1¹⁄₁₆ × *" | 3 | Stop molding |

**Materials:** #6 × 1⅝" and 2" wood screws, #6 × 1" brass wood screws, 16-ga. × ¾" and 1" brass brads, 1½ × 3" brass butt hinges, 6" heavy-duty lid-support hardware, ¾" oak veneer edge tape (25'), ⅜"-dia. oak plugs, wood glue, finishing materials.

**Specialty tools:** Block plane, plastic cutter.

**Note:** Measurements reflect the actual size of dimension lumber.    * Cut to fit.

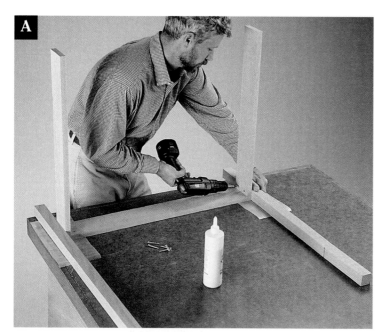

Fasten the apron assembly between the back legs with glue and wood screws.

Attach the front legs to the free ends of the apron sides and side rails.

## Directions: Writing Desk

### JOIN THE LEGS AND APRON.

For all screws used in this project, drill ³⁄₃₂" pilot holes. Counterbore the holes ¼" deep, using a ⅜" counterbore bit.

**1.** Cut the legs (F) to length. Sand the parts smooth.

**2.** Set the legs together, edge to edge, with their ends flush. Draw reference lines across the legs, 8" and 30¼" up from one end. These lines mark the positions of the apron and rail assemblies.

**3.** Cut the apron sides (A) and apron back (C) to length.

**4.** Butt the ends of the apron sides against the face of the apron back. Attach the pieces with glue, and drive 2" wood screws through the apron back and into the sides. Make sure the outside faces of the sides are flush with the ends of the apron back.

**5.** Set a pair of legs on your worksurface, about 30" apart,

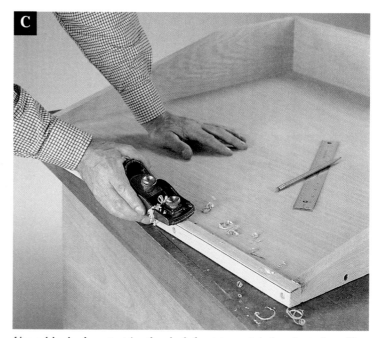

Use a block plane to trim the desk front to match the slanted profiles of the desk sides.

with the reference lines facing each other. Position the apron assembly between the legs so the top edges of the assembly are flush with the top reference lines. The back face of the apron should be flush with the back edges of the legs. Drive 1⅝" wood screws through the

apron sides and into the legs **(photo A).** Position the screws so they do not strike the screws in the apron assembly.

### INSTALL THE FRAME RAILS.

**1.** Cut the side rails (B), back rail (D) and kick rail (E) to length.

**2.** Attach the side rails to the

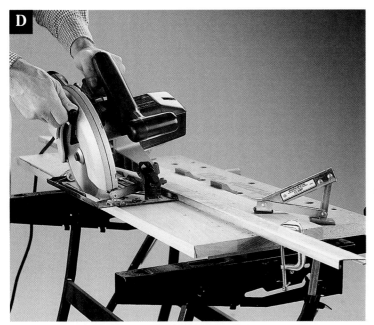

Use a circular saw and a straightedge as a guide to make a slight bevel on the front edge of the desk top.

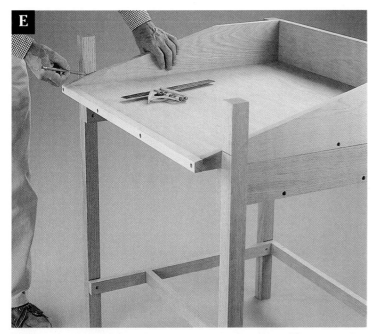

Trace the angles of the desk sides onto the front legs. Then, trim the legs to follow the sides.

**TIP**

*When planing hardwood, always follow the grain. If your planing strokes are resulting in ragged cuts rather than smooth shavings, switch the direction of your planing strokes.*

lines. Keep the back face of the back rail flush with the back edges of the legs, and attach the assembly with glue. Drive 1⅝" wood screws through the side rails and into the legs.

**5.** Position the front legs on the apron sides and side rails, keeping the edges flush with the reference lines **(photo B).** The front edges of the legs should be flush with the ends of the apron sides and side rails. Make sure the parts are square, and fasten the legs with glue. Drive 1⅝" wood screws through the apron sides and side rails and into the legs.

MAKE THE SHELF.
**1.** Cut the shelf (G) to size.
**2.** Apply self-adhesive edge tape to one long edge of the shelf, using a household iron. Trim and sand the taped edges.
**3.** Position the shelf between the apron sides so it butts against the face of the apron back. The shelf should be flush with the bottom edges of the apron assembly, and the taped edge of the shelf should face forward. Attach the shelf to the apron with glue, and drive 1⅝" wood screws through the apron sides and back and into the edges of the shelf.

BUILD THE DESK BOX.
**1.** Cut the desk sides (H) to length.
**2.** To make the slanted cuts on the top edges, mark points on one long edge of each desk side, 8¼" in from one end.

back rail with glue. Drive 2" wood screws through the back rail and into the ends of the side rail. Make sure the outside faces of the side rails are flush with the ends of the back rail.
**3.** Position the kick rail between the side rails so its front face is 7" in from the front ends of the side rails. Make sure the top and bottom edges are flush. Attach the kick rail with glue, and drive 2" wood screws through the side rails and into the ends of the kick rail.
**4.** Position the rail assembly between the legs with the bottom edges on the lower reference

Draw reference lines on the opposite end of each side, 1" up from the bottom edge. Draw straight cutting lines connecting the marks. Cut along the lines with a circular saw, using a straightedge as a cutting guide.

**3.** Cut the desk back (I) and desk bottom (K) to size.

**4.** To cut the desk front (J), use a circular saw and a straightedge as a cutting guide to rip-cut a 1"-wide strip from a $1 \times 4$ or $1 \times 6$.

**5.** Attach the desk sides to the desk back, flush with the ends of the desk back. Apply glue and drive 2" wood screws through the back and into the edges of the sides.

**6.** Position the desk bottom between the desk sides, keeping the front and bottom edges flush. Attach the bottom with glue, and drive 1⅝" wood screws through the desk sides and back and into the bottom.

**7.** Fasten the desk front to the front edge of the desk bottom with glue and 1⅝" wood screws. The ¾"-thick edge should be flush with the bottom face of the desk bottom.

**8.** To trim the desk front to match the slanted profiles of the desk sides, draw reference lines on each end of the desk front, extending the slanted profiles of the desk sides. Use a combination square to draw a reference line across the front face of the desk front, connecting the ends of the reference lines. Use a block plane to trim the profile of the desk front to match the angles of the desk sides **(photo C).** To avoid damaging the desk sides, start the trimming with the plane and finish with a sander.

*Permanently fasten the top and side pieces of the frame around the worksurface.*

### MAKE THE DESK TOP.

**1.** Cut the desk top (L) to length.

**2.** The desk top has a bevel cut along one long edge where it meets the worksurface (M). To make the cut, adjust the blade angle on a circular saw to cut a ⅛" bevel on the front edge of the desk top. First make test cuts on scrap pieces. Clamp a straightedge guide to the desk top, and make the bevel cut on one long edge of the workpiece **(photo D).**

### INSTALL THE DESK BOX.

**1.** Stand the leg assembly up. Set the desk assembly on top of the side aprons, making sure the back edges are flush.

**2.** To cut the front legs to match the slanted profiles of the desk sides, first trace the angles of the desk sides onto the front legs **(photo E).** Remove the desk assembly, and use a circular saw to cut the front legs along the cutting lines.

**3.** Replace the desk, and make sure the front legs are cut at, or

slightly below, the desk side profiles. Fasten the desk assembly with glue, and drive 1⅝" wood screws through the desk sides and into the legs.

**4.** Position the desk top on the flat section of the desk sides so the back edge of the desk top overhangs the back of the legs by ⅛". The top should overhang the outside faces of the back legs by ½" on each side. Make sure the beveled edge faces forward and slants in from top to bottom. Attach the desk top with glue, and drive 1⅝" wood screws through the top and into the edges of the desk sides and back.

**5.** Cut the side trim (P) pieces to fit between the legs on the sides and back, covering the joint where the desk assembly meets the aprons. Tack the side trim over the joint, using ¾" brass brads.

### MAKE THE WORKSURFACE.

The molding nailed to the top of the plywood worksurface holds

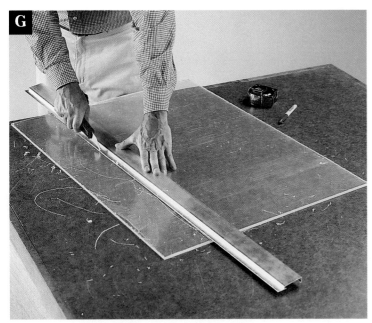

G

*Score the acrylic sheet repeatedly, using a plastic cutter and a straightedge as a guide.*

the acrylic protector in place. One piece of the molding is removable, allowing you to re-place the acrylic if it gets worn.

**1.** Cut the worksurface (M) to size. Apply edge tape to all four edges of the board.

**2.** Cut the top molding (N) to fit around the edges of the worksurface. Miter-cut the cor-ners of the molding pieces to make miter joints.

**3.** Use glue and ¾" brads to attach the top molding to the sides and top of the worksur-face **(photo F).**

**4.** Drive 1" brads through one molding piece and into the other at each joint, lock-nailing the pieces. To secure the bot-tom piece of molding, clamp it in place on the worksurface. From underneath the worksur-face, drill 1¼"-deep pilot holes, ⁹⁄₁₆" in from the front edge. Use a piece of tape on your drill bit as a depth guide to avoid drilling through the face of the molding. Counterbore the holes. Drive 1" brass wood

screws through the pilot holes and into the molding.

## MAKE THE TOP PROTECTOR.

Cut the top protector (O) to size, using a plastic cutter and a straightedge as a cutting guide. Make repeated cuts to score the material deeply **(photo G).**

Then, holding the straightedge next to the score line, bend the sheet to break it at the line.

## APPLY FINISHING TOUCHES.

**1.** Fill all screw holes with oak plugs. Set the nails with a nail set, and fill the nail holes with wood putty. Finish-sand all of the surfaces, and apply a finish to the project. We used three coats of clear tung oil.

**2.** Attach 1½ × 3" brass butt hinges to the top edge of the worksurface, and fasten it to the desk top **(photo H).** Because the worksurface is fairly heavy, you may need to support it from behind as you fasten the hinges.

**3.** Install a 6" heavy-duty lid sup-port on one desk side inside the storage compartment. Fasten the arm of the support to the worksurface, near the top edge of the bottom face.

**4.** Remove the screws holding the removable top molding piece, and insert the top pro-tector into the frame. Attach the molding.

H

*Attach the worksurface to the beveled edge of the desk top with evenly spaced hinges.*

# Secretary Topper

*Transform a plain table, desk or cabinet top into a fully equipped secretary with this box-style topper.*

I n the furniture world, a secretary is a free-standing, upright cabinet with a drop-down worksurface that conceals numerous storage cubbies when raised. The traditional secretary also has two or three large drawers at the bottom. With this secretary topper, we zeroed in on the cubby-hole feature, creating a simple storage unit that will convert just about any flat surface into a functioning secretary.

The fixed shelves are designed to accommodate papers up to legal size, while the adjustable shelf can be positioned to hold address and reference books. The vertical slats with the cutout dividers are good for storing incoming or outgoing mail. And the handy drawer is an ideal spot to keep stamps, sealing wax and other small desktop items.

We made this simple wood project from oak and oak plywood. If you are building a secretary topper to complement an existing piece of furniture, try to match the wood type and finish of the piece.

NOTE: This secretary topper is sized to fit on top of the Writing Desk featured on pages 84 through 89.

## CONSTRUCTION MATERIALS

| Quantity | Lumber |
|---|---|
| 1 | ¼" × 2 × 3' oak plywood |
| 2 | 1 × 10" × 8' oak |
| 1 | ½ × 8" × 6' oak |
| 1 | ¼ × 2" × 7' oak mull casing |

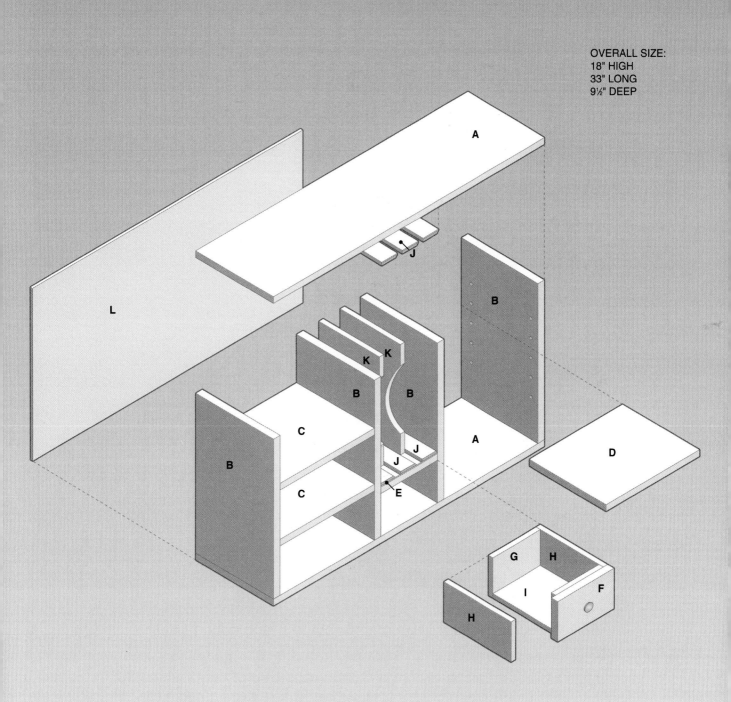

OVERALL SIZE:
18" HIGH
33" LONG
9½" DEEP

## Cutting List

| Key | Part | Dimension | Pcs. | Material |
|---|---|---|---|---|
| **A** | Top/bottom | ¾ × 9¼ × 33" | 2 | Oak |
| **B** | Partition | ¾ × 9¼ × 16½" | 4 | Oak |
| **C** | Fixed shelf | ¾ × 9¼ × 11½" | 2 | Oak |
| **D** | Adjustable shelf | ¾ × 9¼ × 11¼" | 1 | Oak |
| **E** | Bin top | ¾ × 9¼ × 7" | 1 | Oak |
| **F** | Drawer front | ¾ × 4⅛ × 6¾" | 1 | Oak |

## Cutting List

| Key | Part | Dimension | Pcs. | Material |
|---|---|---|---|---|
| **G** | Drawer end | ½ × 4⅛ × 5¾" | 2 | Oak |
| **H** | Drawer side | ½ × 4⅛ × 8¼" | 2 | Oak |
| **I** | Drawer bottom | ½ × 5¾ × 7¼" | 1 | Oak |
| **J** | Bin spacer | ¼ × 2 × 9" | 6 | Mull casing |
| **K** | Divider | ½ × 7¼ × 11½" | 2 | Oak |
| **L** | Back panel | ¼ × 17⅞ × 32¾" | 1 | Plywood |

**Materials:** #6 × 1⅝" wood screws, 16-ga. × ¾" and 1" brads, ¼"-dia. shelf pins (4), ¾"-dia. brass knob (1), ⅜"-dia. oak plugs, adhesive felt pads (6), wood glue, finishing materials.

**Note:** Measurements reflect the actual size of dimension lumber.

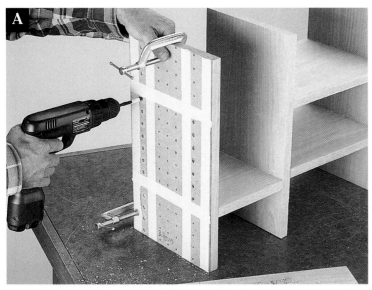

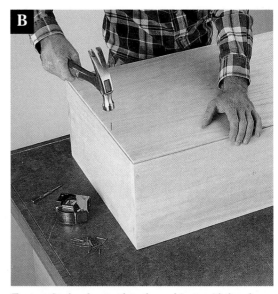

*Use pegboard as a drilling template to align the shelf pin holes in the partitions.*

*Fasten the back panel to the cabinet with brads, keeping the framework square.*

### Directions: Secretary Topper

For all screws used in this project, drill ³⁄₃₂" pilot holes. Counterbore the holes ¼" deep, using a ⅜" counterbore bit.

#### MAKE THE SHELF FRAMEWORK.

**1.** Cut the partitions (B), fixed shelves (C) and bin top (E) to length. Sand the parts smooth.
**2.** Draw reference lines across the faces of two partitions, 5" up from the bottom edge and 5¾" down from the top edge. Use glue to fasten the shelves between the two partitions, keeping their bottom edges flush with the reference lines. Drive 1⅝" wood screws through the partitions and into the ends of the shelves.
**3.** Draw reference lines on the outside face of the left partition, 4¼" up from the bottom edge. Use glue and 1⅝" wood screws to fasten the bin top to the partition, with its bottom edge on the reference line. Make sure the front and rear edges are flush.
**4.** Fasten an unattached parti-

tion to the free end of the bin top with glue and 1⅝" wood screws, keeping the front and back edges flush.
**5.** The left section of the topper features an adjustable shelf. To drill holes in the partitions for the shelf pins, clamp a piece of pegboard to one face, and use it as a drilling template **(photo A).** Drill ¼"-dia. × ⅜"-deep holes into the partition. Wrap masking tape around your drill bit as a depth marker to keep you from drilling through the pieces. After you drill holes in one partition, use tape to mark the locations of the pegboard holes you used. Repeat the drilling with the opposing partition. Keep the same end up and the same edge in front. Sand the pieces smooth.

#### COMPLETE THE CABINET.

**1.** Cut the top/bottom panels (A) to length.
**2.** Attach a panel to the ends of the partitions at the top and at the bottom of the framework. Apply glue, and drive 1⅝" wood screws through the outside faces of the panels and into the

ends of the partitions.
**3.** Fasten the remaining partition between the top and bottom panels, making sure the outside face is flush with the ends of the panels.
**4.** Cut the back (L) to size, and sand it smooth.
**5.** Fasten the back to the cabinet with ¾" brads **(photo B).** Fasten one end of the back and check for square. Adjust it as needed, and fasten the remaining sides. The panel should be centered on the framework, with a slight reveal at all of the edges.

#### MAKE THE DRAWER.

Cut the drawer parts from ½"-thick × 8"-wide oak stock.
**1.** Cut the drawer ends (G), drawer sides (H) and drawer bottom (I) to size. Sand the parts smooth.
**2.** Fasten the drawer ends between the drawer sides with glue, and drive ¾" brads through the drawer sides and into the drawer ends. Make sure the outside faces of the drawer ends are flush with the ends of the drawer sides.

*Drill pilot holes, and fasten the drawer bottom with ¾" brads.*

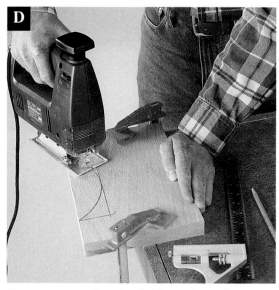

*Gang-cut curves into the dividers, using a jig saw.*

**3.** Position the drawer bottom inside the drawer ends and sides. Drill ¹⁄₁₆" pilot holes through the sides and ends, and fasten the bottom with ¾" brads **(photo C)**. Do not use glue to fasten the bottom.
**4.** Cut the drawer front (F) to size from 1 × 10 stock, and sand it smooth.
**5.** Center the drawer front on one drawer end. With the edges flush, attach the drawer front with glue, and drive 1" brads through the end and into the front.

## INSTALL VERTICAL DIVIDERS.

**1.** Cut the bin spacers (J) and dividers (K) to length.
**2.** Draw a curve on the front edge of one divider, starting 2¼" in from the top and bottom edges, and making it 2" deep at the center. Clamp the dividers together with their edges flush. Gang-cut them along the cutting line with a jig saw **(photo D)**. Gang-sand the pieces, using a drum sander attachment on an electric drill.
**3.** The bin spacers have bevels

on their front edges. Mount a belt sander to your workbench, and clamp a scrap guide to the worksurface to stabilize the parts as you sand the ends of the dividers **(photo E).**
**4.** Use ¾" brads to fasten two of the bin spacers to the bin top, flush against the partitions and butted against the back panel. Fasten two more bin spacers to the top panel.
**5.** Insert the dividers. Fasten the last bin spacers between them.

## APPLY FINISHING TOUCHES.

**1.** Cut the adjustable shelf (D) to length.
**2.** Fill all screw holes with glued oak plugs. Set all nails with a nail set, and fill the holes with wood putty. Remove the dividers, and finish-sand all the parts. Apply a finish.
**3.** Attach a ¾" brass knob to the drawer front. Insert the shelf pins and adjustable shelf. Attach self-adhesive felt pads to the bottom of the topper.

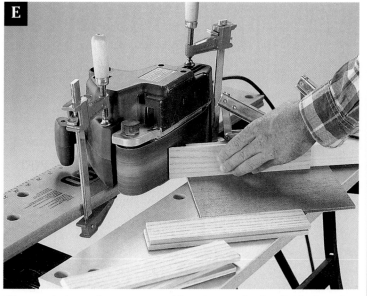

*Clamp a belt sander to your workbench to make the divider bevels.*

# Nesting Office

*The basic building blocks of a home office, designed to
fit together in one small space.*

## CONSTRUCTION MATERIALS

| Quantity | Lumber |
|----------|--------|
| 3 | 2" × 2" × 8' oak |
| 4 | 1" × 4" × 8' oak |
| 2 | 1" × 2" × 8' oak |
| 4 | ¾" × 2 × 4' oak plywood |
| 1 | ⅜" × 1¹⁄₁₆" × 6' oak stop molding |
| 2 | ¾" × ¾" × 8' oak cove molding |

The desk and credenza are the two principal furnishings needed in any home office. This nesting office pair features both components at full size. But because they fit together, they can be stored in about the same amount of space as a standard medium-size desk. Made of oak and oak plywood, both pieces are well constructed and pleasing to the eye. The desk has a large writing surface, and the credenza is a versatile rolling storage cabinet with a hanging file box and shelves for storage of books, paper and other materials. Flip-up tops let you use the credenza as an auxiliary writing or computer surface while storing office supplies below.

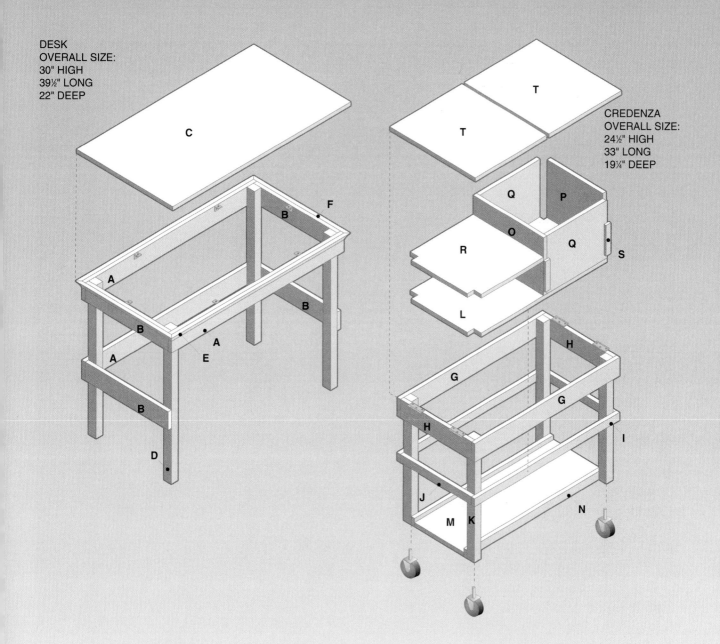

DESK
OVERALL SIZE:
30" HIGH
39½" LONG
22" DEEP

CREDENZA
OVERALL SIZE:
24½" HIGH
33" LONG
19¼" DEEP

| Key | Part | Dimension | Pcs. | Material |
|-----|------|-----------|------|----------|
| **Cutting List** | | | | |
| A | Desk side | ¾ × 3½ × 38" | 3 | Oak |
| B | Desk end | ¾ × 3½ × 19" | 4 | Oak |
| C | Desktop | ¾ × 22 × 39½" | 1 | Plywood |
| D | Desk leg | 1½ × 1½ × 29¼" | 4 | Oak |
| E | Side molding | ¾ × ¾ × *" | 2 | Cove molding |
| F | End molding | ¾ × ¾ × *" | 2 | Cove molding |
| G | Credenza side | ¾ × 3½ × 33" | 2 | Oak |
| H | Credenza end | ¾ × 3½ × 16" | 2 | Oak |
| I | Middle rail | ¾ × 1½ × 33" | 2 | Oak |
| J | End rail | ¾ × 1½ × 16" | 2 | Oak |

| Key | Part | Dimension | Pcs. | Material |
|-----|------|-----------|------|----------|
| **Cutting List** | | | | |
| K | Credenza leg | 1½ × 1½ × 21¼" | 4 | Oak |
| L | Middle shelf | ¾ × 16 × 31½" | 1 | Plywood |
| M | Bottom shelf | ¾ × 11½ × 31½" | 1 | Plywood |
| N | Bottom rail | ¾ × 1½ × 31½" | 2 | Oak |
| O | Divider | ¾ × 11¼ × 16" | 1 | Plywood |
| P | End panel | ¾ × 11¼ × 13" | 1 | Plywood |
| Q | Side panel | ¾ × 11¼ × 13⅞" | 2 | Plywood |
| R | Bin bottom | ¾ × 15⅜ × 16" | 1 | Plywood |
| S | Stop | ⅜ × 1¹⁄₁₆ × 7" | 6 | Stop molding |
| T | Bin lid | ¾ × 16⅜ × 19¼" | 2 | Plywood |

**Materials:** #6 × 1" and 1⅝" wood screws, 16-ga. × 1" brads, 1½ × 3" brass butt hinges (4), 2½" swivel casters (4), 1¼" brass corner braces with ⅝" brass wood screws (6), brass lid supports (4), ¾" oak veneer edge tape (50'), ⅜"-dia. oak plugs, wood glue, finishing materials.

**Note:** Measurements reflect the actual size of dimension lumber.     * Cut to fit.

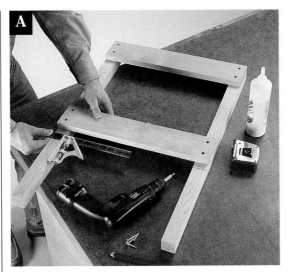

*Check with a combination square to make sure the desk legs are square to the ends.*

*Glue oak plugs into the screw holes to cover the screws.*

## Directions: Nesting Office

For all screws used in this project, drill ³⁄₃₂" pilot holes. Counterbore the holes ¼" deep, using a ³⁄₈" counterbore bit.

MAKE THE DESK-LEG PAIRS.
**1.** Cut the desk ends (B) and desk legs (D) to length. Sand the pieces smooth.
**2.** Lay the legs on a flat surface, arranged in pairs. Lay the desk ends across the legs to form the leg pair assemblies. One desk end in each leg pair should be flush with the tops of the legs, and the bottom of the other desk end should be 10½" up from the bottoms of the legs. Apply glue to the mating surfaces, then clamp the leg pair assemblies together. Check the assemblies with a square to make sure the legs are square to the end boards **(photo A)**. Fasten the pieces together by driving 1⅝" wood screws through the desk ends and into the legs.

ASSEMBLE THE DESK BASE.
**1.** Cut the desk sides (A) to

*Fasten the desktop to the desk base with brass corner braces.*

length and sand them smooth.
**2.** Drill a pair of pilot holes about 1½" in from each end of each desk side board. Before drilling the pilot holes, check the leg pairs to make sure the pilot holes will not run into the screws joining the end boards and the legs.
**3.** Apply glue to the mating ends of one side board, and clamp it in place so it spans between the leg pairs, flush with the tops of the legs and the outside faces of the desk ends. Check to make sure the leg pairs are square to the desk

side. Drive 1⅝" wood screws through the pilot holes. Install the other top desk side, using the same method.
**4.** Use glue and 1⅝" wood screws to attach the lower side board to the legs so the top is flush with the tops of the end boards in the leg pairs. After the glue has set, insert glued oak plugs into all screw holes **(photo B)**. Sand the plugs flush with the surface.
**5.** Sand the entire desk base with medium-grit sandpaper to smooth the surfaces and dull any sharp edges.

Install strips of oak cove molding along the underside of the desktop.

**TIP**

*Plain file boxes can be easily converted to hanging file boxes by installing a self-standing metal hanger system. Sold at office supply stores, the thin metal standards and support rods are custom-cut to fit the box, then assembled and set in place. The metal tabs on the hanging folders fit over the metal support rods.*

### ATTACH THE DESKTOP.

Fasten the plywood desktop to the base with corner braces. These allow the desktop to expand and contract without splitting the wood.

**1.** Cut the desktop (C) to size.

**2.** Sand the edges smooth, and wipe them clean.

**3.** Cut strips of self-adhesive edge tape to fit the edges. Use a household iron set at low to medium heat to press the veneer onto the edges. After the adhesive cools, trim any excess tape with a utility knife. Sand the edges of the tape smooth with fine-grit sandpaper.

**4.** Place the desktop on your worksurface with the top face-down, and center the desk base on the desktop. The desktop should overhang the base by ¾" on all sides. Clamp the base in place, and arrange 1¼" brass corner braces along the inside edges of the desk side and end boards. Use two braces on each side and one at each end. Drill pilot holes, and drive ⅝" brass wood screws to attach the desktop **(photo C).**

### ATTACH THE DESK MOLDING.

Fit the side and end molding pieces underneath the desktop, and fasten them to the desk sides and ends.

**1.** Cut the side molding (E) and end molding (F) pieces to fit the desk dimensions, miter-cutting the ends at a 45° angle.

**2.** Drill ¹⁄₁₆" pilot holes through the molding pieces, and position them against the bottom of the desktop. Apply glue to the molding, including the mitered ends, and attach the pieces with 1" brads **(photo D).**

### MAKE THE CREDENZA BASE.

The credenza base is similar to the desk base. Build the leg pairs first, then join them together with long side boards. Remember to check the frame parts for square before you fasten them.

**1.** Cut the credenza sides (G), credenza ends (H), middle rails (I), end rails (J) and credenza legs (K) to length.

Attach the credenza ends and end rails to the legs with glue and wood screws.

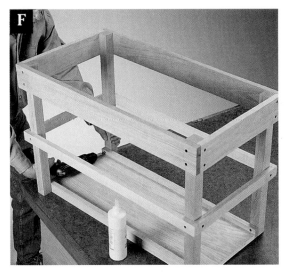
Fasten the bottom shelf by driving wood screws through the bottom rails and into the legs.

Cut notches at each corner of the middle shelf so it will fit between the credenza legs.

**2.** Arrange the legs in pairs with the end rails and credenza ends positioned across them. The credenza ends should be flush with the outside edges and tops of the legs. The end rails should be flush with the outside edges of the legs, with the bottom edges of the rails 12" down from the tops of the legs. Apply glue to the mating surfaces, and clamp the parts together. Make sure the assemblies are square, then drive 1⅝" wood screws through the ends and rails and into the legs **(photo E).**

**3.** Set the leg pairs on one side edge, spacing them about 30" apart. Position a credenza side so its top edge is flush with the tops of the credenza ends. The ends of the side board should be flush with the outside faces of the credenza ends. Fasten the side piece with glue, and drive 1⅝" wood screws through the side and into the legs.

**4.** Attach the middle rail, flush with the end rails in the leg assemblies, using the same methods. Attach the other credenza side and middle rail to complete the base.

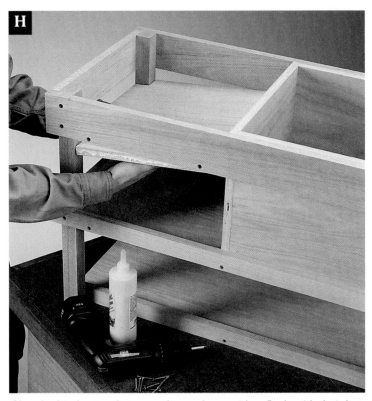
Glue the bin bottom between the credenza sides, flush with their bottom edges, and secure it with screws.

MAKE THE
CREDENZA SHELVES.

**1.** Cut the middle shelf (L), bottom shelf (M) and bottom rails (N) to size. Apply self-adhesive edge tape to both short edges of the bottom shelf.

**2.** Position a bottom rail against each long edge of the bottom shelf. Make sure the ends are flush and the bottom edges of the rails are flush with the bottom face of the shelf. Fasten the parts with glue, and drive 1⅝" wood screws through the bottom rails and into the edges of the bottom shelf.

**3.** Position the bottom shelf be-

Attach strips of oak stop molding to cover the exposed plywood edges of the bins on the outside of the credenza.

tween the credenza legs so the bottom edges are flush. Drive 1⅝" wood screws through the bottom rails and into the credenza legs **(photo F).**

**4.** Use a jig saw to cut a 1½ × 1½" notch in each corner of the middle shelf so it will fit between the credenza legs **(photo G).**

**5.** To attach the middle shelf between the middle rails and end rails, apply glue to the inside edges of the rails, and slide the shelf into position. The shelf should be flush with the bottom edges of the rails. Drive 1⅝" wood screws through the middle and end rails and into the middle shelf.

## MAKE THE CREDENZA BINS.

The credenza bins include a file box for hanging file folders and a supply storage box. Both bins have a flip-up lid.

**1.** Cut the divider (O), end panel (P), side panels (Q) and bin bottom (R) to size.

**2.** Cut 1½ × 1½" notches in both corners at one end of the bin bottom so it will fit between the credenza legs.

**3.** Position the side panels on top of the middle shelf so their outside edges are flush against the legs. Apply glue and drive 1" wood screws through the side panels and into the credenza sides and middle rails.

**4.** Postion the end panel between the legs, with its bottom edge flush against the middle shelf. Apply glue and drive 1" wood screws through the end panel and into the credenza end and end rail.

**5.** Slide the divider into place so it butts against the inside edges of the side panels and is flush with the tops of the side panels. Fasten the divider with glue, and drive 1⅝" wood screws through the divider and into the edges of the side panels.

**6.** From the outside of the credenza, drill evenly spaced pilot holes for the bin bottom in the credenza sides and end, ⅜" up from the bottom edges of the boards. Apply glue to the edges of the bin bottom and slip it into place, flush with the bottom edges of the credenza sides and ends **(photo H).** Drive 1⅝" wood screws through the sides and ends and into the edges of

the bin bottom.

**7.** Cut the stops (S) to length.

**8.** Drill 1/16" pilot holes through the stop pieces. Position the stops to conceal the joints and the edges of the panels that make up the large credenza bin. Use glue and 1" brads to attach the stops **(photo I).**

**9.** Cut the lids (T) to size from a single plywood panel. Apply edge tape to all of the edges. Do not attach the lids until after the finish has been applied.

## APPLY FINISHING TOUCHES.

**1.** Insert glued oak plugs into all visible screw holes in the desk and credenza. Sand the plugs flush with the surface. Set all nails with a nail set, and fill the nail holes with wood putty.

**2.** Finish-sand both furnishings with 180- or 220-grit sandpaper. Then, apply the finish of your choice. You may find it easier to finish the desk if you remove the desktop first. It is important that you finish the underside as well as the top. We used only a clear topcoat for a light, contemporary look. You may prefer to use a light or medium wood stain first.

**3.** When the finish has dried, reattach the desktop. Fasten 1½ × 3" brass butt hinges to the bottom faces of the credenza lids, 2¼" in from the side edges. The backs of the hinge barrels should be flush with the back edges of the lids when closed. Attach the bin lids to the credenza by fastening the hinges to the credenza ends. Attach sliding lid supports to the lids and inside faces of the credenza sides to hold the lids open for access to the bins.

**4.** Attach a 2½" swivel caster to the bottom end of each credenza leg.

# Waste-basket

*A unique decorative accent that won't go to waste in your home office.*

Sure, you probably don't give wastebaskets a second thought, but in any home office they are a necessity. When you need a small trash bin for paper refuse, you don't want a giant, heavy-duty receptacle sitting in the middle of your room. But if you go to the store to buy a wastebasket, often your only options are molded, plastic containers. This project is simple, and the finished product is guaranteed to be useful and attractive.

One unique feature on this wastebasket is the use of decorative diagonal kerfs, or slots, cut into the oak plywood sides. It's an easy technique to use, and it gives the wastebasket a detailed look. We also planed the leg corners to soften the overall appearance and eliminate sharp edges. A plywood bottom is fitted into the wastebasket, which is designed to hold a 9"-dia. paint can or a plastic trash bag as a liner.

This is a great little piece that adds character to a home office or any other room in your house. Compact and unobtrusive, this wastebasket can brighten a forgotten corner or complement other furniture in the room.

## CONSTRUCTION MATERIALS

| Quantity | Lumber |
| --- | --- |
| 1 | ¾" × 4 × 4' red oak plywood |
| 1 | 2 × 2" × 6' red oak |
| 1 | ¾ × ¾" × 3' pine stop molding |

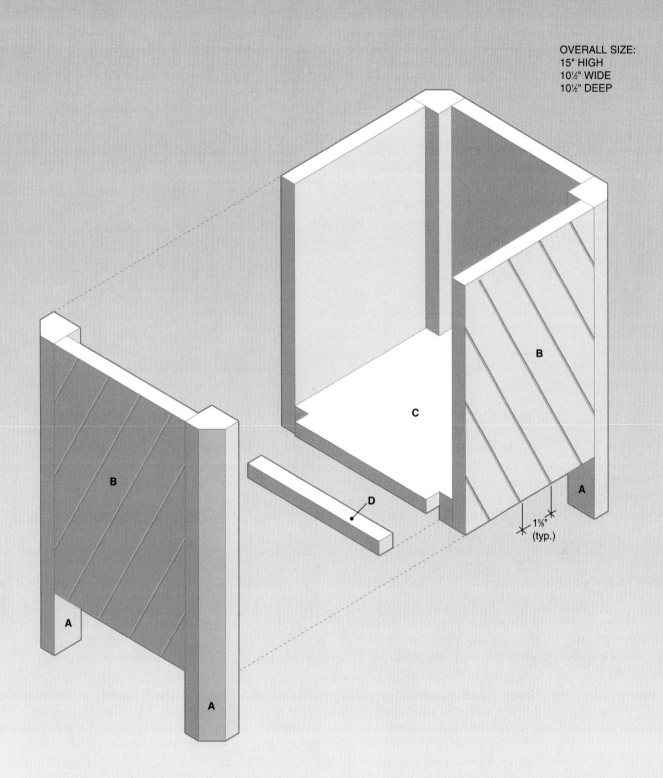

OVERALL SIZE:
15" HIGH
10½" WIDE
10½" DEEP

B

A

B

A

A

C

D

B

A

1⅝"
(typ.)

| Cutting List | | | | |
|---|---|---|---|---|
| Key | Part | Dimension | Pcs. | Material |
| A | Leg | 1½ × 1½ × 15" | 4 | Oak |
| B | Side panel | ¾ × 7½ × 12" | 4 | Plywood |

| Cutting List | | | | |
|---|---|---|---|---|
| Key | Part | Dimension | Pcs. | Material |
| C | Bottom | ¾ × 9 × 9" | 1 | Plywood |
| D | Cleat | ¾ × ¾ × 7½" | 4 | Stop molding |

**Materials:** 3d and 4d finish nails, ¾" oak veneer edge tape (6'), 24 × 32" piece of ¾" plywood, wood glue, finishing materials.

**Specialty tools:** Block plane.

**Note:** Measurements reflect the actual size of dimension lumber.

*Use a plane to trim away one edge of each leg.*

*Use a piece of ¾" plywood with a cutout the same size as a side panel as a jig for cutting the kerfs.*

## Directions: Wastebasket

### MAKE THE LEGS AND SIDE PANELS.

**1.** Cut the legs (A) to length. Sand the pieces smooth.

**2.** To angle the trim cuts on the legs, use a combination square to mark lines ¾" down from one corner along two adjacent sides of each leg. Clamp a leg to your worksurface. Use a block plane to remove wood evenly from the edges **(photo A)**. Use a belt sander to sand the wood down to the lines and to smooth out the plane marks.

**3.** Cut the side panels (B) to size.

### MAKE THE KERF JIG AND LAY OUT THE KERF LINES.

Cut the decorative kerfs on the side panels, using a circular saw and a simple jig. The jig is a piece of ¾" scrap plywood, approximately 24 × 32", with a cutout in the center.

**1.** To make the jig, center a side panel on the scrap plywood, and trace around the edges of the piece. Make the cutout with a jig saw **(photo B)**.

**2.** To draw the cutting lines, set a side panel into the jig cutout, and mark points at 1⅝" intervals along the bottom edge of the panel. Draw cutting lines at a 45° angle to the bottom edge, extending the lines all the way across the panel and the jig. Measure at several places to make sure the lines are parallel.

**3.** To give the side panels a more interesting appearance, we cut two panels with kerfs that run upward from left to right, and two with kerfs that

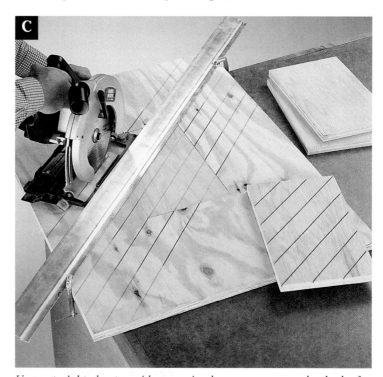

*Use a straightedge to guide your circular saw as you make the kerf cuts in the jig and side panels.*

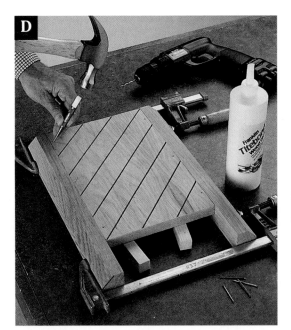

Glue and toenail the side panels to the legs.

As you assemble the wastebasket, check frequently to make sure it is square.

run upward from right to left. The kerfs form peaks where the adjacent sides meet. Mark each panel individually, and remember to change the direction of the lines for two of the panels.

## CUT THE KERFS.

**1.** Place a side panel into the jig. Clamp a long straightedge to the jig so the saw blade will line up with one cutting line. Set the blade depth at ¼". Cut along the line, making sure to start and finish the cut well past the edges of the side panel **(photo C).** NOTE: The saw may cause some splintering along the edges of the kerfs. To minimize this, use a sharp saw blade, and move the saw slowly while making the cuts.

**2.** Moving the straightedge to follow the cutting lines, cut the kerfs in all four panels.

**3.** Use a household iron to apply strips of self-adhesive edge tape to the top and bottom edges of each side panel. Trim any excess tape with a utility knife, and sand the edges smooth.

**4.** Practice assembling the side panels, using alternating patterns (see *Diagram,* page 101).

## ATTACH THE LEGS AND SIDES.

**1.** Cut the cleats (D) to length.

**2.** Lay one side panel on top of two ¾" spacers (the cleats will work). Butt a leg against each side edge, keeping the tops and outside edges flush. Glue and clamp the pieces together. Drill 1/16" pilot holes, and toenail 4d finish nails through the side and into the legs **(photo D).**

**3.** Repeat with the matching side. Make sure the kerf cuts run the same way.

**4.** Attach a cleat to the inside face of each side panel, flush with the bottom edge. Apply glue and drive 3d finish nails through the cleats and into the side panels.

## ASSEMBLE THE WASTEBASKET.

**1.** Assemble the basket by joining the remaining side panels to the legs and gluing and toe-

nailing the unfastened joints. Make sure the project is square and that the faces of the side panels are flush with the outside edges of the legs **(photo E).**

**2.** Cut the bottom (C) to size.

**3.** Cut ¾ × ¾" notches into each corner of the bottom, so it will fit into the opening formed by the sides and legs. Apply glue to the tops of the cleats, and insert the bottom panel.

## APPLY FINISHING TOUCHES.

Set all nails with a nail set. Finish-sand the wastebasket, and apply the finish of your choice. We left the wood unstained and applied two coats of satin-gloss polyurethane.

---

TIP

*When planing, follow the grain of the wood. Don't try to remove too much wood at one time; smooth, easy strokes will yield the best results.*

# Room Divider

*Crafted from cedar boards and lauan plywood, this portable room divider makes it easy to create a new living space.*

## CONSTRUCTION MATERIALS

| Quantity | Lumber* |
| --- | --- |
| 3 | 1 × 4" × 8' cedar |
| 3 | ¾ × ¾" × 8' mahogany cove molding |
| 1 | ¼" × 4 × 4' lauan plywood |

*Materials for a single room divider section.

Strips of lauan plywood are woven together and set in rustic cedar frames to make this room divider. Held together with brass hinges, the sections of the divider can be arranged to fit almost any room. Use it as a partition to make a romantic dining nook in a large living area. Or, position the room divider near a sunny window to establish a tranquil garden retreat without adding permanent walls. There are many creative uses for this versatile decorative barrier.

The instructions for building the room divider show you how to make one section. Add as many additional sections as your space needs require.

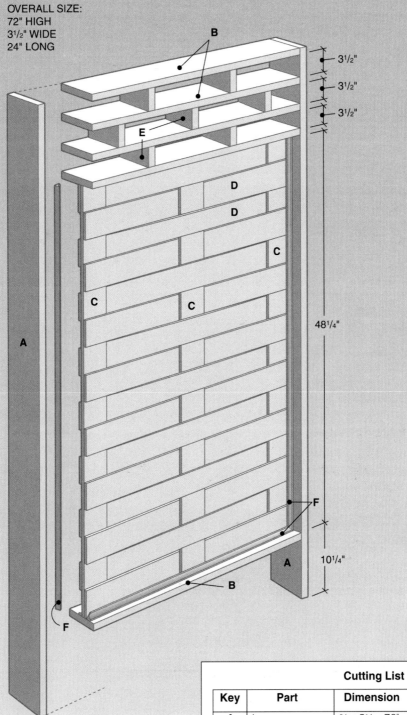

OVERALL SIZE:
72" HIGH
3½" WIDE
24" LONG

B

3½"

3½"

3½"

E

D

D

C

C

C

A

48¼"

F

B

A

10¼"

F

## Cutting List

| Key | Part | Dimension | Pcs. | Material |
|-----|------|-----------|------|----------|
| **A** | Leg | ¾ × 3½ × 72" | 2 | Cedar |
| **B** | Stretcher | ¾ × 3½ × 22½" | 5 | Cedar |
| **C** | Vertical slat | ¼ × 3 × 48" | 3 | Plywood |
| **D** | Horizontal slat | ¼ × 3 × 22½" | 16 | Plywood |
| **E** | Divider | ¾ × 3½ × 3½" | 7 | Cedar |
| **F** | Retaining strip | ¾ × ¾" × * | 8 | Cove molding |

**Materials:** 2" deck screws, 2d finish nails, 2" brass butt hinges, wood glue, finishing materials.

**Note:** Measurements reflect the actual size of dimension lumber.

*Cut to fit.

## Directions: Room Divider

### MAKE THE FRAME.

The frame consists of two legs and five stretchers. Starting from the bottom, the first and second stretchers form the top and bottom borders of the woven panel.

**1.** Cut the legs (A) and stretchers (B) to length.

**2.** Measure and mark the positions for the stretchers on the inside faces of the legs. To make sure the measurements are exactly the same on both legs, tape the pieces together, edge to edge. Make sure the top and bottom edges are flush. Measure and mark a reference line 10¼" from the bottom ends of both legs. These lines mark the top edge of the bottom stretcher. Next, measure and mark lines 48¼" up the legs from the first reference lines **(photo A).** These lines mark the bottom edge of the second stretcher. The top stretcher should be positioned between the legs, flush with the top ends. Mark the remaining stretcher positions as desired. We arranged them equally between the top and second stretchers, about 3½" apart.

**3.** To complete the frame, drill two ³⁄₃₂" pilot holes through the outside faces of the legs at the center position of each stretcher. Counterbore the holes ⅛" deep, using a ⅜" counterbore bit. Glue the ends of the stretchers and position them between the legs. Clamp the frame together and measure diagonally from corner to corner to make sure the frame is square. Fasten the stretchers to the legs with 2" deck screws.

*Tape the legs together with their edges flush, and gang-mark the stretcher positions on the inside faces.*

*Weave the 16 horizontal slats through the three vertical slats to make the divider panel.*

### MAKE THE DIVIDER PANEL.

The divider panel consists of 19 strips of ¼"-thick lauan plywood woven together without fasteners or glue. This step is easy to complete if you work on a flat surface.

**1.** Cut the vertical slats (C) and horizontal slats (D) to size. Sand the edges smooth.

**2.** Lay the vertical slats on your worksurface. Weave the horizontal slats between the vertical slats in an alternating pattern to form the panel **(photo B).**

### INSTALL THE DIVIDER PANEL.

To hold the divider panel in the frame, fasten retaining strips along the inside faces of the legs and stretchers on both sides of the panel.

**1.** Use a miter box or a power miter saw to cut the retaining

*Attach the retaining strips with 2d finish nails.*

*Connect the divider sections with brass butt hinges.*

strips so they are snug against the opposite face of the panel.
**4.** Fill all visible screw holes with tinted wood putty, and sand the legs smooth.

APPLY FINISHING TOUCHES.
Inserting the dividers is the final construction step for the room divider section. These pieces are purely decorative and can be spaced apart in any pattern. Cut them to fit snug between the top stretchers so they won't need fasteners.
**1.** Measure the distance between the top stretchers, and cut the dividers (E) to length. Sand the dividers smooth.
**2.** Set the dividers between the stretchers, positioning them in a way that is visually pleasing.
**3.** Once you have made several room divider sections, join them with evenly spaced 2" butt hinges **(photo D).** To attach the hinges, clamp the sections together with scrap wood spacers in between. The spacers should have the same thickness as the barrels of the hinges. Use cardboard pads to prevent the feet of the clamps from damaging the soft wood of the frames.
**4.** Cedar lumber, mahogany trim and lauan plywood do not require a protective finish, so we left them unfinished. If you prefer a glossier, more formal look, apply a coat of tung oil to the parts before assembly.

strips (F) to length from ¾"-thick mahogany cove molding. Miter-cut the retaining strips to fit the inside of the frame.
**2.** Mark reference lines along the inside faces of the legs, and on the faces of the stretchers at either end of the divider panels, 1⅜" in from one edge. Position the molding on the outside

of the reference lines, so one flat face is flush with the line. Attach the retaining strips to the frame with 2d finish nails **(photo C).** Set the nails with a nail set.
**3.** Place the woven panel against the retaining strip frame, and secure the panel by attaching the other retaining

# Cedar Chest

*This compact cedar chest has the potential to become
a cherished family heirloom.*

## CONSTRUCTION MATERIALS

| Quantity | Lumber |
|----------|--------|
| 3 | 1 × 2" × 8' cedar |
| 1 | 1 × 3" × 10' cedar |
| 1 | 1 × 6" × 8' cedar |
| 3 | 1 × 8" × 8' cedar |
| 1 | 2 × 2" × 8' cedar |
| 1 | ¾" × 2 × 4' plywood |

The cedar chest has a long history as a much-appreciated graduation gift. The appreciation will be even greater for a cedar chest you have built yourself. And short of a packing crate, you won't find a simpler chest to build anywhere.

Despite its simplicity, this cedar chest has all the features of a commercially produced chest costing hundreds of dollars. The framed lid is hinged in back and can be locked open with an optional locking lid support. A removable tray fits inside the chest for storing delicate items. The main compartment is fitted with aromatic cedar panels to keep sweaters or your favorite linen treasures safe from moth damage and musty odors.

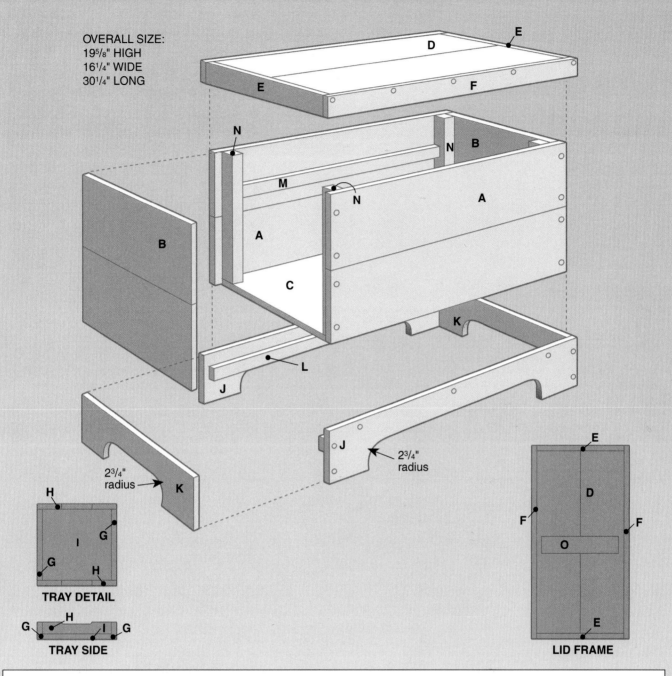

OVERALL SIZE:
19⅝" HIGH
16¼" WIDE
30¼" LONG

2¾" radius

2¾" radius

TRAY DETAIL

TRAY SIDE

LID FRAME

| Key | Part | Dimension | Pcs. | Material |
|-----|------|-----------|------|----------|
| **A** | Side | ⅞ × 7¼ × 28" | 4 | Cedar |
| **B** | End | ⅞ × 7¼ × 12½" | 4 | Cedar |
| **C** | Bottom | ¾ × 12½ × 26¼" | 1 | Plywood |
| **D** | Top | ⅞ × 7¼ × 28½" | 2 | Cedar |
| **E** | End lip | ⅞ × 1½ × 14½" | 2 | Cedar |
| **F** | Side lip | ⅞ × 1½ × 30¼" | 2 | Cedar |
| **G** | Tray side | ⅞ × 2½ × 12¾" | 2 | Cedar |
| **H** | Tray end | ⅞ × 2½ × 11¾" | 2 | Cedar |

Cutting List

| Key | Part | Dimension | Pcs. | Material |
|-----|------|-----------|------|----------|
| **I** | Tray bottom | ⅞ × 2½ × 12¾" | 4 | Cedar |
| **J** | Side plate | ⅞ × 5½ × 29¾" | 2 | Cedar |
| **K** | End plate | ⅞ × 5½ × 14¼" | 2 | Cedar |
| **L** | Base cleat | ⅞ × 1½ × 28" | 2 | Cedar |
| **M** | Chest cleat | ⅞ × 1½ × 23¼" | 2 | Cedar |
| **N** | Corner post | 1½ × 1½ × 13¾" | 4 | Cedar |
| **O** | Top cleat | ⅞ × 2½ × 12" | 1 | Cedar |

Cutting List

**Materials:** 1¼" and 2" deck screws, 2d finish nails, 1½ × 2" brass butt hinges (2), lid support, optional hardware accessories, aromatic cedar panels, panel adhesive, ⅜"-dia. cedar plugs, wood glue, finishing materials.

**Note:** Measurements reflect the actual size of dimension lumber.

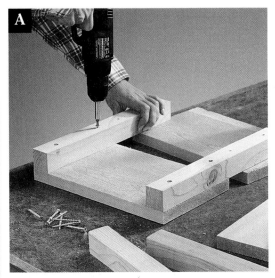

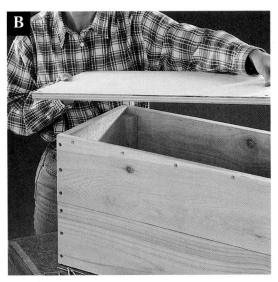

*Drive screws through the posts and into the ends.*

*Install the bottom onto the corner posts and fasten it to the sides and ends of the chest.*

## Directions: Cedar Chest

For all screws used in this project, drill ³⁄₃₂" pilot holes. Counterbore the holes ¼" deep, using a ⅜" counterbore bit.

### BUILD THE BOX FRAME.
**1.** Cut the chest sides (A), chest ends (B) and corner posts (N) to length. Sand the pieces smooth with medium-grit sandpaper.
**2.** Use glue and 2" deck screws to fasten two chest ends to each pair of corner posts, with their tops and side edges flush **(photo A).** When using cedar that is rough on one side, be sure that exposed surfaces are consistent in texture. For this project, make sure all rough surfaces are facing inside.

*Attach the top cleat to the undersides of the tops, making sure it is centered between the ends and the sides.*

**3.** Once the chest ends and corner posts are attached, apply glue to the outside edges of the corner posts, and fasten the chest sides to the chest ends by driving 2" deck screws through the chest sides and into the edges of the chest ends. Make sure the top and side edges are flush. If the box frame is assembled correctly, there will be a ¾"-wide space between the bottom of the corner posts and the bottom edges of the box frame.
**4.** Cut the bottom (C) to size.

**5.** Turn the box frame upside down. Fasten the bottom to the corner posts, ends and sides with glue and 2" deck screws **(photo B).**
**6.** Seal the inside surfaces with an oil finish or sealer to prevent warping and splitting.

### BUILD THE TOP ASSEMBLY.
**1.** Cut the top pieces (D) and the top cleat (O) to length. Cut the end lips (E) and side lips (F) to length. Sand the pieces smooth.

*Smooth the jig saw cuts on the radius cutouts using a drum sander attachment and drill.*

*Set the box frame into the base, and fasten it with evenly spaced screws.*

**2.** Use bar or pipe clamps to hold the tops together, edge to edge, with their ends flush. Use a combination square to measure and mark the top cleat position on the inside faces of the tops. Make sure the top cleat is centered, with its side edges 13" from the ends of the tops and with its ends centered between the side edges of the tops. Attach the cleat to the tops with glue and 1¼" deck screws **(photo C)**.
**3.** Attach the side lips and end lips to the edges of the tops with glue and 2" deck screws. Make sure the top edges of the lips and tops are flush.

### BUILD THE BASE.
**1.** Cut the side plates (J) and end plates (K) to length.
**2.** Use a compass and a straightedge to draw the carved cutouts on the side and end plates. Make marks along the bottom edge of the side plates, 6¾" in from each end. Set a compass to draw a 2¾" radius curve. Hold the compass point on the mark, as close as possible to the bottom edge, and draw the curve onto the face of the side plate. Then, using a straightedge, draw a straight line 2¾" from the bottom edge of the side plate, intersecting the tops of the curves. Repeat these steps to draw the cutouts on the end plates, but hold the compass point 5⅞" from the ends. Make the cutouts with a jig saw.
**3.** Use a drill and a drum sander attachment to smooth the curves of the cutouts **(photo D)**. Finish-sand the side plates and end plates.
**4.** Fasten the end plates between the side plates with glue. Drive 2" deck screws through the faces of the side plates and into the ends of the end plates.
**5.** Cut the two base cleats (L) to length.
**6.** Use glue to fasten the base cleats to the inside faces of the side plates, 2¾" from the bottom edges, flush with the top of the cutouts. Drive 1¼" deck screws through the cleats and into the side plates.

### ATTACH THE BOX FRAME AND BASE.
**1.** Test-fit the box frame in the base, making sure it sits squarely on top of the cleats.
**2.** Apply glue to the mating surfaces, and attach the base by driving evenly spaced 1¼" deck screws through the end plates and side plates and into the box frame **(photo E)**.

> **TIP**
>
> *When constructing pieces that fit inside of other pieces (as the chest fits inside the base), build the inside piece first. The outer parts can always be cut larger or smaller to fit the inner ones.*

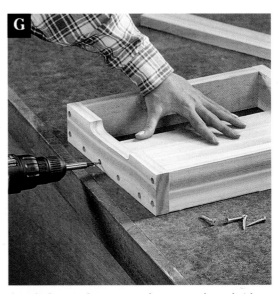

*Tape the tray ends together. Then, draw a slot across the joint to mark identical handle cutouts.*

*Attach the tray bottoms to the tray ends and sides with glue and screws.*

## MAKE THE TRAY.

**1.** Cut the tray sides (G), tray ends (H) and tray bottom (I) pieces to length.

**2.** Lay out the tray handles by placing the tray ends side by side, with the ends flush. Tape the pieces together. Mark a 1½"-wide × 5"-long slot with ¾"-radius curves centered on each end of the slot where the two pieces meet **(photo F).** Make the cuts with a jig saw. Use a drum sander attachment on a drill to smooth out the radius cuts.

**3.** Attach the tray sides between the tray ends with glue and 2" deck screws.

**4.** Fasten the tray bottoms between the tray sides and ends with glue and 2" deck screws **(photo G).** Finish-sand the entire tray, and smooth out any sharp edges.

## INSTALL AROMATIC CEDAR PANELS.

**1.** Cut aromatic cedar liner panels to fit the inside of the chest. Use panels that are no thicker than ¼".

**2.** Attach the liner panels to the sides, ends and bottom with panel adhesive and 2d finish nails **(photo H).** Set the nails with a nail set.

> ### TIP
>
> *Aromatic cedar paneling, often described as "closet liner," has a strong cedar scent that keeps away insects that can damage stored items. The paneling is sold in board packages (usually covering 14 square feet) or in thin sheets that resemble particleboard.*

## MAKE AND INSTALL THE CHEST CLEATS.

**1.** Cut the chest cleats (M) to length. Finish-sand the cleats.

**2.** Install the chest cleats so their top edges are 3½" from the tops of the chest sides. They should fit snugly between the corner posts. Attach the cleats with glue, and drive 1¼" deck screws through the cleats and into the sides.

## INSTALL THE TOP ASSEMBLY.

**1.** Place the top assembly over the chest box, and use masking tape to mark where the lower edge of the lip contacts the back side. Install two 1½ × 2" brass butt hinges on the back of the chest box, 6" in from each end. Mount the hinges so the leaves are above the contact line and the barrels are below the contact line.

**2.** Place the chest and top assembly on a flat worksurface. Prop the chest box against the top so the unfastened leaves of the hinges rest on the inside of the lip of the top assembly. Insert spacers equal to the thickness of the hinge barrel between the chest and lip. (Ordinary wood shims work well for this.) Fasten the hinges to the lip using the screws provided with the hinge hardware **(photo I).** Test the lid assembly and hinges for proper operation and fit.

**3.** Install a locking lid support between the lid assembly and

**H**

*Install aromatic cedar panels to the sides, ends and bottom, using panel adhesive and 2d finish nails.*

**TIP**

*Use the right tools and techniques when applying stencils. A special brush, called a stippling brush, is recommended for stencils (they resemble old-style shaving brushes). Use special stenciling paint, which is very dry so it does not leak under the stencil. Attach the stencil securely, and dab the dry paint onto the surface with the stippling brush. Do not remove the stencil until the paint has dried.*

the chest box to hold the lid in an open position during use. For just a little more money, you can purchase hardware accessories called soft-down supports, which let the lid close gently instead of slamming down.

**4.** Install chest handles and brass corner protectors, if desired.

## APPLY FINISHING TOUCHES.

**1.** Fill all exposed counterbore holes with cedar plugs. Apply glue to the edges of the plugs and tap them in place with a hammer. Sand the plugs flush with the surrounding surface. Finish-sand all of the outside surfaces of the chest.

**2.** Set the tray on the chest cleats and slide it back and forth to test the fit. Adjust the fit, if necessary, using a belt or palm sander and medium-grit sandpaper. Finish-sand the tray to remove any sanding scratches and roughness.

**3.** Finish the chest and tray as desired. We chose a traditional clear finish to provide a rustic, natural appearance. To apply this type of finish, first brush on a coat of sanding sealer to ensure even absorption (a good idea with soft wood like cedar). Then, apply two light coats of tung-oil finish, and buff the surface to a medium gloss with a buffing pad. Apply finish to the chest cleat pieces but leave the cedar panels bare.

**4.** After the finish is applied, dried and buffed, you may want to stencil a design or monograms onto the chest. If you choose to monogram the chest, look for plain stencils that are 1" to 2" tall, to keep in scale with the size of the chest. Very ornate typestyles are hard to stencil, and generally are not in tune with the rustic look of a cedar chest (see *Tip*, above). If you are interested in stenciling a design or emblem onto the chest, also look for a simple pattern. Almost any nature motif (like pinecones) is a good fit.

**I**

*Install brass butt hinges on the chest box and lid assembly. Use wood shims as spacers to help align the hinges.*

# Nightstand

*A back rail adds style to our nightstand and keeps you from knocking bedside items to the floor. Put our nightstand at your bedside for a classic touch of bedroom beauty.*

PROJECT
POWER TOOLS

The nightstand is a classic piece of furniture that will never go out of fashion. Our nightstand has a simple design with a solid, traditional look. The arched back rail and base pieces add style and grace to the nightstand, while the handy drawer gives you a great place to store bedside items.

Assembling this little beauty is easy. The box frame is made by attaching the sides, back and shelves. It is topped with a decorative back rail and wings. These pieces do more than dress up the nightstand—they reduce the risk of knocking over that insistent alarm clock when you lurch to shut it off in the morning.

Once the top sections are complete, you can make and attach the arched base. The drawer comes next. We avoided expensive metal track glides and instead used friction-reducing plastic bumpers and tack-on glides for easy installation and convenience.

Our nightstand is built from edge-glued "ponderosa" pine panels that you can purchase at most building centers.

### CONSTRUCTION MATERIALS

| Quantity | Lumber |
| --- | --- |
| 2 | 1 × 16" × 8' edge-glued pine |
| 1 | 1 × 4" × 4' pine |

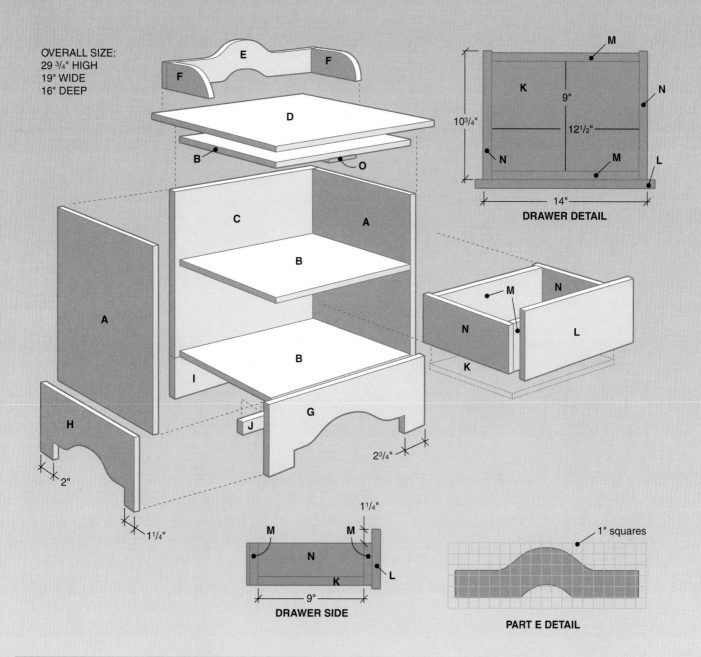

OVERALL SIZE:
29 ¾" HIGH
19" WIDE
16" DEEP

**DRAWER DETAIL**

**DRAWER SIDE**

**PART E DETAIL**

1" squares

| **Cutting List** | | | | |
|---|---|---|---|---|
| **Key** | **Part** | **Dimension** | **Pcs.** | **Material** |
| **A** | Side | ¾ × 13¼ × 17" | 2 | Pine |
| **B** | Shelf | ¾ × 13¼ × 14½" | 3 | Pine |
| **C** | Back | ¾ × 16 × 17" | 1 | Pine |
| **D** | Top | ¾ × 16 × 19" | 1 | Pine |
| **E** | Back rail | ¾ × 4½ × 17½" | 1 | Pine |
| **F** | Wing | ¾ × 2½ × 5½" | 2 | Pine |
| **G** | Base front | ¾ × 8 × 17½" | 1 | Pine |
| **H** | Base side | ¾ × 8 × 14" | 2 | Pine |

| **Cutting List** | | | | |
|---|---|---|---|---|
| **Key** | **Part** | **Dimension** | **Pcs.** | **Material** |
| **I** | Base back | ¾ × 4 × 16" | 1 | Pine |
| **J** | Base cleat | ¾ × 2 × 16" | 1 | Pine |
| **K** | Drawer bottom | ¾ × 9 × 12½" | 1 | Pine |
| **L** | Drawer front | ¾ × 5 × 15¾" | 1 | Pine |
| **M** | Drawer end | ¾ × 3½ × 12½" | 2 | Pine |
| **N** | Drawer side | ¾ × 3½ × 10¾" | 2 | Pine |
| **O** | Stop cleat | ¾ × 1½ × 3" | 1 | Pine |

**Materials:** 1¼", 1½", and 2" deck screws, 6d finish nails, wooden knobs (2), plastic drawer stop, tack-on drawer glides, stem bumpers, wood glue, finishing materials.

**Note:** Measurements reflect the actual size of dimension lumber.

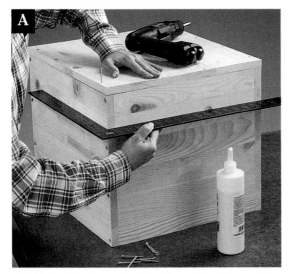

Attach the back to one side. Then, check for square.

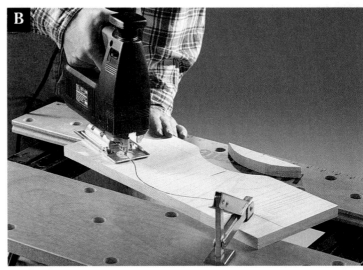

Trace the back rail pattern and cut the piece to shape with a jig saw.

## Directions: Nightstand

For all screws used in this project, drill ³⁄₃₂" pilot holes. Counterbore the holes ⅛" deep, using a ⅜" counterbore bit.

BUILD THE BOX FRAME.
**1.** Cut the sides (A) and shelves (B) to size, and finish-sand the pieces. Use glue and 2" deck screws to fasten the top and bottom shelves between the sides. Attach one shelf flush with the top ends of the sides and the other shelf flush with the bottom ends. Make sure the screws are centered and the front and back shelf edges are flush with the side edges.
**2.** Cut the back (C) to size, and sand it smooth. Attach it along the back edge of one side with glue and 2" deck screws **(photo A).**
**3.** Use a framing square to

Fasten the wings to the back rail with glue and screws.

check the outside of the box to be sure the sides are square with the shelves. If they are not, apply pressure to one side to draw the pieces square. This can be done by hand or by attaching a bar or pipe clamp diagonally from one side to the other. When the pieces are square, clamp them in place, and finish attaching the back to the remaining sides and shelves.

MAKE THE BACK RAIL AND WINGS.
**1.** Cut the back rail (E) and wings (F) to size.
**2.** Transfer the grid on page 115 to a piece of stiff cardboard to make a cutting template for the back rail (see *Tip*).
**3.** Use the template to trace the shape onto the back rail. Cut the piece to the finished shape, using a jig saw **(photo B).** Sand the back rail smooth.
**4.** Place the cardboard template onto the face of one of

TIP

*When transferring a grid diagram, you can enlarge the diagram on a photocopier and trace it onto a piece of cardboard to form a tracing template.*

*Draw reference lines on the top. Then, drill pilot holes and attach the back rail and wings.*

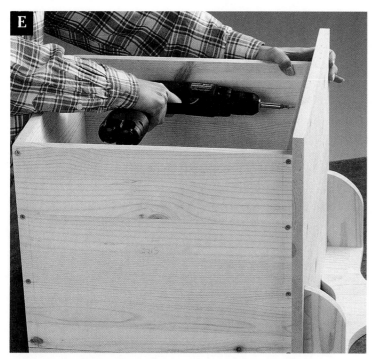

*Attach the top assembly to the top shelf with glue and screws.*

the wings. Trace along the template arc to make a smooth curve at the wing end. Cut the curve with a jig saw. Then, use the cut piece to trace an identical curve onto the other wing. Cut the second wing, and gang-sand the two wings smooth.

**5.** Drill pilot holes in the back rail ⅜" in from the ends. Fasten the wings to the back rail with

glue and 1½" deck screws **(photo C).**

COMPLETE THE TOP SECTION.
**1.** Cut the top (D) to size, and sand it smooth.
**2.** Center the back rail and wings onto the top with the back rail flush with the top's back edge. Draw a 5½"-long line marking the outside edge

of each wing. The lines should be ¾" in from the side edges of the top.
**3.** Drill pilot holes through the top, ⅜" inside each line for attaching the wings **(photo D).** Attach the back rail and wings to the top with glue, and drive 1½" deck screws through the bottom face of the top and into the back rail and wings.
**4.** Center the top assembly over the top shelf, with the back edges flush. Attach the top assembly by driving 1¼" deck screws through the top shelf and into the top **(photo E).**

ATTACH THE MIDDLE SHELF.
**1.** Draw reference lines across the inside faces of the sides, 5½" down from the top edges of the sides.
**2.** Position the top of the middle shelf below the reference lines with its front edge flush with the front edges of the sides. Fasten the shelf with glue, and drive 2" deck screws through the sides and into the edges of the shelf. This shelf supports the drawer, so make sure it is square to the sides.

MAKE THE BASE CUTOUTS.
**1.** Cut the base front (G), base sides (H), base back (I) and base cleat (J) to size.
**2.** To make the decorative cutout on the base front, draw vertical lines 2¾" in from each end. Using the template you made for the back rail, center

*Use a combination square to mark the finish nail position on the base front and sides.*

the top of the arc 3" down from the top edge of the base front. Trace the curved line along the top of the template until it intersects the two vertical lines (see *Diagram*, page 115). Cut out the detail with a jig saw, and sand the piece smooth.

**3.** Make the cutout on one of the base sides, using the template. Draw a vertical line on the base side piece, 1¼" in from the front end and 2" in from the rear end. Center the arc of the template 3" from the top of the base side, and trace the curve to meet the vertical lines. Cut the piece with a jig saw and sand it smooth.

**4.** Use the finished base side to trace an identical pattern onto the other base side. Make the cutout with a jig saw, and sand

the piece smooth.

ASSEMBLE THE BASE.
**1.** Butt the front ends of the base sides against the base front so the top edges are flush and the outside faces of the base sides are flush with the ends of the base front. Drill ¹⁄₁₆" pilot holes through the base front and into the sides. Attach the pieces with glue and 6d finish nails.

**2.** Position the base back between the base sides so that its top edge is ½" below the top edges of the base sides and the back edges are flush. Attach the base back with glue, and drive 6d finish nails through the sides and into the ends of the base back.

**3.** Attach the base cleat to the

inside face of the base front with glue, and drive 1¼" deck screws through the cleat and into the base front. Leave a ½" space between the top edge of the cleat and the top edge of the base front.

ATTACH THE FRAME.
**1.** Draw a reference line for finish nails, ¼" below the top edge of the base front and sides **(photo F).**
**2.** Set the nightstand box frame into the base so it rests on the base back and base cleat.
**3.** Drill evenly spaced ¹⁄₁₆" pilot holes along the reference lines. Fasten the base by driving 6d finish nails through the base front and sides and into the sides and bottom shelf.

BUILD THE DRAWER.
**1.** Cut the drawer bottom (K), drawer front (L), drawer ends (M) and drawer sides (N) to size. Sand the parts smooth.
**2.** Position the drawer bottom between the drawer ends, keeping the bottom edges and the ends flush. Attach the pieces with glue, and drive 1½" deck screws through the drawer ends and into the drawer bottom.
**3.** Align the drawer sides so their front edges are flush with the front face of the front drawer end. Fasten the sides to the bottom and ends with glue and 1½" deck screws **(photo G).** The rear ends of the drawer sides should overhang the rear drawer end by ¼".
**4.** Draw a reference line along the inside face of the drawer front ¼" above the bottom edge. Lay the drawer front flat on your worksurface. Center the drawer from side to side on the drawer front with its bottom

edge on the reference line. Apply glue, and drive 1¼" deck screws through the drawer end and into the drawer front **(photo H).**

## INSTALL THE STOP CLEAT AND DRAWER KNOBS.

Used in conjunction with a store-bought drawer stop, the stop cleat prevents the drawer from pulling completely out of the nightstand. A drawer stop is a small plastic bracket with an adjustable stem that catches the stop cleat when the drawer is opened.

**1.** Cut the stop cleat (O) to size.
**2.** Center the cleat on the bottom face of the top shelf so its front edge is ¾" in from the front edge of the top shelf. The length of the cleat should run parallel to the front edge of the shelf, and its 1½" face should contact the shelf face.
**3.** Attach the stop cleat with glue, and drive 1¼" deck screws through the cleat and into the top shelf.
**4.** Fasten the drawer knobs to the drawer front. Be sure to space the knobs evenly, and center them from top to bottom on the drawer front.

## APPLY FINISHING TOUCHES.

**1.** Set all nails with a nail set, and fill the nail and screw holes with wood putty. Finish-sand the entire project.
**2.** Paint the nightstand inside and out, including the drawer. Apply a polyurethane topcoat to protect the painted finish.

## INSTALL THE HARDWARE.

You have a number of options in making the drawer a functioning element of the nightstand. For instance, you can use metal glides that attach per-

*Fasten the drawer sides to the drawer ends and drawer bottom with glue and screws.*

manently to the drawer and frame. We used inexpensive plastic glides and stem bumpers. You can buy these glides and bumpers at any building center. Always follow manufacturer's directions when installing hardware.

**1.** The Teflon-coated glides we used have metal points, and they are installed like thumbtacks. Align the glides along the path of the drawer, and tack them in place.
**2.** Drill holes for the stem bumpers into the drawer bottom. Apply glue to the bumpers, and insert them into the holes.
**3.** To install the drawer stop, drill a ³⁄₁₆"-dia. hole on the rear drawer end, ½" below the top edge. Apply glue to the drawer stop and attach it to the drawer end.
**4.** Insert the drawer. With the drawer open slightly, reach in and rotate the drawer stop until it is in position to catch the stop cleat.

*Align the drawer front, and attach the pieces by driving screws through the drawer end.*

# Armoire

*With a simple, rustic appearance, this movable closet
can blend into almost any bedroom.*

## Construction Materials

| Quantity | Lumber |
|----------|--------|
| 3 | ¾" × 4 × 8' birch plywood |
| 1 | ¼" × 4 × 8' birch plywood |
| 1 | 1 × 2" × 8' pine |
| 6 | 1 × 3" × 8' pine |
| 1 | 1 × 6" × 8' pine |
| 1 | 1½"-dia. × 2' fir dowel |

Long before massive walk-in closets became the norm in residential building design, homeowners and apartment-dwellers compensated for cramped bedroom closets by making or buying armoires. The trim armoire design shown here reflects the basic styling developed during the heyday of the armoire, but at a scale that makes it usable in just about any living situation. At 60" high and only 36" in width, this compact armoire still boasts plenty of interior space. Five shelves on the left side are sized to store folded sweaters and shirts. And you can hang several suit jackets or dresses in the closet section to the right.

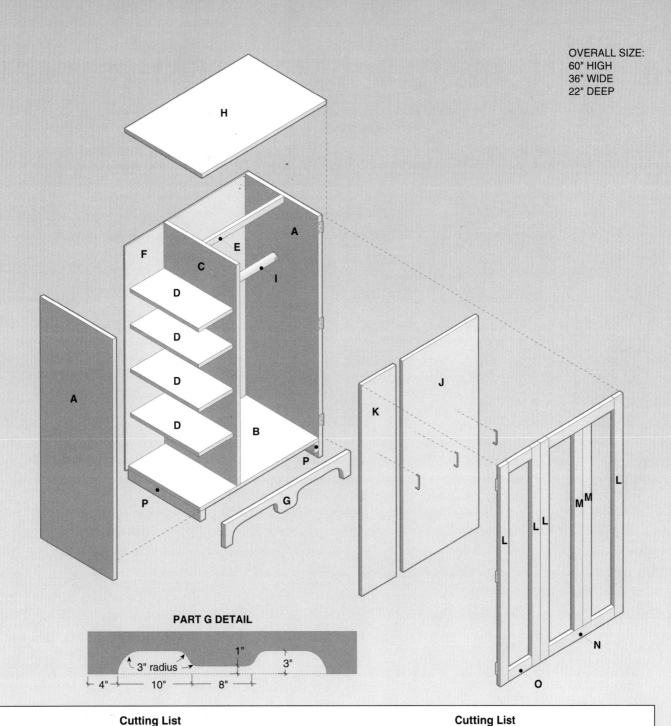

**OVERALL SIZE:**
60" HIGH
36" WIDE
22" DEEP

**PART G DETAIL**

3" radius
3" radius
1"
3"
4"
10"
8"

## Cutting List

| Key | Part | Dimension | Pcs. | Material |
|-----|------|-----------|------|----------|
| **A** | Side panel | ¾ × 21 × 59¼" | 2 | Plywood |
| **B** | Bottom panel | ¾ × 21 × 34½" | 1 | Plywood |
| **C** | Center panel | ¾ × 21 × 53¾" | 1 | Plywood |
| **D** | Shelf | ¾ × 10⅞ × 20¼" | 4 | Plywood |
| **E** | Stringer | ¾ × 1½ × 22⅞" | 1 | Pine |
| **F** | Back | ¼ × 36 × 54½" | 1 | Plywood |
| **G** | Front skirt | ¾ × 5½ × 36" | 1 | Pine |
| **H** | Top panel | ¾ × 22 × 36" | 1 | Plywood |

## Cutting List

| Key | Part | Dimension | Pcs. | Material |
|-----|------|-----------|------|----------|
| **I** | Closet rod | 1½ × 22⅞" | 1 | Fir |
| **J** | Closet door panel | ¾ × 22⁷⁄₁₆ × 52⅛" | 1 | Plywood |
| **K** | Shelf door panel | ¾ × 10⁷⁄₁₆ × 52⅛" | 1 | Plywood |
| **L** | Door stile | ¾ × 2½ × 53⅝" | 4 | Pine |
| **M** | False stile | ¾ × 2½ × 48⅝" | 2 | Pine |
| **N** | Closet door rail | ¾ × 2½ × 18¹⁵⁄₁₆" | 2 | Pine |
| **O** | Shelf door rail | ¾ × 2½ × 6¹⁵⁄₁₆" | 2 | Pine |
| **P** | Cleat | ¾ × 1½ × 21" | 2 | Pine |

**Materials:** #6 × 1¼" wood screws, 3d and 6d finish nails, closet rod hangers (2), wrought-iron hinges and pulls, magnetic door catches, ¾" birch veneer edge tape (50'), wood glue, finishing materials.
**Note:** Measurements reflect the actual size of dimension lumber.

*Apply veneer edge tape to the exposed plywood edges. Trim off excess tape with a sharp utility knife.*

### Directions: Armoire

#### PREPARE THE PLYWOOD PANELS.

Careful preparation of the plywood panels that become the sides, bottom, top and shelves is key to creating an armoire with a clean, professional look. Take the time to make sure all the parts are perfectly square.

Then, apply self-adhesive veneer edge tape to all plywood edges that will be visible. (If you plan to paint the armoire, you can simply fill the edges with wood putty and sand them smooth before you apply the paint.)

**1.** Cut the side panels (A), bottom panel (B), center panel (C) and shelves (D) to size, using a circular saw and a straightedge as a cutting guide. We used birch plywood because it is easy to work with and takes wood stain well. Smooth the surfaces of the panels with medium-grit sandpaper.

**2.** Apply self-adhesive veneer edge tape to the front edges of the center panel, side panels and shelves. Cut the strips of edge tape to length and position them over the plywood edges. Then, press the strips with a household iron set on a low-to-medium heat setting. The heat from the iron activates the adhesive.

**3.** Trim the excess tape with a sharp utility knife **(photo A).** Sand the trimmed edges and surfaces of the edge tape with medium-grit sandpaper.

#### ASSEMBLE THE CARCASE.

The *carcase* for the armoire (or any type of cabinet) is the main cabinet box. For this project, the carcase includes the

*Clamp the bottom panel between the sides and fasten it to the cleats with glue and finish nails.*

*Fasten the shelves between the side panel and center panel with glue and finish nails.*

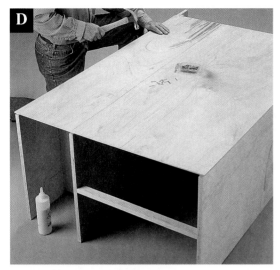

Nail the ¼"-thick back panel to the back edges of the carcase to help keep it square.

Lay out the decorative cutout at the bottom of the front skirt board, using a compass to make the curves. Then, cut with a jig saw.

side, bottom and center panels. Fasten the panels together with wood glue and finish nails. Make sure all of the joints are square and the edges are flush.

**1.** Lay out the cleat positions on the lower sections of the side panels. Measure up 4¾" from the bottom edges of the side panels, and draw a reference line across the inside face of each side panel.

**2.** Cut the cleats (P) to length.

**3.** Position the cleats just below the reference lines. Secure them with glue, and drive 3d finish nails through the cleats and into the side panels.

**4.** Stand the side panels upright on their bottom edges. Apply a bead of wood glue to the top of each cleat. Place the bottom panel between the side panels on top of the cleats, and clamp it in place. Make sure the taped front edges of the side panels and bottom panel are flush. Drive 6d finish nails through the bottom panel and into each cleat. Then, drive nails through the side panels and into the edges of the bottom panel **(photo B).**

**5.** Lay the assembly on its back edges. Use a pair of shelves as spacers to set the correct distance between the center panel and the left side panel (as seen from the front of the carcase). Make sure the taped panel edges are at the front of the carcase. Fasten the center panel to the bottom panel with glue, and drive 6d finish nails through the bottom panel and into the edge of the center panel.

### INSTALL THE SHELVES.

**1.** Draw reference lines for the shelves on the inside face of the left side panel and on the left face of the center panel. Measure up from the top of the bottom panel, and draw lines at 13", 23⅜", 33¾" and 44⅛". Use a framing square to make sure the lines are perpendicular to the front and back edges of the panels.

**2.** Arrange the shelves so the tops are just below the reference lines, flush with the back edges of the carcase (creating a ¾" recess in front of each shelf). Attach the shelves with glue, and drive 6d finish nails

through the side panel and center panel, and into the edges of the shelves **(photo C).** Brace each panel from behind as you drive the nails.

### ATTACH THE STRINGER AND BACK PANEL.

**1.** Cut the stringer (E) to length.

**2.** Fasten the stringer between the center panel and side panel with glue and 6d finish nails. The stringer should be centered between the fronts and backs of the panels and flush with the tops.

**3.** Cut the back panel (F) to size from ¼"-thick plywood.

**4.** Measure the distances between opposite corners of the carcase to make sure it is square (the distances between corners should be equal). Adjust the carcase as needed. Then, position the back panel over the back edges of the carcase so the edges of the back panel are flush with the outside faces and top edges of the side panels. Fasten the back panel by driving 3d finish nails through the back and into the edges of the side, center and bottom panels **(photo D).**

*Mount the top panel so it covers the top edge of the back panel and overhangs the front edges of the side panels by ¾".*

*Attach strips of 1 × 3 to the fronts of the door panels to create a frame.*

## MAKE AND ATTACH THE FRONT SKIRT.

**1.** Cut the front skirt (G) to length.

**2.** To lay out the curves that form the ends of the decorative cutouts on the skirt board (see *Diagram*, page 121), start by making a mark 7" in from each end. Use a compass to draw a 3"-radius curve to make the outside end of each cutout, holding the point of the compass on the 7" mark, as close as possible to the bottom edge of the board. Then, make a mark 11¾" in from each end of the skirt board. Holding the compass point at the bottom edge, draw a 3"-radius curve to mark the top, inside end of each cutout. Measure 16⅜" in from each end of the skirt board, and mark points that are 1¾" down from the top edge of the board. Set the point of your compass at each of these points and draw 3"-radius curves that mark the bottom, inside ends of the cutouts. Then, at the middle of the bot-

tom edge of the board, measure up 1" and draw a line parallel to the bottom edge, intersecting the inside ends of the cutout lines. Finally, draw lines parallel to the bottom edge of the board, 3" up, to create the top of each cutout. Make the cutout on the skirt board with a jig saw **(photo E).** Sand the saw cuts smooth with medium-grit sandpaper.

**3.** Position the skirt board against the front of the armoire carcase to make sure the ends of the skirt are flush with the outside faces of the side panels and the top of the skirt is flush with the top of the bottom panel. Fasten the front skirt to the front edges of the side panels and bottom panel with glue and 6d finish nails.

## MAKE AND ATTACH THE TOP PANEL.

**1.** Stand the armoire upright, and measure the distance between the outside faces of the side panels—it should be 36".

**2.** Cut the top panel (H) to size.

**3.** Test-fit the top panel to make sure the edges are flush with the outside faces of the side panels. The back edge should be flush with the outside face of the back panel, and the front edge of the top should overhang the front of the carcase panels by ¾". Apply veneer edge tape to all four edges of the top panel (see *Prepare the Plywood Panels*, page 122).

**4.** Fasten the top panel to the center panel, side panels and stringer with glue and 6d finish nails, making sure it is in the same position as it was when you test-fit the piece **(photo F).**

## BUILD THE DOORS.

**1.** Cut the closet door panel (J) and shelf door panel (K) to size. Sand the edges and surfaces of the door panels to smooth out the saw blade marks and any rough spots. Apply edge tape to the edges of each door panel. Trim off the excess tape, and sand the edges smooth.

**2.** Cut the door stiles (L), false

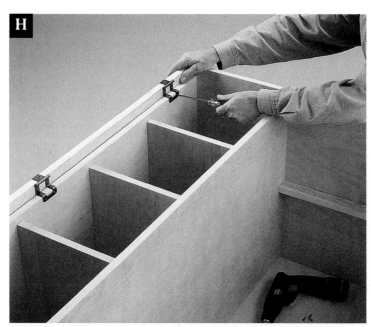

Hang the armoire doors with pairs of hinges attached to the door stiles and the front edges of the side panels.

stiles (M), closet door rails (N) and shelf door rails (O) to length. *(Rails* are the horizontal frame pieces; *stiles* are the vertical frame pieces.)

**3.** Position the rails and stiles on the front faces of the door panels so they overhang all edges of the panels by ¾". Make sure the rails and stiles meet at right angles to make perfectly square frames. Attach the rails and stiles to both door panels with glue, and drive 3d finish nails through the frame pieces and into the panels.

**4.** Turn the door panels over on your worksurface. To reinforce the joints between the stiles and rails and the door panels, drill ⁵⁄₆₄" pilot holes through the panels and into the stiles and rails. Counterbore the holes ⅛" deep, using a ⅜" counterbore bit. Fasten the pieces together with 1¼" wood screws **(photo G).**

**5.** To hang the doors, first mark points along the outside edge of each outer door stile, 8" down from the top and 8" up

from the bottom. Mount door hinges to the edges of the stiles at these points. Then, position the doors in place, and fasten the hinges to the side panels **(photo H).** Be sure to adjust the hinges to allow for a ⅛"-wide gap between the doors. Also leave a slight gap between the top end of the doors and the top panel and between the bottom of the doors and the front skirt.

APPLY THE FINISH.
It is easiest to finish the parts of the armoire before you attach the rest of the hardware.

**1.** Set all nails with a nail set. Fill all nail and screw holes with wood putty, and sand the dried putty flush with the surface. Sand all of the wood surfaces with medium (150-grit) sandpaper. Finish-sand the surfaces with fine sandpaper (180- or 220-grit).

**2.** Wipe the wood clean. Then, brush on a coat of sanding sealer so the wood will accept the wood stain evenly. Be sure

to read the manufacturer's directions before applying any finishing products. Apply a wood stain and let it dry completely. Then, apply several coats of topcoating product— we used two thin coats of water-based, satin polyurethane. If you prefer, you can leave the wood unstained and simply apply a protective topcoat.

INSTALL THE HARDWARE.
**1.** Install door pulls on the door panels, 25" up from each bottom rail and centered between the stiles. We used hammered wrought-iron pulls for a rustic appearance.

**2.** Mount closet rod hangers to the sides of the closet compartment, 11" down from the top panel. Cut the closet rod (I) to length, and set it into the closet rod hangers. (Applying finishing materials to the closet rod is optional.)

**3.** To keep the doors closed tight when not in use, install magnetic door catches and catch plates on the upper inside corners of the doors and at the corresponding locations on the bottom of the top panel. For extra holding power, also install catches at the bottoms of the doors.

> **TIP**
>
> *An armoire is basically a freestanding closet. But with a few modifications, it can become a custom furnishing that meets a variety of specific needs. To improve its usefulness as a dressing cabinet, attach a full-length dressing mirror to the inside of one of the doors. Rearrange the shelf positions, drill a few holes in the back, and you have a beautiful entertainment center. Or, add more shelves and tuck the armoire in your kitchen to be used as a portable pantry.*

# Mission Lamp Base

*The beauty and texture of oak combine with a simple style and charm in this traditional table lamp.*

PROJECT
POWER TOOLS

### CONSTRUCTION MATERIALS

| Quantity | Lumber |
|----------|--------|
| 1 | 1 × 8" × 2' oak |
| 2 | 1 × 2" × 10' oak |
| 1 | 1 × 3 × 12" oak |

This decorative lamp base provides just the right accent for a family room tabletop or bedside stand. It's made of red oak, and the design is simple and stylish. The clean, vertical lines of the oak slats are rooted in the popular Mission style.

The oak parts are joined with glue and nails, so the lamp base goes together with a minimum of time and fuss.

Once the base is assembled, just insert the lamp hardware, which you can buy at any hardware store. Lamp hardware kits include all of the components you need—harp, socket, cord and tubing. Make sure to follow manufacturer's directions when installing the hardware.

When you're finished, buy an attractive shade, either contemporary or classic, and set the lamp on a nightstand or table.

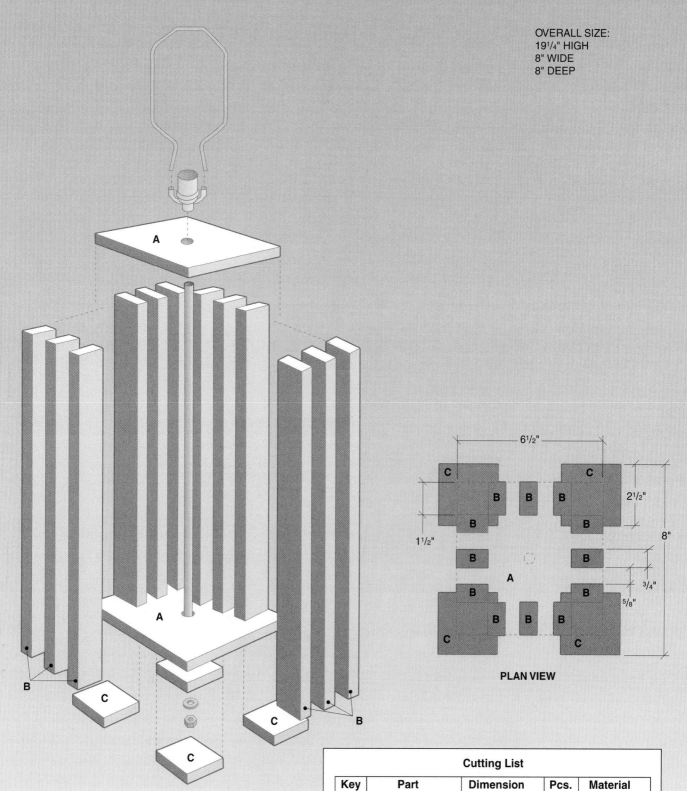

OVERALL SIZE:
19¼" HIGH
8" WIDE
8" DEEP

**PLAN VIEW**

**Cutting List**

| Key | Part | Dimension | Pcs. | Material |
|-----|------|-----------|------|----------|
| **A** | Plate | ¾ × 6½ × 6½" | 2 | Oak |
| **B** | Slat | ¾ × 1½ × 17" | 12 | Oak |
| **C** | Foot | ¾ × 2½ × 2½" | 4 | Oak |

**Materials:** 3d and 6d finish nails, lamp hardware kit, felt pads, wood glue, finishing materials.

**Note:** Measurements reflect the actual size of dimension lumber.

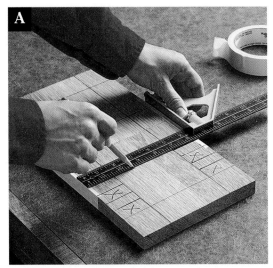

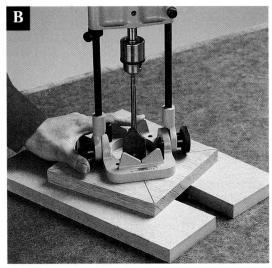

*Tape the plates edge to edge, and use a square to lay out the slat positions.*

*Use a portable drill guide to make accurate center holes in the plates.*

*Drill pilot holes through the plates for finish nails.*

**4.** Use the same technique to drill a ⅜"-dia. hole through the center of the counterbore and the center of the other plate for the lamp tube. To prevent splintering when the drill bit exits the other side, use a backer board when drilling holes through your workpiece.
**5.** Drill ¹⁄₁₆" pilot holes for finish nails through the plates to secure the slats **(photo C).** Each slat should have two finish nails attaching it to each plate.

### Directions: Mission Lamp Base

PREPARE THE PLATES.
**1.** Cut the plates (A) to size, and sand the pieces smooth with medium-grit sandpaper.
**2.** Set the plates flat on your worksurface, edge to edge, with their ends flush, and tape

them together. Following the *Diagram* on page 127, lay out the slat placement, using a combination square to ensure the lines are square and identical on both plates **(photo A).**
**3.** Draw diagonal lines from corner to corner, on the opposite sides of each plate, to locate the centers of the pieces. Drill a 1"-dia. × ¼"-deep counterbore hole on the bottom center of the lower plate, using a spade bit **(photo B).** Use a portable drill stand to hold the drill straight. This hole will receive a washer when you assemble the lamp.

CUT AND ATTACH THE SLATS.
**1.** Cut the slats (B) to length. Only a portion of each slat will be fully visible on the completed lamp, so choose the best sides and edges of the slats to be exposed.
**2.** Finish-sand the slats. Be careful not to round the end edges.
**3.** Attach the slats to the top plate, one at a time. First, apply glue to the top end of the slat. Then, drive 6d finish nails through the pilot holes in the top plate and into the end of the slat **(photo D).** For best results, fasten each slat with one nail, and check the positioning. Then, make any necessary ad-

justments, and drive the second nail.

**4.** Fasten the bottom ends of the slats to the lower plate, using glue and 6d finish nails. Make sure the counterbore for the lamp hardware is on the bottom.

CUT AND ATTACH THE FEET.
**1.** Cut the feet (C) to size from the leftover 1 × 8 stock.
**2.** Gang-sand the pieces to a uniform shape, and finish-sand them with fine-grit sandpaper.
**3.** Draw reference lines on each foot to mark its position on the base plate. Measure ¾" from the outside edge of two adjacent sides, and draw lines across the face of the foot, parallel to the side edges. These lines show where the four feet meet the plate corners (see *Diagram*).
**4.** Drill two ⅟₁₆" pilot holes for finish nails through each foot. Apply glue, and follow the reference lines to position the feet on the bottom face of the bottom plate. The two outside edges of the feet should overhang the corner edges of the plate by ¾".
**5.** Secure the feet by driving 3d finish nails through the feet and into the bottom plate.

APPLY FINISHING TOUCHES.
**1.** Set all nails in the lamp base with a nail set. Fill the nail holes with tinted wood putty, and sand the putty flush with the surface. Then, finish-sand the entire project.
**2.** Finish the lamp as desired (see *Tip*, page 128). We used a light oak stain and added two coats of wipe-on tung oil for a protective topcoat.
**3.** When the finish has dried, attach self-adhesive felt pads to

*Attach the slats to the top plate with glue and 6d finish nails.*

*Install the threaded lamp tube, and secure it to the bottom plate with a washer and nut.*

the bottom of the feet to prevent scratching on tabletop surfaces.

INSTALL THE HARDWARE.
With the wood parts assembled, install the lamp kit components to complete the project. Always follow manufacturer's instructions when installing hardware.
**1.** Begin by cutting the lamp tube to length so that it extends from plate to plate. Insert the tube through the holes in the plates.
**2.** Attach the harp to the top plate. Then, secure the tube to the bottom plate with a washer and nut **(photo E).**
**3.** Thread the cord through the tube, and wire the ends to the socket according to the manufacturer's directions.

# Pine Pantry

*Turn a remote corner or closet into a kitchen pantry
with this charming pine cabinet.*

## CONSTRUCTION MATERIALS

| Quantity | Lumber |
|----------|--------|
| 2 | 1 × 10" × 10' pine |
| 3 | 1 × 8" × 8' pine |
| 1 | 1 × 8" × 10' pine |
| 1 | 1 × 6" × 8' pine |
| 1 | 1 × 4" × 8' pine |
| 5 | 1 × 3" × 8' pine |
| 1 | 1 × 2" × 10' pine |
| 1 | ¾" × 4 × 8' plywood |
| 1 | ¼" × 4 × 8' plywood |

This compact pantry cabinet is ideal for keeping your kitchen organized and efficient. It features a convenient turntable shelf, or "Lazy Susan," on the inside of the cabinet for easy access to canned foods. A swing-out shelf assembly lets you get the most from the pantry's space. Its roominess allows you to store most of your non-refrigerated food items.

But the best feature of the pantry is its appearance. The rugged beauty of the cabinet hides its simplicity. For such an impressive-looking project, it is remarkably easy to build, so even if you don't have a traditional pantry in your home, you can have a convenient, attractive storage center.

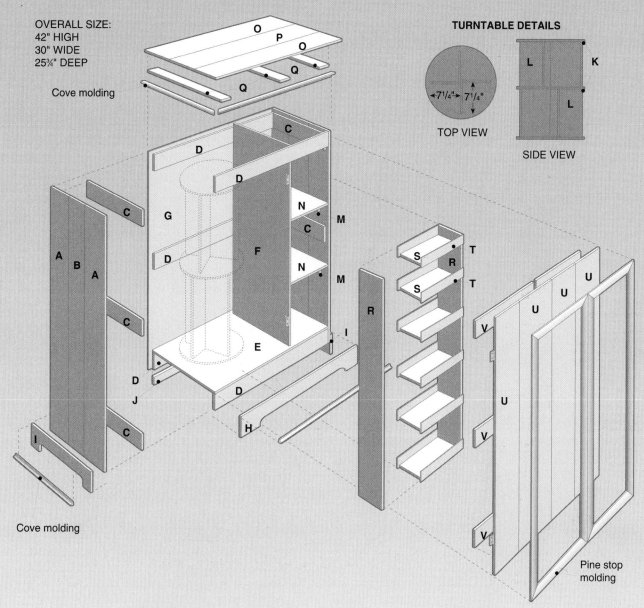

**OVERALL SIZE:**
42" HIGH
30" WIDE
25¾" DEEP

Cove molding

Cove molding

**TURNTABLE DETAILS**

←7¼"→ ←7¼"→

TOP VIEW

SIDE VIEW

Pine stop molding

| Key | Part | Dimension | Pcs. | Material |
|-----|------|-----------|------|----------|
| **A** | Side board | ¾ × 9¼ × 39¼" | 4 | Pine |
| **B** | Middle board | ¾ × 5½ × 39¼" | 2 | Pine |
| **C** | Panel cleat | ¾ × 2½ × 22½" | 6 | Pine |
| **D** | Stretcher | ¾ × 2½ × 26½" | 5 | Pine |
| **E** | Floor | ¾ × 24 × 26½" | 1 | Plywood |
| **F** | Divider | ¾ × 22½ × 36" | 1 | Plywood |
| **G** | Back | ¼ × 28 × 39¼" | 1 | Plywood |
| **H** | Base front | ¾ × 3½ × 29½" | 1 | Pine |
| **I** | Base side | ¾ × 3½ × 24¼" | 2 | Pine |
| **J** | Base back | ¾ × 1½ × 28" | 1 | Pine |
| **K** | Turntable shelf | ¾ × 16"-dia. | 3 | Plywood |

| Key | Part | Dimension | Pcs. | Material |
|-----|------|-----------|------|----------|
| **L** | Supports | ¾ × 7¼ × 12" | 8 | Pine |
| **M** | Shelf cleat | ¾ × 1½ × 22" | 4 | Pine |
| **N** | Fixed shelf | ¾ × 9 × 23" | 2 | Plywood |
| **O** | Top board | ¾ × 9¼ × 30" | 2 | Pine |
| **P** | Middle board | ¾ × 7¼ × 30" | 1 | Pine |
| **Q** | Top cleat | ¾ × 2½ × 22¼" | 3 | Pine |
| **R** | Swing-out end | ¾ × 6 × 32" | 2 | Pine |
| **S** | Swing-out shelf | ¾ × 6 × 10" | 6 | Pine |
| **T** | Swing-out side | ¼ × 2 × 11½" | 12 | Plywood |
| **U** | Door board | ¾ × 6⅝ × 35" | 4 | Pine |
| **V** | Door cleat | ¾ × 2½ × 11" | 6 | Pine |

**Cutting List** (both tables titled "Cutting List")

**Materials:** #6 × 1¼", 1½" and 2" wood screws, 2d, 4d and 6d finish nails, 16-ga. × 1" wire nails, turntable hardware, cabinet handles, 3 × 3" brass hinges (2), cabinet door hinges (4), ¾" cove molding, ⅜ × 1¼" stop molding, glue, finishing materials.

**Note:** Measurements reflect the actual size of dimension lumber.

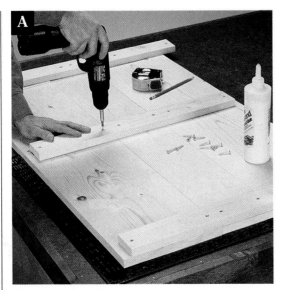

*Fasten cleats to the side and middle boards, forming the cabinet sides.*

*Attach front and back stretchers at the top and bottom, and a middle stretcher at the back.*

### Directions: Pine Pantry

For all screws used in this project, drill ⁵⁄₆₄" pilot holes. Counterbore the holes ⅛" deep, using a ⅜" counterbore bit.

MAKE THE CABINET SIDES.
**1.** Cut the side boards (A), middle boards (B) and panel cleats (C) to length. Sand all of the parts smooth.
**2.** Position a middle board between two side boards with the ends flush. As you assemble the sides, butt the boards against a framing square to keep them in line. Position a panel cleat flat across the boards so the bottom edge of the cleat is flush with the bottom edges of the boards. The ends of the cleat should be ¾" from the outside edges of the side boards. Fasten the cleat to the boards with glue, and drive 1¼" wood screws through the cleat and into the side and middle boards.
**3.** Attach the next panel cleat to the boards so its top edge is 21½" up from the bottom edge of the first cleat **(photo A).** Maintain a ¾" distance from the

cleat ends to the board edges.
**4.** Install the top panel cleat with its top edge 1" down from the board tops.
**5.** Repeat these steps to make the other cabinet side.

ATTACH THE SIDES.
**1.** Cut the side stretchers (D) to length.
**2.** Connect the cabinet sides by attaching the stretchers to the ends of the panel cleats. Position bottom stretchers at the front and back of the cabinet, keeping their top and bottom edges flush with the top and bottom edges of the panel cleats. The top two stretchers are each positioned a little differently—while the back stretcher is flush with the tops and bottoms of the panel cleats, the front stretcher is flush with the top edges of the cabinet sides. Apply glue and drive 1½" wood screws through the stretcher faces and into the ends of the cleats.
**3.** Attach the remaining stretcher at the back of the cabinet, flush with the panel cleats on the middle of the cabinet

sides **(photo B).**

ATTACH THE FLOOR.
**1.** Cut the floor (E) to size. Sand the top face smooth, and fill any voids in the front edge of the floor with wood putty.
**2.** Position the floor on top of the bottom stretchers and panel cleats, with the floor's front edge flush with the face of the front stretcher. Glue the parts. Drive 1½" wood screws through the floor and into the stretchers and panel cleats.

ATTACH THE DIVIDER.
**1.** Cut the divider (F) and shelf cleats (M) to size.
**2.** Draw a reference line across the floor from front to back, 9" from the right cabinet side. This line marks the position of the divider's shelf-side face. Measure and mark shelf cleat position lines on the right cabinet side, 10" and 20¾" up from the cabinet floor. Draw corresponding lines on the divider. These lines mark the top edges of the shelf cleats.
**3.** Use glue and 1¼" wood screws to fasten the shelf cleats

Install the divider 9" in from the right side of the cabinet.

Check for square by measuring diagonally between the corners to make sure the distances are equal.

to the divider and side with their top edges at the lines. Keeping all back edges flush, drive the screws through the cleats and into the divider and side panel.

**4.** Apply glue to the bottom edge of the divider. Insert the divider into the cabinet with its cleated face toward the cleated cabinet side. Drive 1½" wood screws up through the cabinet floor and into the divider edge. Drill ¹⁄₁₆" pilot holes through the top stretchers and drive 6d finish nails through the top stretchers and into the divider edges **(photo C).**

## ATTACH THE BACK.

**1.** Cut the back (G) to size, and position it on the cabinet.
**2.** Drive evenly spaced 1" wire nails through the back and into the edge of one side panel.
**3.** Measure diagonally across the opposite corners to check if the cabinet is square **(photo D).** Square the cabinet, if needed, by applying pressure to opposite corners. When the diagonal measurements are equal, complete the nailing of the

back to the stretchers and the remaining side panel.

## ATTACH THE FIXED SHELVES.

**1.** Cut the fixed shelves (N) to size. Sand them smooth.
**2.** Position the shelves on the shelf cleats, with their ends butted against the cabinet back. Attach the shelves with glue, and drive 1½" wood screws through the shelves and into the cleats.

## MAKE THE BASE.

Three of the four base boards have cutouts that create a foot at each corner.
**1.** Cut the base front (H), base sides (I) and base back (J) to length. Sand the parts smooth.
**2.** Use a compass to draw 1¾"-radius semicircles, centered 7¼" from each end of the base front. Hold the point of the compass as close as possible to the bottom edge. Using a straightedge, draw a straight line connecting the tops of the semicircles. Repeat these steps on the base sides, but center the semicircles 4¾" from the

front end and 5½" from the back end. Cut along the lines with a jig saw.
**3.** Mark lines on the rear edges of the base sides, ½" from the bottom edge. These lines mark the position of the bottom edge of the base back.
**4.** Attach the base sides to the base front with glue, and drive 4d finish nails through the base front and into the ends of base sides.
**5.** Attach the base back between the base sides at the reference lines, using glue and 4d finish nails.

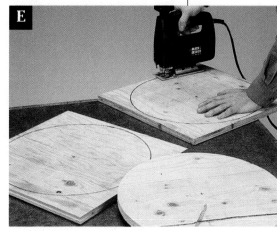

Cut the round turntable shelves with a jig saw. Each turntable shelf has an 8" radius.

*Assemble the turntable supports in three pairs, joined at right angles.*

*Using glue and 4d finish nails, attach the swing-out shelf sides.*

### ATTACH THE CABINET AND BASE.

**1.** With the cabinet on its back, slide the base over its bottom end until the base back meets the bottom cleats. The base should extend 2" beyond the cabinet's bottom edges. Drive 2" wood screws through the bottom cleats and side boards and into the base sides.

**2.** Drive 1¼" wood screws through the front stretcher and into the base front.

### BUILD THE TURNTABLE SHELVES.

**1.** Cut the turntable shelves (K) to size. To cut the circular shape, mark the center of the turntable shelves, and use a compass to draw a 16"-dia. circle. Cut the shelves to shape with a jig saw, and sand the cuts smooth **(photo E).**

**2.** Cut the turntable supports (L) to length.

**3.** Attach pairs of turntable supports at right angles by applying glue and driving 1½" wood screws through one support's face and into the other sup-

port's edge, forming simple butt joints **(photo F).**

**4.** To attach the turntable supports to the turntable shelves (see *Diagram*, page 131), use a straightedge to draw a line across the shelves, directly through their centerpoints. Place one pair of supports along the line with the joint at the centerpoint. Make sure the support pair forms a right angle. Then, draw the outline of the supports on the shelf. Position another support pair on the other side of the line and draw the outline. Drill pilot holes through the shelves, centered within the outlines, and fasten the turntable shelves to the turntable supports with glue and 1½" wood screws. The supports should have their spines meeting at the centerpoint of the turntable. Offset the upper and lower sets of supports on the opposite sides of the middle shelf to allow room for driving the screws.

**5.** Attach the turntable hardware to the bottom face of the bottom turntable shelf, follow-

ing manufacturer's directions. The turntable must be centered on the shelf, or the assembly will not rotate smoothly. Install the turntable assembly after you apply the finish to the pantry.

### BUILD THE SWING-OUT RACK.

**1.** Cut the swing-out shelves (S), swing-out ends (R) and swing-out sides (T) to size. Sand the parts smooth.

**2.** Starting from one end, draw lines 6" apart up the swing-out ends. These lines mark the positions of the bottom faces of the swing-out shelves. Apply glue to the shelf edges. Then, attach them to the swing-out ends by driving 1½" wood screws through the ends and into the shelf edges. The bottom shelf should be flush with the bottom of the end edges.

**3.** Attach the swing-out shelf sides (T) on the edges of the shelves with glue and 4d finish nails **(photo G).**

### MAKE THE TOP.

**1.** Cut the top boards (O), mid-

*Use a circular saw with a straightedge as a guide to rip-cut the door boards to size.*

*Attach pine stop molding to create a frame around the edges of the door boards.*

dle board (P) and top cleats (Q) to length. Sand them smooth.

**2.** Attach a top cleat across the inside faces of the boards, 1¾" from each end. Make sure that the ends of the boards are flush and that the cleats are centered from front to back. Apply glue and drive 1¼" wood screws through the cleats and into the top and middle boards. Fasten the middle cleat so its right edge is 11½" from the right end of the top.

**3.** Position the top on the cabinet so it overhangs the front and sides of the cabinet by 1". Fasten the top by driving 4d finish nails into the cabinet sides and toenailing through the middle cleat and into the divider.

## BUILD THE DOORS.

**1.** Cut the door boards (U) and door cleats (V) to size **(photo H).** Sand them smooth.

**2.** Lay the boards in pairs, with their ends flush. Center the top and bottom cleats, keeping them 2" in from the top and bottom ends. Apply glue and drive 1¼" wood screws through the cleats and into the door

boards. Attach the middle cleat, centered between the top and bottom cleats.

**3.** Miter-cut ⅜" stop molding to frame the front faces of the doors. Fasten the molding with glue and 2d finish nails **(photo I).**

## APPLY FINISHING TOUCHES.

**1.** Miter-cut ¾" cove molding to fit around the base and top (see *Diagram*). Attach the molding with glue and 2d finish nails.

**2.** Set all nails with a nail set, and fill the nail and screw

holes with wood putty. Finish-sand the pantry, and apply the finish of your choice.

**3.** Attach two evenly spaced 3 × 3" butt hinges to the edge of the swing-out rack. Mount the rack to the divider, using ¼"-thick spacers between the rack and divider **(photo J).**

**4.** Install the turntable assembly on the floor of the pantry.

**5.** Attach hinges and handles to the doors. Mount the doors to the cabinet sides.

*With spacers in place to help align the parts, attach the swing-out rack to the divider with 3 × 3" butt hinges.*

# Wine & Stemware Cart

*This solid oak cart with a lift-off tray allows you to transport and serve your wine safely and provides an elegant place to display your vintage selections.*

## CONSTRUCTION MATERIALS

| Quantity | Lumber |
|---|---|
| 2 | 1 × 12" × 6' oak |
| 1 | 1 × 4" × 8' oak |
| 1 | 1 × 4" × 6' oak |
| 1 | 1 × 3" × 2' oak |
| 1 | 1 × 2" × 4' oak |
| 1 | ½ × 2¾" × 2' oak* |
| 1 | ½ × 3¾" × 4' oak* |

*Available at woodworker's supply stores.

With our versatile oak wine and stemware cart, you can display, move and serve wine and other cordials from one convenient station. This cart can store up to 15 bottles of wine, liquor, soda or mix, and it holds the bottles in the correct downward position to prevent wine corks from drying out.

The upper stemware rack holds more than a dozen long-stemmed wine or champagne glasses, and a removable serving tray with easy-to-grip handles works well for cutting cheese and for serving drinks and snacks. Beneath the tray is a handy storage area for napkins, corkscrews and other items. Sturdy swivel casters make this wine rack fully mobile over tile, vinyl or carpeting.

OVERALL SIZE:
40³/₈" HIGH
23¹/₂" WIDE
11¹/₄" DEEP

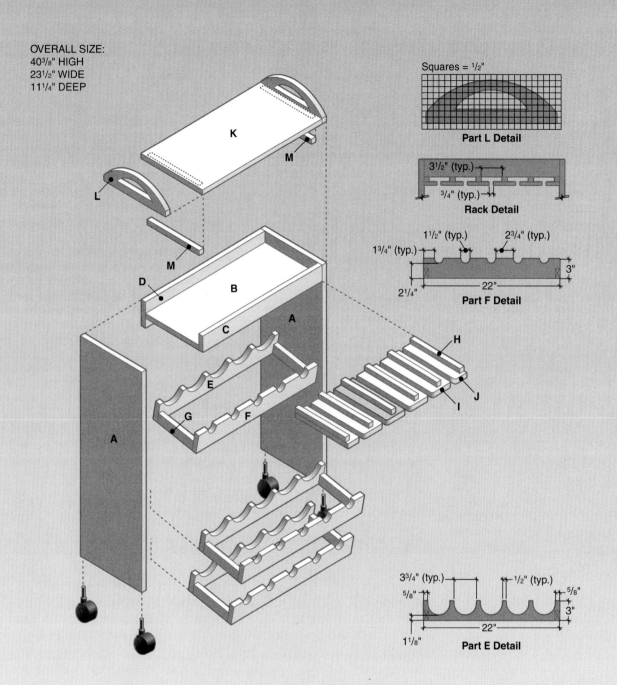

Squares = ¹/₂"

**Part L Detail**

3¹/₂" (typ.)

³/₄" (typ.)

**Rack Detail**

1³/₄" (typ.)   1¹/₂" (typ.)   2³/₄" (typ.)

3"

2¹/₄"   22"

**Part F Detail**

3³/₄" (typ.)   ¹/₂" (typ.)   ⁵/₈"

⁵/₈"   3"

1¹/₈"   22"

**Part E Detail**

| Cutting List | | | | |
|---|---|---|---|---|
| **Key** | **Part** | **Dimension** | **Pcs.** | **Material** |
| **A** | Side | ¾ × 11¼ × 34" | 2 | Oak |
| **B** | Top | ¾ × 9¾ × 22" | 1 | Oak |
| **C** | Front stretcher | ¾ × 2½ × 22" | 1 | Oak |
| **D** | Back stretcher | ¾ × 4 × 22" | 1 | Oak |
| **E** | Wine rack, back | ¾ × 3 × 22" | 3 | Oak |
| **F** | Wine rack, front | ¾ × 3 × 22" | 3 | Oak |
| **G** | Wine rack, cleat | ¾ × 1½ × 6½" | 6 | Oak |

| Cutting List | | | | |
|---|---|---|---|---|
| **Key** | **Part** | **Dimension** | **Pcs.** | **Material** |
| **H** | Stemware slat | ¾ × ¾ × 9¼" | 6 | Oak |
| **I** | Stemware plate | ½ × 3½ × 9¾" | 4 | Oak |
| **J** | End plate | ½ × 2⅛ × 9¾" | 2 | Oak |
| **K** | Tray | ¾ × 11¼ × 22" | 1 | Oak |
| **L** | Tray handle | ¾ × 3½ × 11¼" | 2 | Oak |
| **M** | Tray feet | ¾ × ¾ × 9½" | 2 | Oak |
| | | | | |

**Materials:** #6 × 1", 1¼" and 1½" wood screws, ⅜"-dia. oak plugs, casters (4), wood glue, finishing materials.

**Note:** Measurements reflect the actual size of dimension lumber.

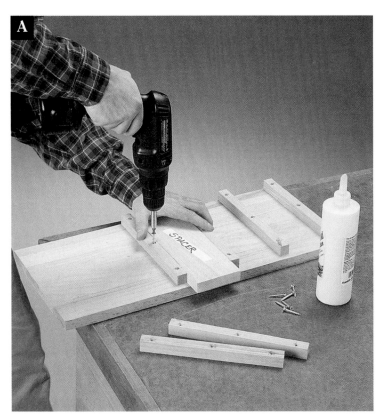

*Use a spacer to keep the slats aligned properly, and attach them with glue and screws.*

*Use a drum sander attached to your portable drill to smooth the jig saw cuts on the wine racks.*

### Directions: Wine & Stemware Cart

CONSTRUCT THE SIDES AND STEMWARE RACK ASSEMBLY. Before fastening frame parts together, make sure the assembly is square (see *Tip*).

**1.** Cut the cart sides (A), top (B) and back stretcher (D) from 1 × 12 oak. Cut the front stretcher (C) from 1 × 3 oak and the stemware slats (H) from 1 × 4 oak. Cut the plates (I) and end plates (J) from ½"-thick oak.

TIP

*To check for square, measure your project from one corner diagonally to its opposite corner. Repeat the procedure for the other two corners. If the two diagonal lines are equal, your assembly is square.*

**2.** Clamp a belt sander to your worksurface, and use it as a grinder to round over the front corners of the stemware plates, and one front corner of each end plate.

**3.** Sand all of the pieces smooth.

**4.** Place the top flat on your worksurface. Arrange the slats on its bottom face, flush with the back edge. Space the slats 3½" apart, using a piece of scrap wood as a spacer **(photo A).** Keep the outer slats flush with the ends of the top. Drill ³⁄₃₂" pilot holes through the slats, and counterbore the holes ⅛" deep, using a ⅜" counterbore bit. Attach the slats with glue and 1¼" wood screws.

### BUILD THE WINE RACKS.

First assemble the wine racks as individual units. Then, attach them to the sides of the cart.

**1.** Cut the wine rack backs (E) and fronts (F) from 1 × 4 oak, and cut the cleats (G) from 1 × 2 oak.

**2.** To lay out the cutouts on the wine rack front and back pieces (see *Diagram*, page 137), mark points along one long edge of each board, and use a compass to draw the semicircles. Measuring from one end, mark points at 2½", 6¾", 11", 15¼" and 19½".

**3.** The rack back has 1⅞"-radius semicircles, and the rack front has ¾"-radius semicircles. Set the point of the compass on each reference mark, as close as possible to the edge, and draw the semicircles. Carefully make the cutouts with a jig saw.

**4.** Position the cleats between the rack fronts and backs, and drill two pilot holes through the faces of the fronts and backs

*Measure ½" along the front and 2½" along the back of each side, and connect the marks for the bottom rack alignment.*

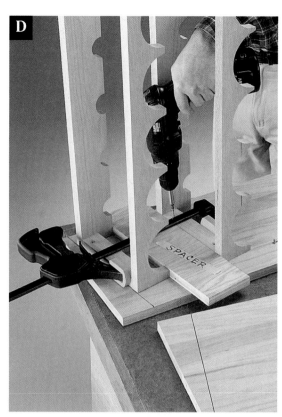

*Clamp a 4 × 10" spacer between the bottom and middle racks for proper positioning.*

*Drive screws through the slats to secure the top to the sides.*

and into the ends of the cleats. Counterbore the holes ¼" deep. Join the pieces with glue and 1½" wood screws.

**5.** Fill the counterbores with glued oak plugs. Sand the plugs flush with the surface, and smooth any rough edges.

Clamp each completed rack to your worksurface, and sand the cutouts smooth with a drum sander **(photo B).**

ATTACH THE WINE RACKS.

**1.** On the inside face of each side piece, measure up ½" from

the bottom, and make a mark at the front edge. Then, measure up 2½" from the bottom, and make a mark at the back edge. Draw an angled reference line between the marks **(photo C).**

**2.** With one of the side pieces lying flat on your worksurface, position a wine rack so the bottom edge is on the reference line and the front edge is set back ¾" from the front edge of the side piece. Drill pilot holes through the rack cleats, and counterbore the holes ⅛" deep. Attach the rack to the side with glue and 1¼" wood screws.

**3.** Attach the middle and top racks in the same manner, using a 4 × 10" spacer to position them correctly **(photo D).**

**4.** Use bar or pipe clamps to hold the remaining side piece in position. Make sure the bottom rack is on the reference line, and use the spacer to set the positions of the middle and top racks. Fasten the racks to the side piece.

**5.** Arrange the stretchers between the sides so their top and outside edges are flush with the tops and outside edges of the sides. Drill pilot holes through the sides and into the ends of the stretchers. Counterbore the holes ¼" deep. Attach the stretchers with glue and 1½" wood screws.

ATTACH THE TOP ASSEMBLY.
**1.** Lay the cart on its side, and clamp the top between the side pieces. The bottom face of the top should be flush with the bottom edge of the front stretcher.
**2.** Measure the distance between the top and the top ends of the sides to make sure the top is level. Drill pilot holes through the outer slats and into the sides, and counterbore the holes ⅛" deep. Apply glue to the edges of the top and to the outside edges of the outer slats. Position the top, and drive 1¼" wood screws through the outer slats and into the sides **(photo E).**
**3.** Drill three evenly spaced pilot holes, counterbored ¼" deep, through both stretchers and into the edges of the top, and secure the pieces with 1½" wood screws.

COMPLETE THE RACK
AND FIT THE CASTERS.
Attach the stemware plates to the slats to complete the stemware rack.
**1.** Set the cart upside down on your worksurface. Position an end plate onto an outside slat, with its square side flush against the side panel and its

Use a ¾"-thick spacer to guide the placement of the stemware plates.

square end flush against the back stretcher. Drill two pilot holes down through the end plate, taking care to avoid the screws in the slat beneath. Counterbore the holes ⅛" deep, and fasten the plate with glue and 1" wood screws.
**2.** Repeat these steps to position and attach the remaining plates. Use a ¾"-thick spacer

between the plates to ensure uniform spacing **(photo F).**
**3.** Drill holes into the bottom edges of the cart sides, and test-fit the casters **(photo G).** Position the holes so they are centered on the edge from side to side and are no less than 1" from the front and back side edges. For the casters to work properly, the holes must be per-

*Drill holes for the casters in the bottom edges of the sides.*

*Drill a pilot hole, and cut the inside handle profile with a jig saw. Use scrap wood as a backer board to prevent splintering.*

pendicular to the bottom edges of the sides.

MAKE THE TRAY.
The wine cart tray is simply an oak board with handles attached to the sides and narrow feet attached below.
**1.** Cut the tray (K) from 1 × 12 oak, and cut the tray handle (L) blanks from 1 × 4 oak. Cut the ¾ × ¾" feet (M) from leftover 1 × 12.
**2.** Transfer the pattern for the handles onto one of the blanks (see *Diagram*).
**3.** Using a backer board to prevent splintering, drill a starter hole on the inside portion of the handle. Then, use a jig saw to cut along the pattern lines **(photo H).**
**4.** Trace the outline of the shaped handle onto the re-

maining handle blank. Cut the pattern on the second handle. Clamp the two handles together, and gang-sand them so their shapes are identical.
**5.** Position the tray between the handles, and drill three evenly spaced pilot holes through the side of each handle. Counterbore the holes ¼" deep. Attach the handles to the ends of the tray with glue and 1½" wood screws.
**6.** Position the tray feet on the bottom edge of the tray, ⅛" in from the side edges and ⅞" from the front and back edges. Drill pilot holes through the feet, and counterbore the holes ⅛" deep. Attach the feet with glue and 1" wood screws.

APPLY FINISHING TOUCHES.
**1.** Glue oak plugs into all

> ### TIP
> *Applying a thin coat of sanding sealer before staining helps the wood absorb stain evenly and can eliminate blotchy finishes. Sanding sealer is a clear liquid, usually applied with a brush. Read the package labels of the different products you plan to use to make sure the finishes are compatible.*

visible ¼"-deep counterbore holes, and sand the plugs flush with the surface. Finish-sand the entire cart.
**2.** Apply your choice of stain (we used a rustic oak) and a polyurethane topcoat.
NOTE: If you will be using the tray as a cutting board, be sure to apply a nontoxic finish.
**3.** When the finish is dry, install the casters on the bottom of the cart.

# Utility Cart

*Form and function combine in this richly detailed rolling cart.*

## CONSTRUCTION MATERIALS

| Quantity | Lumber |
|---|---|
| 2 | 1 × 2" × 6' oak |
| 2 | 1 × 4" × 6' oak |
| 1 | 2 × 4" × 4' pine |
| 1 | 1 × 4" × 6' pine |
| 1 | ¾" × 4 × 8' oak plywood |
| 2 | ⅜ × ⅝" × 6' dentil molding |
| 4 | ⅜ × ¾" × 6' stop molding |
| 8 | ⅜ × 2¼" × 3' beaded casing |
| 4 | ¾" × 2 × 3' melamine-coated particleboard |

Y ou'll appreciate the extra space, and your guests will admire the classic style of this movable cabinet. The cart features decorative dentil molding around a scratch-resistant 22½ × 28½" countertop that provides additional work-surface space for preparing special dishes. Two storage or display areas, framed by beaded corner molding, can hold food, beverages, dinnerware and appliances. Underneath, the cart has casters, so it easily rolls across floors to the preparing or serving area. Time and again, you'll find this versatile cart a great help in the kitchen, dining room or other entertainment areas of your home.

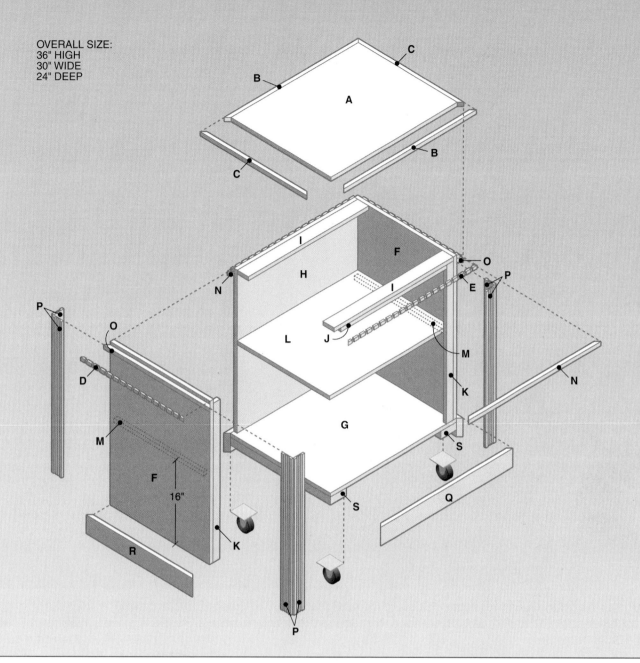

OVERALL SIZE:
36" HIGH
30" WIDE
24" DEEP

## Cutting List

| Key | Part | Dimension | Pcs. | Material |
|---|---|---|---|---|
| A | Top | ¾ × 22½ × 28½" | 1 | Particleboard |
| B | Long upper trim | ¾ × ¾ × 30" | 2 | Stop mld. |
| C | Short upper trim | ¾ × ¾ × 24" | 2 | Stop mld. |
| D | Short dentil | ⅜ × ⅝ × 23¼" | 2 | Dentil mld. |
| E | Long dentil | ⅜ × ⅝ × 29¼" | 2 | Dentil mld. |
| F | Side panel | ¾ × 22½ × 30⅞" | 2 | Plywood |
| G | Bottom | ¾ × 22½ × 28½" | 1 | Plywood |
| H | Back | ¾ × 27 × 30⅞" | 1 | Plywood |
| I | Stretcher | ¾ × 3½ × 27" | 2 | Pine |
| J | Brace | ¾ × 1½ × 24" | 1 | Oak |

## Cutting List

| Key | Part | Dimension | Pcs. | Material |
|---|---|---|---|---|
| K | Post | ¾ × 1½ × 30⅛" | 2 | Oak |
| L | Shelf | ¾ × 20¾ × 27" | 1 | Plywood |
| M | Cleat | ¾ × ¾ × 20¼" | 2 | Stop mld. |
| N | Long lower trim | ¾ × ¾ × 30" | 2 | Stop mld. |
| O | Short lower trim | ¾ × ¾ × 24" | 2 | Stop mld. |
| P | Corner trim | ⅜ × 2¼ × 29½" | 8 | Bead. csg. |
| Q | Long base | ¾ × 3½ × 30" | 2 | Oak |
| R | Short base | ¾ × 3½ × 24" | 2 | Oak |
| S | Caster mount | 1½ × 3½ × 22½" | 2 | Pine |
| | | | | |

**Materials:** #6 × 1", 1¼", 1⅝" and 2" wood screws, 16-ga. × 1" brads, 3d finish nails, 2" casters (4), ¾" shelf nosing or oak veneer edge tape (30"), ⅜"-dia. oak plugs, wood glue, finishing materials.

**Note:** Measurements reflect the actual size of dimension lumber.

*Use a ¾" piece of scrap wood as a spacer to inset the cleats ¾" from the back edges of the side panels.*

*Drive screws through the top of the stretcher to secure the oak brace.*

### Directions: Utility Cart

For all screws used in this project, drill ³⁄₃₂" pilot holes. Counterbore the holes ¼" deep, using a ⅜" counterbore bit.

#### PREPARE THE SIDES AND BOTTOM.

**1.** Cut the side panels (F), bottom (G), back (H) and cleats (M) to size. Sand them smooth.
**2.** Drill four evenly spaced pilot holes along the long edges of each side panel, ⅜" in from each edge.
**3.** Flip each side over and, on the inside face, place a cleat so the bottom edge is 16" from the bottom of the side panel. Attach the cleats with glue, and

drive 1" wood screws through the cleats and into the side panels. Make sure the ends of the cleats are inset ¾" from the back edges of the side panels **(photo A).**
**4.** Drill pilot holes along the side and back edges of the bottom, keeping the holes ⅜" in from the edges.

#### ASSEMBLE THE CABINET.

**1.** Position the back between the side panels. Attach it with glue, and drive 1⅝" wood screws through the pilot holes in the side panels and into the edges of the back.
**2.** Apply glue to the bottom edges of the side panels and back. Attach the bottom by

driving 1⅝" wood screws through the bottom and into the edges of the sides and back. The side and back edges of the bottom piece should be flush with the outside faces of the side panels and back.
**3.** Cut the stretchers (I), brace (J), posts (K) and shelf (L) to size. Sand the parts smooth.
**4.** Position the front stretcher between the side panels, flush with the top and front edges of the side panels. Attach the stretcher with glue, and drive 1⅝" wood screws through the side panels and into the ends of the stretcher. Apply glue to the back edge and ends of the rear stretcher, and butt it against the back, flush with the

Use glue and brads to attach shelf nosing to the front edge of the shelf.

Fasten the dentil molding around the top edge of the cabinet with glue and brads.

top edge. Drive screws through the side panels and back and into the stretcher.

**5.** Set the posts in place, faces flush with the front side edges. Attach them with glue, and drive 1⅝" wood screws through the pilot holes in the sides and into the edges of the posts.

**6.** Apply glue to the brace, and clamp it to the front stretcher so their front edges are flush. Drive 1" wood screws through the stretcher and into the brace **(photo B).**

**7.** Clamp the shelf vertically to your worksurface. Cut a strip of shelf nosing to match the length of the front edge. Apply glue, and attach the nosing to the shelf with 1" brads **(photo C).**

**8.** Apply glue to the tops of the cleats, and set the shelf into place, butting the back edge against the back. Drive 3d finish nails through the shelf and into the cleats.

## ATTACH THE UPPER MOLDING.

**1.** Cut the short dentils (D), long dentils (E), long lower trim (N) and short lower trim (O) to length.

**2.** Make 45° miter cuts on the ends of each piece of molding, always angling the cuts inward. When cutting the miters for the dentil molding, make sure to cut through the blocks, or "teeth," so the return piece will match at the corners (see *Tip*, page 147).

**3.** Fit the dentil pieces, with the gap edge up, flush to the top

> **TIP**
>
> *Instead of fastening shelf nosing to the shelf edge, an option is to apply self-adhesive oak veneer edge tape. Cut the tape to length, and press it onto the wood, using a household iron to activate the adhesive. When cool, trim away excess tape with a sharp utility knife.*

edge of the cabinet. Drill ¹⁄₁₆" pilot holes through the molding, and attach it with glue and 1" brads **(photo D).**

**4.** Attach the lower trim pieces snug against the bottom of the dentil molding, using glue and 3d finish nails. Set the nails with a nail set **(photo E).**

## ATTACH THE BASE MOLDING.

**1.** Cut the caster mounts (S) to length.

**2.** Lay the cart on its back, and attach the caster mounts to the bottom of the cart, flush with the edges of the bottom. Apply glue and drive 2" wood screws through the mounts and into the bottom. Angle the screws slightly to avoid breaking through the top face of the bottom with the tip of the screw.

**3.** Miter-cut the long bases (Q) and short bases (R) to length.

**4.** Attach the trim to the cabinet, keeping the top edges flush with the top face of the bottom. Apply glue to all mating surfaces, and drive 1¼" wood screws through the trim pieces and into the edges of the bottom.

**5.** Cut the corner trim (P) pieces to length.

**6.** Apply glue to a corner trim piece, and clamp it in place over a post so the inside edges are flush **(photo F).** Drill ¹⁄₁₆" pilot holes through the corner piece, and nail it to the post and side panel with 1" brads.

**7.** When the glue is dry, complete the corner by attaching another trim piece with glue and brads. The edges of the trim pieces should touch but should not overlap. Attach the corner trim to the remaining corners.

*Attach the lower trim underneath the dentil molding, and set the nails with a nail set.*

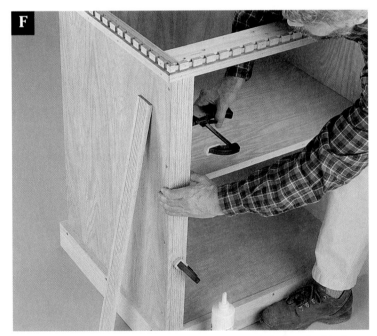

*Clamp the corner molding in place to ensure a tight bond with the posts as the glue dries.*

## MAKE THE TOP.

**1.** Mark the dimensions for the top (A) on a piece of melamine-coated particleboard. Apply masking tape over the cut lines, and mark new cut lines onto the tape. Use a sharp utility knife and a

G

Score the cutting lines on the melamine with a sharp utility knife to prevent chipping.

TIP

*The size of the "teeth" in dentil molding can vary, as can the gaps between the teeth. You might want to purchase extra molding to allow for cutting adjustments that may be necessary to form the corners properly.*

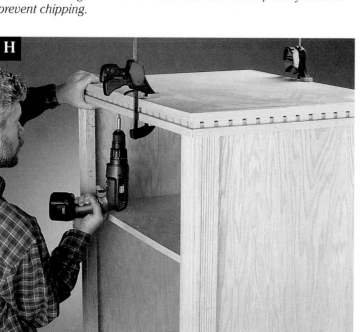

H

Apply glue and clamp the top in place. Then, secure it by driving screws through the stretchers.

straightedge to score the board along the cut lines. This will help prevent chipping and splintering from the saw blade **(photo G).** To minimize chipping when making the cut, use a sharp blade on your circular saw. Cut the top to size, using the straightedge clamped in place as a guide. Then, remove the masking tape.

**2.** Cut the long upper trim (B) pieces and short upper trim (C) pieces to length, mitering the ends at 45°.

**3.** Drill pilot holes through the trim pieces, and attach them to the edges of the top with glue and 1" brads. Make sure the tops of the trim pieces are flush with the top face of the top.

**4.** Center the top over the cabinet, and attach it with glue. Drive 1" wood screws up through the stretchers and into the underside of the top **(photo H).**

APPLY FINISHING TOUCHES.

**1.** Lay the utility cart on its back, and attach the casters to the caster mounts.

**2.** Set all nails with a nail set, and fill the nail holes with wood putty. Fill the screw holes on the base trim with glued oak plugs. Finish-sand the utility cart.

**3.** Finish the cart with the stain or sealer of your choice. We used a rustic oak stain to enhance the grain of the wood.

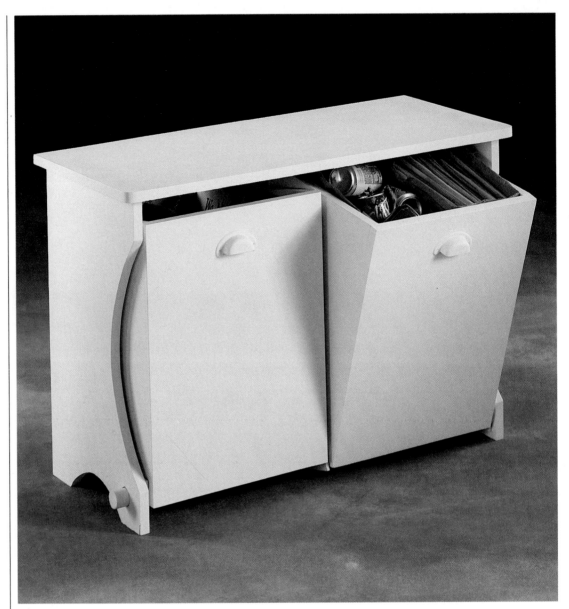

# Recycling Center

*Recycling is no longer a chore when this convenient recycling center is a fixture in your kitchen.*

## CONSTRUCTION MATERIALS

| Quantity | Lumber |
|----------|--------|
| 1 | ¾" × 4 × 8' birch plywood |
| 1 | 1¼"-dia. × 36" birch dowel |
| 3 | ¼ × 3 × 3" Masonite® or scrap wood |

Finding adequate storage for recyclables in a kitchen or pantry can be a challenge. Gaping paper bags of discarded aluminum, newspaper, glass and plastic are an unsightly nuisance. Our recycling center eliminates the nuisance and makes recycling easy. The recycling center holds up to four bags of recyclables, keeping the materials in one place and out of sight. Arches create four feet on the bottom of the cabinet and a bold detail on the front edges. The two spacious bins pivot forward on a dowel for easy deposit and removal of recyclables, and the broad top of the cabinet serves as a handy low shelf.

OVERALL SIZE:
23³/₄" HIGH
34³/₄" WIDE
14³/₄" DEEP

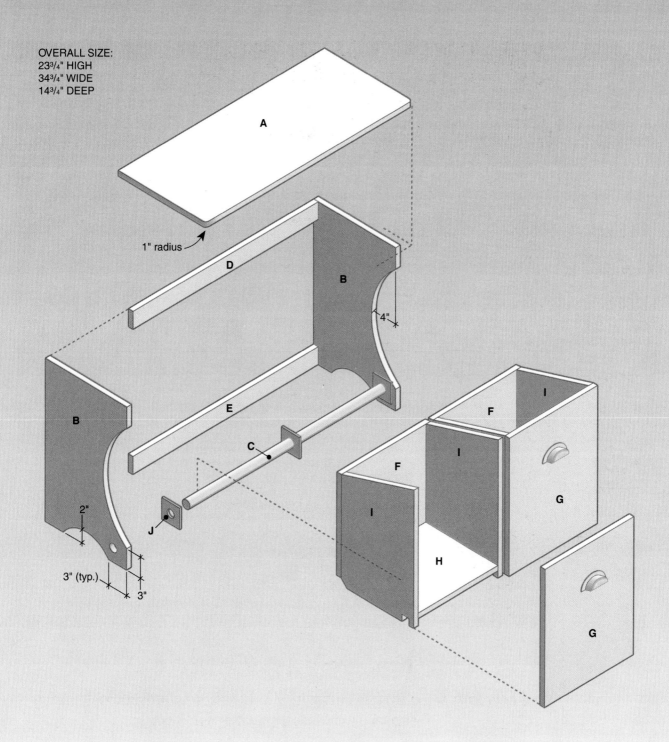

1" radius

4"

2"

3" (typ.)

3"

| Cutting List | | | | |
|-----|------|-----------|------|-------------|
| Key | Part | Dimension | Pcs. | Material |
| A | Top | ¾ × 14¾ × 34¾" | 1 | Plywood |
| B | End | ¾ × 13¾ × 23" | 2 | Plywood |
| C | Dowel | 1¼"-dia. × 34" | 1 | Birch dowel |
| D | Top stretcher | ¾ × 2½ × 31" | 1 | Plywood |
| E | Bottom stretcher | ¾ × 2½ × 31" | 1 | Plywood |

| Cutting List | | | | |
|-----|------|-----------|------|-------------|
| Key | Part | Dimension | Pcs. | Material |
| F | Bin back | ¾ × 15 × 16½" | 2 | Plywood |
| G | Bin front | ¾ × 15 × 19½" | 2 | Plywood |
| H | Bin bottom | ¾ × 12¼ × 13½" | 2 | Plywood |
| I | Bin side | ¾ × 12¼ × 19½" | 4 | Plywood |
| J | Spacer | ¼ × 3 × 3" | 3 | Masonite |

**Materials:** #4 × ⅜", #6 × 1½" and #8 × 2" wood screws, 4d finish nails, 10" metal chains (2), screw hooks (2), drawer pulls (2), paste wax, wood glue, finishing materials.
**Note:** Measurements reflect the actual size of dimension lumber.

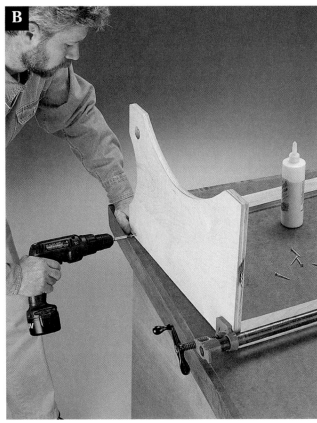

*Drill pilot holes for the anchor screws through the bottom edges and into the dowel holes.*

*Apply glue and drive screws through the ends and into the stretchers. Use bar clamps to ensure square joints.*

## Directions:
## Recycling Center

For all #6 wood screws used in this project, drill ⁵⁄₆₄" pilot holes. Counterbore the holes ⅛" deep, using a ⅜" counterbore bit.

MAKE THE TOP AND ENDS.
**1.** Cut the top (A) and ends (B) to size. Sand the edges smooth with medium-grit sandpaper.
**2.** To create rounded front corners on the top, mark reference points 1" in from the side and front edges at each front corner. Set a compass to 1", and

draw the roundovers, holding the compass point on the reference marks. Sand the corners down to the curved lines with a belt sander.
**3.** An easy way to draw the arches on the end pieces is to use a thin, flexible piece of metal, plastic or wood as a tracing guide. Along the front edge of each piece, make marks 3" in from each corner. Make a mark on the side face of each piece, 4" in from the center point of the front edge. Tack finish nails at these three points. Hook the flexible guide

behind the center nail, then flex each end and set them in front of the edge nails so the guide bows in to create a smooth curve. Trace the arches with a pencil, and remove the guide and nails.
**4.** Draw the curves for the bottom edges using the same technique. Along the bottom edges, measure 3" in from the bottom corners and 2" up from the center point of the bottom edge. Tack finish nails at the marks, set the guide and trace the arches.
**5.** Make the cuts for the bottom and front arches with a jig saw. Sand the cuts smooth with medium-grit sandpaper.
**6.** Mark the location for the dowel hole on each end piece, 2¼" in and 2" up from the bottom front corner. Set the end

---

TIP

*When checking a cabinet for square, measure diagonally from corner to corner. If the measurements are equal, the cabinet is square. If not, apply pressure to one side or the other with your hand or clamps until the cabinet is square.*

Draw reference lines on the top to use for positioning when attaching it to the sides.

Anchor the dowel by driving screws through the predrilled holes and into the dowel.

pieces with their inside faces down onto a backer board to prevent splintering during drilling. Drill the dowel holes, using a 1¼" spade bit.

**7.** The dowel will be pinned in the holes on each end by an anchor screw. Drill pilot holes for the anchor screws, using a ³⁄₃₂" bit **(photo A).** Align the drill bit with the center of the dowel hole, and drill through the bottom edge of the end piece and into the dowel hole.

### ASSEMBLE THE CABINET FRAME.

Attach the stretchers between the ends to form the back of the cabinet frame.

**1.** Cut the dowel (C), the top stretcher (D) and the bottom stretcher (E) to size. Sand all of

the parts smooth.

**2.** Apply glue to the ends of the stretchers and position them between the ends so they are flush at the back edges and corners. Clamp the parts together and measure diagonally

between opposite corners to make sure the assembly is square (see *Tip,* opposite page). Then, drive 1½" wood screws through the end pieces and into the ends of the stretchers **(photo B).**

---

**TIP**

*Careful planning can prevent valuable wood from being wasted. With the exception of the dowel and the spacers, all of the parts for this project can be cut from a 4 × 8' piece of birch plywood (see pattern below):*

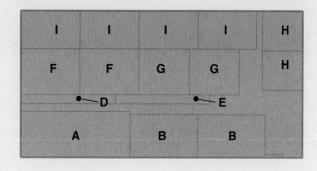

*Clamp the bin sides to your worksurface, and use a jig saw to cut the notches and bevels.*

*Position the bin bottom flush with the dowel notch, and attach it with glue and screws.*

**3.** Set the cabinet on its back. Lay the top piece flat on your worksurface, bottom-side-up. Butt the back edge of the top against the top stretcher so the ends overhang the cabinet equally on both sides. Mark the bottom face of the top piece to indicate where it will rest on the cabinet ends **(photo C).**

**4.** Set the cabinet upright and position the top, aligning the reference lines with the outside faces of the ends. The back edge of the top should be flush with the back face of the top stretcher. Attach the top with glue, and drive 1½" wood screws through the top and into the edges of the ends and top stretcher.

INSERT THE DOWEL.
Place spacers along the dowel to separate the bins, ensuring smooth operation.

**1.** Make the three spacers (J) by cutting 3" squares from Masonite or scrap ¼" material. Masonite is a good choice because it has hard, smooth surfaces that create little friction.

**2.** Mark the center points of the spacers, and drill holes with a 1¼" spade bit to accommodate the dowel.

**3.** Apply paste wax to the dowel for lubrication. Slide the dowel through one end piece. Then, install the spacers, and slide the dowel end through the hole in the other end. Position the dowel so it protrudes an equal distance from both ends. Anchor the dowel in position by driving #8 × 2" wood

screws through the pilot holes on the bottom edges of the ends and into the dowel **(photo D).**

MAKE THE BIN SIDES.
The bin sides have a notch near the bottom front edge so they can rock safely on the dowel. There are bevels on the top edges and at the bottom rear corners to provide clearance.

**1.** Cut the bin sides (I) to size. Sand the pieces smooth.

**2.** Use a jig saw to cut a 1¼"-wide, 1"-high notch, located ¾" from the bottom front corner of each bin side (see *Detail,* opposite page).

**3.** To make the short bevel on the bottom, measure and draw marks along the bottom and back edges, 1" from the bottom rear corner. Draw a diagonal cut line between these two marks, and cut off the corner with a jig saw.

**4.** To make the long bevel on the top edge, measure down 2" from the top back corner, and draw a mark. With a straight-edge, draw a diagonal cut line from the mark to the upper front corner, and make the cut with a jig saw **(photo E).** Sand all of the cuts smooth.

## ASSEMBLE THE BINS.

**1.** Cut the bin backs ( F), bin fronts (G) and bin bottoms (H) to size. Sand the pieces smooth.

**2.** Position a front over the ends of two sides so their tops and outside edges are flush. Attach the bin front to the bin sides with glue, and drive 1½" wood screws through the bin front and into the edges of the bin sides.

**3.** Position a bin bottom between the sides so it is recessed 1" and is flush with the top of the dowel notches. Attach the sides to the bottom with glue and 1½" wood screws **(photo F).**

**4.** Set the bin back over the edges of the bin sides, keeping the top edges flush. Attach the back with glue, and drive 1½" wood screws through the back and into the edges of the bin sides and bottom.

**5.** Repeat this process to assemble the other bin.

## ATTACH THE CHAIN.

To prevent the bins from falling forward when adding or removing recyclables, our design uses chain and screw hooks to attach the bins to the top. The chains can easily be detached when the recycling center needs cleaning.

**1.** Center and attach the screw

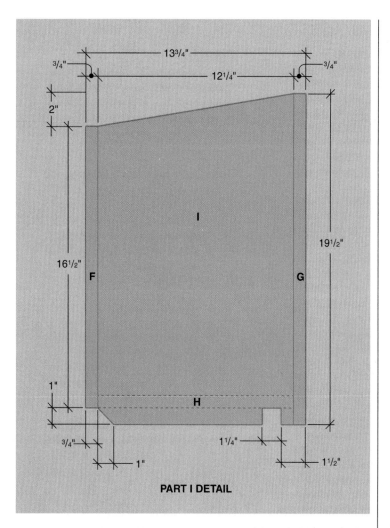

**PART I DETAIL**

> **TIP**
>
> *Ensure a smooth finish by working in a well-ventilated, dust-free area. Airborne dust can ruin a painted finish. Avoid painting a project in an area where woodworking tools have recently operated, and wipe the sanded surfaces to remove all dust.*

hooks on the top edge of the bin backs. Attach 10" chains with #4 × ⅜" wood screws to the underside of the top, 8" from the front edge and 8" from the inside faces of the ends.

**2.** Place the bins in the cabinet, with spacers in between and on both sides. For smoother movement, sand the notches as necessary.

## APPLY FINISHING TOUCHES.

**1.** Fill all screw holes with wood putty. Finish-sand the cabinet and bins with fine-grit sandpaper. For a finish, choose an enamel with a medium gloss or eggshell finish to make cleaning easy.

**2.** When the finish is dry, install a metal drawer pull on the front of each bin.

# Gateleg Table

*Swing-out tabletop supports transform this wall-hugging oak
bistro table into a family-size table.*

### CONSTRUCTION MATERIALS

| Quantity | Lumber |
|---|---|
| 6 | 1 × 4" × 8' oak |
| 3 | 1 × 2" × 6' oak |
| 1 | ¾" × 4 × 8' oak plywood |

The fashionable oak gate-
leg table is a necessity in
apartments, cabins and
homes where space is tight.
Typically, a gateleg table is
used as either a modest side
table or, when fully extended,
as a dinette-style table that seats
four. But this space-saving table
has loftier ambitions. With the
end leaves down, the tabletop
measures 19 × 48" to provide
plenty of space for two diners
or for use as a bistro-style serving table. When the end leaves
are raised, this table expands to
a spacious 67 × 48", giving you
enough space for six diners
with full table settings. And all
this versatility is offered in a
lovely oak package with slat
styling in the base.

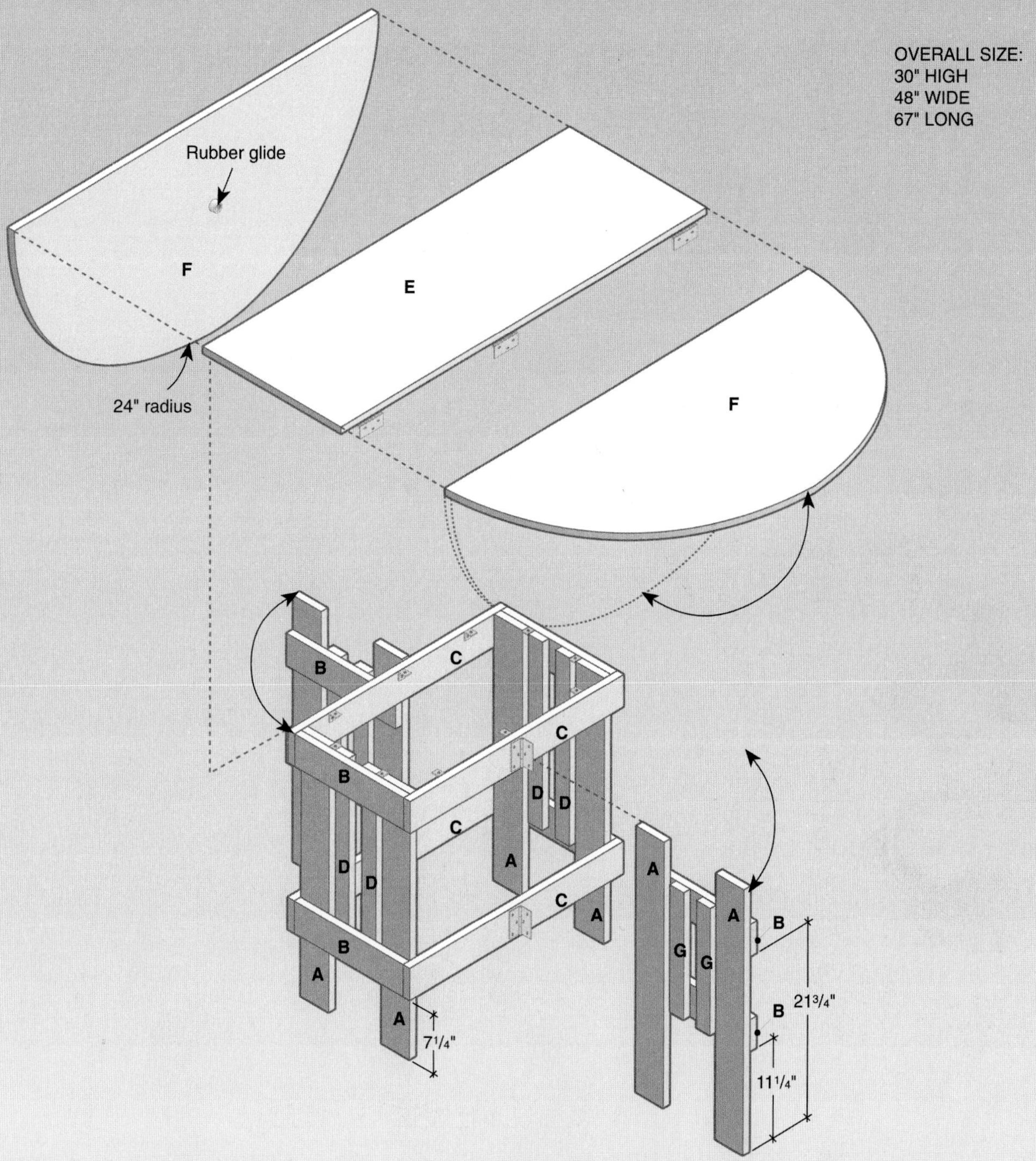
OVERALL SIZE:
30" HIGH
48" WIDE
67" LONG
Rubber glide
F
E
F
24" radius
B
C
C
B
C
D
D
D
D
A
C
A
B
A
A
7¹/₄"
A
A
G
G
B
B
21³/₄"
11¹/₄"

**Cutting List**

| Key | Part | Dimension | Pcs. | Material |
|---|---|---|---|---|
| A | Leg | ¾ × 3½ × 29¼" | 8 | Oak |
| B | Cross rail | ¾ × 3½ × 14½" | 8 | Oak |
| C | Base rail | ¾ × 3½ × 28" | 4 | Oak |
| D | Base slat | ¾ × 1½ × 21" | 4 | Oak |

**Cutting List**

| Key | Part | Dimension | Pcs. | Material |
|---|---|---|---|---|
| E | Table panel | ¾ × 19 × 48" | 1 | Plywood |
| F | Table leaf | ¾ × 24 × 48" | 2 | Plywood |
| G | Gate slat | ¾ × 1½ × 14" | 4 | Oak |
| | | | | |

**Materials:** #6 × ½", 1" and 2" brass wood screws, 1¼" brass corner braces (10), 1½ × 3" brass butt hinges (10), ⅞"-dia. rubber glides (2), ¾" oak veneer edge tape (40'), ⅜"-dia. oak plugs, wood glue, finishing materials.

**Note:** Measurements reflect the actual size of dimension lumber.

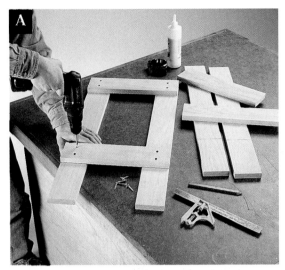

*Attach cross rails to each pair of legs with glue and wood screws.*

*Position the base slats between the base legs, and attach them to the inside faces of the cross rails.*

## Directions:
## Gateleg Table

For all screws used in this project, drill ³⁄₃₂" pilot holes. Counterbore the holes ¼" deep, using a ³⁄₈" counterbore bit.

BUILD THE LEG PAIRS.
The support system for the gateleg table consists of four pairs of 1 × 4 legs fastened to short 1 × 4 cross rails. Two of the pairs connect with base rails to form the main table base, while each swing-out gate has a single pair of legs.
**1.** Cut the legs (A) and cross rails (B) to length, and sand the pieces smooth.
**2.** To build the main base leg pairs, lay four legs flat on your worksurface, about 7½" apart.
**3.** Position a pair of cross rails over each leg pair so the ends of the cross rails are flush with the outer edges of the legs. Set the bottom edge of the lower cross rail 7¼" up from the bottoms of the legs. Keep the upper cross rail flush with the tops of the legs.
**4.** Attach the cross rails to each leg pair with glue, and drive 1"

*Sand the oak plugs flush with the surfaces, using a belt sander.*

wood screws through the rails and into the legs **(photo A)**. Check with a square to make sure the legs and rails are at right angles to one another before you fasten them together.
**5.** Assemble the leg pairs for the swing-out gates the same way, but position the bottoms of the cross rails 11¼" and 21¾" up from the bottoms of the legs.

INSTALL THE SLATS.
**1.** Cut the base slats (D) and gate slats (G) to length, and

sand the pieces smooth.
**2.** Set the base leg pairs so the cross rails are face-side-down on your worksurface. Position two base slats on each leg pair so the tops of the slats are flush with the tops of the upper cross rails and the slats are spaced evenly, with a 1½" gap between the slats and the legs. Use scrap 1 × 2s as spacers.
**3.** Attach the slats to the cross rails with glue, and drive 1" wood screws through the slats and into the rails **(photo B).**

**D**

*Mark the semicircular cutting line for the table leaves with a bar compass (we made ours from a piece of scrap wood).*

**4.** Set the gate slats on the gate cross rails with the same spacing between slats, so the ends of the slats are flush with the tops and bottoms of the cross rails. Attach the gate slats with glue and screws.

ASSEMBLE THE TABLE BASE.
**1.** Cut the base rails (C) to length, and sand them smooth.
**2.** Drill and counterbore a pair of pilot holes, ⅜" in from both ends of each base rail.
**3.** Apply glue to the ends of the base cross rails. Then, clamp the base rails in position so the ends are flush with the outer faces of the cross rails and the tops are aligned. Check all joints for square, and drive 2" wood screws at each joint.
**4.** After the glue in the joints has dried, insert glued oak plugs into all of the screw holes in the base and gates.
**5.** Sand the plugs flush with the surface. If the plugs protrude more than ⅟₁₆", belt-sand them with an 80- to 120-grit sanding belt, taking care not to round the ends of the rails **(photo C)**.

MAKE THE TABLETOP.
The tabletop consists of three pieces of plywood trimmed with oak veneer edge tape.
**1.** Cut the table panel (E) and table leaves (F) to size.
**2.** Use a bar compass to draw a centered, 24"-radius semicircle on one long edge of each leaf. If you don't own a bar compass, create a makeshift one from a straight piece of scrap wood. To do this, drill a ⅜"-dia. hole, centered ½" in from one

end of the scrap, to hold a pencil. Then, measure 24" from the center of the hole, and mark a point in the center of the board. This is the pivot point of the compass. Next, clamp a table leaf to your worksurface, and clamp a piece of scrap ¾"-thick plywood butted tightly against a long edge of the leaf. Make a mark at the center of this long edge. Drive a 6d finish nail through the mark on the compass board. Then, tap the nail into the seam between the leaf and the scrap board, at the center mark. Insert the pencil into the hole, and draw the semicircle **(photo D)**. To prevent splintering on the top side of the table leaf, draw and cut the semicircle with the bottom face up.
**3.** Cut the leaf with a jig saw,

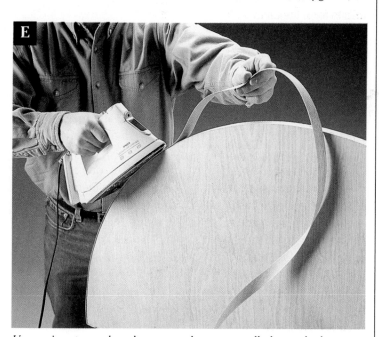

**E**

*Use an iron to apply oak veneer edge tape to all plywood edges.*

*Attach the table panel to the base with corner braces.*

*Attach the leaves to the table panel with brass hinges.*

keeping the blade at the outside edge of the pencil line.

**4.** Using the pencil line as your guide, sand the curve smooth with a belt sander. Keep the sander moving along the edge of the table leaf, and sand just until the pencil line disappears.

**5.** Using the cut table leaf as a template, trace a matching semi-circle onto the other leaf. Cut and sand the second table leaf following the same steps.

**6.** Apply self-adhesive edge tape to all edges of the table panel and table leaves, using a

*Attach rubber glides to the tabletop to work as stops for the gates.*

household iron set at low to medium heat **(photo E).** Trim the excess tape from the edges with a sharp utility knife.

APPLY FINISHING TOUCHES AND ASSEMBLE THE TABLE.

**1.** Finish-sand all of the table parts. Apply a stain, if desired, and a topcoat product (we used water-based polyurethane).

**2.** Position the table panel top-side-down on your worksurface. Center the table base on the underside of the table panel, and attach it with 1¼"

brass corner braces, using ½" wood screws **(photo F).**

**3.** Butt the table leaves against the side edges of the table panel, and attach each leaf with three 1½ × 3" butt hinges **(photo G).** Position the middle hinges slightly off center so they will be out of the way of the gatelegs (see *Diagram*, page 155).

**4.** To attach the gates, fasten a butt hinge to the outer face of each base rail, centered between the base legs. Install the hinges so the gates will swing toward opposite ends of the base from each other.

**5.** Position a gate at each side of the base, making sure the tops of the gates and bases are flush. Attach the free hinge leaves to the edges of the gate legs. The exposed sides of the gate rails should face inside the base when the gates are in the closed position.

**6.** Attach a rubber glide to the bottom face of each leaf to prevent the gates from swinging open too far **(photo H).** The gates should contact the glides when they are perpendicular to the table base.

# Index